A Patient In Time: Jojutsu

Dedicated to my dear wife Maggie

Published in 2015 by FeedARead.com Publishing, Mahon

Copyright © John Robinson

Second Edition (with Feedaread)

A CIP catalogue record for this title is available from the
British Library.

Contents:

A Patient in Time

Preface to the 2013 edition

Well this book has taken a long time coming, a lot of water under the bridge you might say? It is actually devised in two halves, the first comprising of memories of the past, and moments in hospital, the second a memory from out of hospital and into the fires of pre-emptory martial madness. Sure these have been some quite unrestful moments of my life.

But the moments and memories captured within these few meager pages, should hopefully fire you're the reader's imaginations much as they have acted both as the trigger and reference points for my life, at its different stages, both within and without hospital.

The truth be told I am at this point in time in the process of rewriting, and re-ordering portions of this body work, so that it holds together better as both a single entity. But I also need to do this in mindfulness of the at times delicate and cautious, at others brash and even damaging world of martial knowledge and skill base. This is not an easy thing, much less a compelling one. But still it needs to be done, in order for both me and others who have the slightest insight into this diverse world, can honour both the precepts of the arts, ranging for Tae-Kwon-Do, to Hoshin inspired Ninjutsu, and so forth onto my current forte of Aikido, which at the time of writing was still very much in its formative mode.

So conclude this brief end to a beginning, I hope, as always that you enjoy these works. But more over I hope that you can find the time and courage in yourself, to strive to finish reading these works, and after paying full attention to the detail, are able to step down these detours of the journey of my life, much as I have walked.

A Patient in Time
1: From Wence We Came

Joseph lay on the beach the waves gently lapping at his heels. He had spent the past thirty-one years of his life entering the Matrix and now he was leaving it. God what a relief. How much torment and suffering had it taken for him to reach this point? How many innocents had had to lose their lives and, more to the point, how many more would have to go? None he had hoped, but now he was on the beach he just concentrated on the sea and the sand. And yeah it was... nice.

He moved out his arms and they responded to touch if only barely. He found his breathing laboured and inconsistent, as if by some stroke of misfortune he had been hit on the back of the head by a large mallet, and he felt in pain as if he was dying. So as his old life ebbed slowly away from him, he held his breath. And considered all of the things he could have done but didn't, all of the people he should have helped but never did. But he didn't cry, not now. He actually felt cool, calm and relieved to have escaped the monster's jaws for one last time.

He tried to think back to his past but couldn't. He had little awareness of what the future held for him either. And only retained a spiritual hope and faith that this great unknown held the best yet to come. He had left his homeland and this time there would be no turning back. 'That dump can take care of itself', he vaguely contemplated before falling into a deep sleep on the beach.

When he awoke Joseph was covered in cuts and bruises as if he had been in some kind of fight and struggle. But he had never felt less bothered in his life. Crawling out of the woodwork like rats fleeing from a building on fire, he knew that they had come at him and attacked. Then he had had to use both hands and even occasionally also a leg to keep them at bay. But rats he could handle and did, until the vermin had been purged. Now all Joe had to worry about was the soothing beat of the waves and the gentle lapping of his heart. 'Nightmare' he jested. So was it worth it, all of this and for what, another day in paradise?

My story starts with a man who was quite different from the rest. His name is Joseph and this is his story. It all began some quiet thirty-one years ago on a nice warm park bench when Mr and Mrs Robinson met for the first time. There they made passionate love and as a result of this one sweet encounter Joseph was born. As he grew up he was rather a timid and non-de-script build of a lad. But once he was breeched by puberty he began to fill out, until eventually his body was rippled by muscle and his mind with fire. Even though he was born under a water moon, which actually made him a Pisces. And being a fish sign gave him the once learnt and never forgotten swimming trait of a surfer and an athlete, although if you would look at him now you might question where this twinkle of excellence had   got to.

As well as swimming, Joseph especially enjoyed walking, and did this whenever he got the opportunity. He both enjoyed stretching his legs, marching off to new places and feeling the blood course through his veins. He thus held onto his spirit through his legs. The blue skies up above and the brown earth down below, both gave him the inspiration to walk and the means by which to do so. And he loved all of his friends, unlike the executioners who walk around with one hand on the guillotine at all times, Joseph was actually a peaceful man.

Perhaps one of Joe's more remarkable and unusual qualities was the kind of dreams he had. Sometimes at night when he was gently slumbering he imagined far off worlds full of butterflies and songs, and on other occasions he visualised fantastic cities crowned with stone gargoyles and mannequins all about. This is not living, rather it was life, and the way he always dreamed it should be.

'How then', reflected Joseph, 'can I fight the demons without the muscles of Héraclés or the speed of a cheetah? Is there not some other way?' This took him a moment to time out and recollect his thoughts. Then he decided the following: 'I have to work hard and to be my utmost every day whenever I can, and chill coolly whenever I can't. I have to look hard, and not just look for the obvious. To see that there is often another side to the two arguments hence being presented and in this way appreciate that the truth is not always handed to the observer on a platter. Like most things it has to be worked for, fought for, and earned. I have to stay alive, but where there are liars they will die.' This point of Biblical prophecy was actually a tad too much for him in this early hour of the day, and so without so much as taking his eye off the ball, he almost stumbled over in exhaustion. His back was aching, his eyes were sore, his wrists knackered, his fingers cold, his shoulders stooped and so on. He actually craved for just one more cigarette, which he knew was coming. And would provide just a slight sting to nudge his long abused corpse out of this slumber which it now found itself falling into.

He didn't feel the hit that cigarettes had once provided him with. Only a dull warm feeling inside his lungs. But it was enough. I have written books on how to stop smoking, but now that I have relapsed I am not going to lie to you. I enjoy it and whilst I know that it is killing me, it is one of those little pleasures I get out of life and so hence I will give up when I choose to do so and that is that. Kosher?

Smoking is not an anti-climax. I actually can see definite similarities between making love and lighting up, the main difference for me being that one I have got on tap and the other I haven't, more is the pity! Sure it gives me something to look forward to in the morning after dragging myself out of bed, but what I ask you is the big deal. It's only a cigarette? Chew on this the next time you jump on the band-wagon to humiliate and or insult your next-door neighbour who hasn't been as lucky as you in avoiding the addiction for all of these years.

It is right to \<try to\> stop the smoker from getting addicted and so lighting up. But it is their right to do so, and you sure as heck-as-like cannot take this away from them. Okay, children shouldn't be forced to inhale the smoke, and I will never forget the day I met a kid in the local baths who bragged to me that he smoked – what – thirty a day. But this is both nothing to be proud of and the exception to the rule. Let's try and keep it that way. Yet a minute's silence from the noise of the underworld can both provide a refreshing breath of dirty air, and one more dirty ashtray for the cleaners to empty.

2: More Tea Vicar?

As a young man Joseph liked drinking cups of tea, which was fortunate because his dad Peterson liked making them. Day in on day he would beg for a drink of the fabulous brew and day in on day Peterson would make them. Weak at first but stronger as the years went by. One to get him out of bed in the morning, one to help him through the day and one to put him to sleep again once the day was done.

On one day however, overly eager to get a taste of that special poison, Joe crept downstairs before the dawn had even broken. He had a plan to get to the kettle before the teapot had even been filled and in that way prepare for himself a drink even before his dad had put his slippers on. Everything was going according to plan, he got to the top of the stairs and even made it as far as halfway down before disaster struck. His foot slipped on a Banana skin the monkeys had left from last night's midnight orgy, and his body came crashing down smack bang into the tea trolley. You had never seen such a mess! There were tea-bags, banana skins and hot water everywhere. Even the pet cat Lucy poked her head from around the corner to see what all the fuss was about. And when the old man Peterson heard the racket he was ENRAGED!

'WHAT' he yelled 'IS GOING ON?!' and 'STOP THIEF, I'LL HAVE YOUR HEAD FOR A TROPHY STREET-RAT!' This was before he noticed the atypically chequered brown and orange pyjama top and pants of his son and wrested control of his composure. A beat passed before he muttered out something to the effect of, 'Oh, it's only you. Sorry son, I had no idea. You wanted tea at this time, why didn't you just knock on my door and I'm sure I could have made you a drink albeit as it may be half past two in the morning. Well I suppose that can't be helped now. Here hold on, let me get down and help you clear up this mess then we can brew.' Which is exactly what they did.

Fighting in the dark like a rat in a cage or a pig in a rut. It's dark outside and I cannot see my enemy, only hear him creeping under the sounds of my every breath. And smell his sweet aftershave on the nape of my neck. If only you knew how true these few words are to me. How they have dominated the best part of my life from day one and assumed my identity whereas my shadow discovered none. I can feel him close to me on the strike of the night and that is not to say that I don't like him, or even know him. I don't. But I know myself reasonably well and in this respect have a fair assumption as to what he can and cannot do. Perhaps this all sounds like gibberish to you the well informed reader. Or perhaps it sounds like the ramblings of a madman. But I hope and pray that one day you will reach the supreme state of identity, seldom looked for but rarely found, much known as enlightenment between the inner circle of believers. And when you attain this state of inner calm and tranquillity what to do then? You see it is a much mistaken belief that different people's journeys will all reach the same destination. And I have no doubt that some of them do. But I can see no sense in the equation that operandi modus plus individual output has to equate to one and the same. Sure it can. But just as different faiths may or may not share points of vision from the same rainbow, so human beings are forceful entities. And like footballers they will each have their own strengths and weaknesses. Back to the story now.

I feel him close to me on the strike of midnight, that is not to say that I like to feel him, but I can on some days and some days he scares me. Not some quaint fear but a deep and foreboding terror which shuts my mind down and switches my body into overdrive. Being a warrior at heart it is at these moments that I try my best to acquaint myself with the powerful reflexology of the force. But Superman didn't learn how to fly overnight, and nor did Popeye grow his muscles from eating one can of spinach if you catch my drift.

Currently the world is in a mess. And only the people living in it can know what a state of affairs this dump has become. Perhaps mine is a biased view because they have me trapped in a nightmarish labyrinthine prison with no escape in sight and only my own vision to eschew me from this cork-screw, but no difference. I have, and am walking the path and I hope that when I finally die others will be able to take on from where I leave off. If not me then at least someone else's baby. The power is there, it just needs to be made real. I'm not gonna talk like an English teacher when I believe in a universal language beyond sounds or barriers, of turbo-communication for the ultimate goal in sight. Which is a one/two/three step! Even me, baby.

The three greatest moments of my life are none of your business. But suffice to say that they exist and so do I presently, as you do too. Remember that.

Who controls the media, who controls what people say, what they think and what they do? I'm not saying that he or they do, we do live in a democracy give or take the occasional mass hysteria or carefully orchestrated media blackout to eliminate from popular consciousness some of the worst elements of the state's atrocities. Yet whereas I once considered myself a revolutionary I now think that perhaps the title of deviant free radical would be more apt. I am also a conspiracy theorist which is to say that I concur and agree with certain enemy of the state theories. But as a lover I am kind and as a Brit I am responsible. Got that?

We live in a world of poems and poets who are afraid to speak their minds for fear of having their throats cut. I got in here to get away from the voices, but still they follow me everywhere I go. Only the soothing sounds of my friends voices keep my mind at bay, and even then there is only one voice, that of my love, who can calm these turbulent waves completely.

Life is like a game of scrabble, you never know what you're going to get. Git. Pennies making money and money building houses. Houses homing families and families regenerating the community. The communities make up society and society builds up the livelihood of what this planet once was, or rather what it ought to be given half the chance.

I am a firm believer in a perfect world without borders where the rule of law is not subservient to the power of money but rather the Christian ideal. But in order for that to happen people have to stand up to make themselves heard which is unfortunately not the case as we speak. Damn it! I wish all of these Doctors who have done this trouble to me were locked away for three months to a year, simply to give them and their families a taste of their own medicine. And I will spell their how I choose to spell it and not down to some head-strong English know-it-all who couldn't speak another heart if it hit him in the head.

'I love you', epic words softly spoken but irreversible none the less. What I can't do is play football. I never learnt that skill at school. I do know how to play chess and consider myself something of a perfectionist at that poor much-neglected and abused pastime. And I have a couple of small if perfectly developed brown hairs growing on my chest which is something to be proud of if ever there was one!

In his cage the fat golden and happy Buddha quietly sobs and waits for the day when he is set free once again. And this time he vows to leave the cruel megalomania of the industrialised continent for the smooth soothing waters of the warm Indian ocean. And this time also there will be no looking back.

Learning how to speak different languages from French to Swahili is not dissimilar to playing chess I would like to surmise. I only understand a fragment of them, but what I do understand is immensely rewarding. And where does smoking fit into this equation? As the reward at the end of the day? Or how about as the recognition of the uncontrollable power of defeat, crushing and dragging me deep under its dark and murky depths. Suffocating me and restraining my every move. Such is the effect this institution has on me. Sure I am free to write, and to smoke, but big deal. I am not free.

There was once a traveller called Joseph who liked eating lots of pies. He had such a great appetite in fact that he would scoff his face for day in on day until it was blue all over. And even then he continued to munch.

Everywhere he went he liked to sample the local cuisine, so down his regular pub he would try the salad on a Tuesday and the chips on Thursdays, cheese and onion toasties on Wednesdays and cod in batter with chips and mayo on the Mondays and Fridays alternatively. This was the way he liked it and this was what he was. You see just as the old adage goes you are what you eat, and so you see if you eat fat you become fat. Likewise if you stay old in the cold for too long you blood freezes over. Or if you are lucky enough to eat good food for everyday of your life you become a good person. And Joe or Joseph as his friends liked to call him, was thoroughly good through and through. In this way he retained his sanity in the face of overbearing pressure to the opposite direction.

One day when out walking amongst the hills, Joseph came across an old beggar type figure stooped amongst the reeds. 'Ahoy there' he called out, half expecting to be shunned by the old man, and half expecting to be welcomed. So imagine his surprise when this other guy, Tony, welcomed him into his arms.

'Come and sit down with me,' Tony proclaimed whilst simultaneously stretching out his right hand offering Joe a bite to eat from his tasty cheese and pickle morsel. Not one to turn down a snack, Joe jumped at the offer, and began to feast into the tasty morsel. It was tasty and nutritious made from mature Cheddar cheese on wholemeal bread with Irish butter to lubricate and Branston pickle to complete the package. Joe was in fact half way through eating before he noticed the cop car pull up outside on the other side of the road.

'Trouble,' he thought to himself and 'not again' before he prepared to leg it. And sometime later when he was on the run yet again, he realised that he had been grassed in and for what? Stealing half of a cheese and Branston pickle sandwich? Some people get all the luck.

Isn't it funny how time can just slip by, Joseph reflected. One minute everything is running hunky-dory, and the next thing the rug is pulled out from beneath your feet and you find yourself hurtling down at break neck velocity. Until you crash head-first into a pit full of tigers, surrounded by six stone walls, with baying audiences all around yelling for your blood.

What to do in this situation? Well the easy thing would be to unsheathe your scabbard and go for the throats. A braver man may well and try to appease or coerce the beasts into a more peaceful resolution to the situation. However given that tigers are flesh-eaters by their very nature, this would be a foolhardy approach I would suspect. All it would take would be for one half-starved and deranged animal to break from the pack and slice and dice the unsuspecting felon from his chops to his navel, for the game-over whistle to call out and then it really would be game over. Oh well, at least with sword in hand, action can be taken if so ever it need be. That's the thing about swords. They are pretty to look at, but in the right hands a fearsome weapon indeed. I've never actually so much as swung a real sword in real combat myself, but I once watched a TV show demonstrating how this technique is perfected in a dojo, then using bamboo swords for the obvious safety concerns, so I can well respect the amount of time and dedication required it takes to have this thing done properly.

You try to close your eyes and open your heart. But no thought resolves the pain of treachery and so you bleed to sleep, dreaming of just one lousy loving kiss. In the wrong hands this encounter can well turn out to be fatal, as the tears turn to blood and your old carcass shrivels away to nothing. It's alright though, I've not come all this way to just throw the lot out of the window. To crash the TV from a second storey window onto the ground, a large wide screen Panasonic lithium ray tube excavator splinters into a thousand pieces below. And what's with this?

Other people absorb my pain when I'm fighting with a shotgun. And with a sniper rifle the bullet goes in. Even a punch receives little to no after effect until one is returned. Which fortunately for me today, it wasn't. All I have to put up with is a lousy push crushing my already well stressed lower vertebrae back into their right and proper places at the bottom of my spine. Without fighting I would be a peaceful person. With it I am a warrior. Hence the moment, wasn't the first and I very much doubt will be the last we see of the shadow Joe.

Change affects all men in different ways. Like when you are fighting a Dragon and it breathes a shoot of fire, you had better run for cover. Or when it goes for you with its massive talons you had better either duck and or preferably raise your engraved sword to block the scratches. Then after it has tired itself out you could quickly perform a surgically precise series of jab-jab-hook body blows to its torso in order to wear the beast down before finishing the fight with a central snout clout.

That is if you are fighting a dragon. And unfortunately for many of us, we will never get to see a dragon seeing as the conventional type with two wings and a snout died out some million-trillion years ago to be exact. That's not to say that there aren't still dragon people about in this day and age. And I'm not talking about these big multi-millionaire celebrities, not these company top dog fat cats. Although they might be one I somehow rather doubt it. Rather a dragon seldom moves around on the ground at all. He flies using wings. Yes that is a metaphor, but look into the root of it none the less and you can well see the delicate fragrance therein. You see a dragon person, probably drives a car, and keeps his head low when the pigs ride by. Or if he is in with that crew then he may even smile and give them a wave, he may even honk his horn, but somehow I doubt it. Then when they get out of the car they will most likely walk similar to ordinary people. Or exactly the same as ordinary people if we are going to be pedantic. Then one of the dragon's hidden inbuilt faculties is that he can fly, kick into a run with the flash of an adrenaline rush, and run a whole marathon starting right there wherever that may be, and for the whole twenty six miles or whatever, until he touches base camp which will presumably be his preferred destination. I think it must be very hard to run a marathon without this goal of reaching in mind, like running through the streets of once cobbled now dusty Baghdad with nothing but the sun and the stars to give you direction and keep you company. The sailors were good at that in the old days, as were the Greeks in an age or two before. But now it seems to be a shame that the art of independent self-navigation has been lost to all but a few insider soldiers. Oh well, what was once the craze often fades away in latter days.

Still more the folks of times before used to believe the world was a floor just flat no hat, or interstellar combat if it ever came to that.

But now with KO body knockout blows, somebody's gonna pay and somebody's gotta know.

Three line rhyming verse prose. Cute don't you think?

Anyway before we digress too far from the gist of this topic I want us to get back to the thread which I was so happily talking about just a minute before. That is dragon people can fly. In planes if it so suits them, with cars if they put their foot down and even in the mind's eyes of others if certain industrial strength Modus Operandi (the media) are behind them. By this I mean to say that look how the media has convinced the public and MPs of my country (Britain) that it is okay and morally justifiable to bomb that poor dirt hole to destruction (Iraq). That is not a justifiable means to an end but rather a hysterical smash to a completely out of order threat. Or the threat was completely out of line to the punishment dealt out to just one man.

Of course to understand this situation properly we will have to educate ourselves to both the history of the first gulf war, the later extra-range missile crisis, the nature of modern warfare and weapons used by both sides, not to mention the effect the media and the public have on the battlefront and the historical importance of past battlefields – namely Vietnam – in all of this.

I have neither the time nor energy to plug into this lot now, but will say that after a couple of antiwar demonstrations which I marched along on in London I was on both occasions stopped by a couple of (different) Derby lads in the city centre. And both times they saw my Stop the War banner, and informed me that at least one of them had just come back from combat operations in that god-forsaken country. If I remember correctly, the first time I was with a slightly older mate of mine who tried to distance himself from any sign of danger. But I actually recognised the lad from living in a suburb near to where I used to, and so concluded the occasion quite amicably. I can't remember whether we shook hands or not then, but we could well have done.

The next incident happened a couple of months, or was it years, down the road. And this time the men I met seemed to be slightly less receptive to my pastime of feeding the vermin (as they called them) pigeons as well as my pro-active anti-war stance. But again, after exchanging a few brief words, me and the soldier dude came to a truce at least. And I was still half tempted to have a go at his mate but decided the better of it, not the least influenced by the fact that he was twice my size all over and could have quite easily plucked the living senses of this tender shell, had he so desired. Fortunately for me that geezer ended up deciding to go off and break some poor lame pigeon's neck with a firm kick, to put it out of its misery. And I just suppose that I was glad that those boots weren't after all, headed for me!

There was once a child called Joe who lived a pretty life and had watched in dismay at the breakup of his parents' marriage much as a sailor foretells bad tidings on the arrival of dark monsoon storm clouds up ahead. At the young age of sixteen he suffered nasty injuries both on the road and in hospital and, on exiting hospital, it took him well over a decade to right himself again. Some might say that he would never be *right* again, and if by right you mean normal then you too would probably be right. But if by right you mean conformable then you would be wrong, because despite his injuries Joe had gone a long way in restoring his body's natural internal equilibrium on his own and without the help of his parents. That isn't to say that he didn't appreciate everything that they had done for him over the years. Far from it. But there were certain things, such as bringing a new little one into the world, which he knew he had to do on his own.

When he was in hospital he felt like or I could quite validly say metaphorically speaking was, put in a sarcophagus. In as much as the doors were closed around him and he was drugged up to his eye-balls on a beat by beat basis. But if there is one thing that kept him going and that is a good nights sleep (kip). And so with this in mind Joseph was eventually able to persuade the all powerful doctors to administer his medicine in the mornings as a means to run through his body during the day and leave it alone by the time bed-time comes about. He still had enemies, in the government, on the internet, in the base of people's hearts and in their mind's eyes as well. But he had tried, oh how he had tried, to make friends as well. Much like how the eagles fly in the sky, or the swallows hop across the ground, Joseph acquainted himself with sometimes rich sometimes poor entities, or people rather, in the desperate hope that some of them could help him find a way out of the matrix.

Then he found her. With a blinding flash one day the clouds parted and on a chariot of gold driven by two white stallions the love of his life appeared. Dressed in a dress of shimmering silk jade and adorned with rubies and sapphires she beckoned for him to come closer to her. And a few heartbeats later it was all done. The little baby was made. Perfect.

3: Quotations

After having dissected a flower, and despite using the most powerful electron microscope known to man, nowhere can the scientist find its beauty.

Scar tissue can be cause by electrical burns, fire ones, chemicals, and even physical trauma.

Bernie, Staff Nurse

In learning the honest path is there not a commitment to sincerity also? Where is the truth of love but in the eyes of its beholders?

When friends and family gather round from far asunder do we not rejoice?

Please trust me love, I have a plan and I want to help us both.

People have limits. We have to be aware of them and together we are stronger than the combined value of our individual parts.

What can you tell me about the agony of defeat or the pain of misery?

Consider the lilies in the field, the daffodils in the grove or the tulips in the sun. See how they neither toil nor struggle, and look beautiful the whole season round. Rather they play with the wind and drink the rain.

From The Bible

When I grow up I want to be just like a flower.

Little Joe

The only way to have a friend is to be one

Make new friends but treasure the old, those are like silver these are like gold.

Mark Twain

Like a monkey in the trees, listen to the songs of the birds and the bees, determine where and forth each wind blows, follow your heart and play in the snow.

I sang a song into the air, it fell to the ground I know not where; for who has sight so keen and strong, that they can see the flight of a song?

And now the melody from beginning to end I find again in the look of a friend.

Kassia

Laughter is the sun which drives the snow from the bleak midwinter face.

Victor Hugo

When you say goodbye to your past life you will feel a sharp sting in the pit of your stomach. Let it go. Sometimes stinging gives way to remorse. But cry when it is time to cry and be happy when the sun shines. So is the nature of all things, the emotions from life should be let to wave out like the waves return to the sea. And hopefully over a period of time, maybe days, maybe months, maybe years, you will find that cool and vast expanse of sea which you have been looking for. Then you can paddle to wherever you wish to be.

Buddhist fable

On the night of the fight you might feel a slight sting that's pride messing with you. Forget pride, it only hurts; never helps.

Butch from Pulp Fiction

And as your love grows the light you see it by waxes stronger.

Fenélon (a Christian mystic)

Love is one of God's rainbows shining down from heaven to lighten up the dreary days of all of us normal people stuck slap bang in the middle of the rat-race!

Joseph once asked his dad;

'Pa.. if God knows all things then how come he doesn't know when I need a wee?'

His dad replied;

'Son there are some things man is supposed to know and some things that he just ain't. Now be quiet and finish your cornflakes!'

Shiva the sun

Allah my precious one.

The birds and the bees

The sky and the trees

Help out the living

Pay respect to our dead

Kill off the dying

With a bullet to the head

Listen to the song

Play it all through

Give love to your lover

And let her love you

Chase out the rats

Let them scurry away

Go into the back yard

And there may you play

I ain't no good

No good am I

I can't kick a ball

Laugh at me try

But am I bothered

Am I really no

Get on this wagon and come watch me go.

Believe with your heart and see with your ears

Cry with your eyes and watch with your tears.

Hidden words of madness sought in a scholar's dream

Insane sparks of wisdom licked from another tramp's ice-cream.

Count on your fingers the sheep over the style

and pay respect to your neighbours all the while.

4: The Happy Buddha

The Happy Buddha was a kind man with a forgiving heart. He was known across the land as one who regularly fed the birds. Magpies, rooks (more commonly known as blackbirds) and pigeons too. Yes I am talking about the stool variety. He fed the lot. Even complete strangers in the street enjoyed watching this little man take his time out from doing nothing in particular to do nothing in particular. Aka feed the birds. Then one day a single seagull flew up to his hand and gently prised the chip he was holding away from it (his hand). Soon they were all doing this.

Cheeky birds he thought, but he wasn't deterred. Still he fed them. The other bird types still flocked down to eat when they thought the coast was clear. But the Seagulls were the especially naughty ones. On another day he came across a sad and desperate looking pigeon who had broken her wing. Perhaps she had been shot by a kid with an air-rifle, or perhaps she had been run over, or attacked by a Rottweiler. Each is possible but knowing the temperament of the kids on the streets nowadays, and their parents who let them get away with it, I wouldn't be surprised for the former to be the case. Anyhow, on gently tempting the bird to eat Buddha was aghast on the approach of a six foot troll, eager to snap its neck, presumably by stamping on it, or kicking it, and then presumably to eat the carcass raw because that's what trolls do you see. So Buddha protested and saw the troll over back into the dark and heavily overgrown undergrowth from whence it came.

He did see another deformed pigeon another day. Perhaps it was the same one, perhaps not. But whether the troll got its meal is another thing altogether.

Joseph was the son of an epic martial artist, the Dying Phoenix. His dad was renowned the world over for his skill with the nun-chuckers, among other weapons. They both had their enemies, but the Phoenix would take out the more gruesome ones which stood in Joe's way. Then one night when the Phoenix was off busy teaching in Canada, Joseph encountered a large a grisly looking troll, out for a fight. Unsure what to do the kid held back, whereupon the troll pounced. And to be sure there was not much left of our poor hero once he had been done in. He was still breathing but only barely.

If we take a step forward past this deciding fight we can see that Joseph grew up to be a gentle giant. Locked away in a sarcophagus to 'aid' the healing process, all he could do was look this way and that to observe and listen to the world as it operated around him. He was no fool, but foolishness is as foolishness does. And there were many who said that he was foolish for picking a fight with a giant twice his size. Although it never happened that way, how were they to know this?

Eventually Joe decided that he had had enough and began punching at the stone lid. In-fact he punched so hard one day that both his knuckles cracked and his eyes welled up with tears from the agony of brutal exhaustion. When this happened he had to stop. Then another day he found a stick, which with his wits about him he used to jam in between the coffin's lid and its main body. Then a couple or more like a couple of hundred well placed kicks, followed by a full strength shoulder lift, finally got the coffin open. Nobody did it for him, he did it himself.

On the outside the first thing that hit him was the cold, then the rain. Then the light of day. Then on getting accustomed to his strange new surroundings he saw his dad standing there before him with a cheesy grin on his smart looking face.

'Didn't you hear my cries for help, or what about the kicks?' little Joe pleaded

But his dad just smiled. And in his mind's eye the boy knew that the old man hadn't set this test up for him as a means to test his prowess and means to a way of becoming a man, but had seen this as an opportunity to do so, perhaps when it presented itself.

In-fact Joseph knew nothing of the sort. He was not a mind reader. He in the bottom of his heart hoped that the Phoenix had now lost his abilities and was no longer the able warrior whom he had fallen in love with. But that being said, this paternal matrimony was all a bit gay for him and so without any further ado he went up and smacked the little b******.

As Joseph watched the silent and unmarked police car pull up outside his house he knew that his time was up. He instantly ran outside his back door, in a hope to escape from the inevitable. There he was met by the large and overbearing fully uniformed police constables, both ready for a fight. They then proceeded to grab each of his arms and force him to the ground.

The journey to the station was quite uneventful in itself, in the back of the meat wagon. Once there again his demons got the better of him, he shouted and cried for help until he could shout and cry no more. All hell broke loose. Metaphorically speaking the ground shook, the soils broke and Lucifer himself reared his ugly head. His unseen and unspoken teacher from his head had always foretold that this day would come. But he had never expected to actually see this day come to pass. When it did all finally calm down, he decided to be led away peacefully. There is no point in fighting the machine once it is on-top of you. Better to just close your eyes and let it do its dirty worst. And it did.

He had once heard the story of a convict who had taken down a dozen police single-handedly and lived to tell the tale. But this was not so much a grass, as a man with no pride. A man who had been beaten and would be forced to spend the remainder of his abject days living in sin and misery.

Joseph had no such fate in store for the man whom he planned to be. Of course, at the time, things are never quite as simple as they are to read in a book. What I mean to say by this is that little Joe didn't quite go down as easily as I might have you believe. When he was grabbed he wrestled the attacker away, when he was hit he punched back, and when he was looked at like he wasn't even worth the dirt of the shoe which someone trod in, he glared back with such a rage as if hell itself hath no fury. But in the end it was all no good. Then after this fighting was over he was led to the cell where the real psychological torture began.

After that was over, he just had to wait. But not before he had sampled a dish of the local cuisine. I can in all honesty say that I have absolutely no memory at all of what this was. Only that it tasted nice, proper sweet if you catch my drift. It was vegetarian, at least that much is sure. And he had never tasted a tastier meal in all of his years, as I'm sure you can imagine after being starved for some twenty odd hours. Vegetarian, or Indian sweetheart. Mm she did taste sweet!

Then with nothing else better to do he downed the customary single white cup or two of polystyrene water and waited some more. All of this seemed to take place at rather a leisurely pace compared to what he had been through before. But still something was missing from his life, although he couldn't quite put his finger on what it was.

Joseph's time in hospital had its ups and downs. A clear up was when he met new people and made some enemies but mostly allies with them.

It's blatantly not a very nice experience going behind those pearly gates for some three to four months. But you just have to make the most of them. For example the abseiling on Mondays is a bit windy, the rock-climbing on Tuesdays is a bit wet, the Para-diving on Wednesdays cold, the criss-cross-country circuit training on Thursdays hurts my lungs, but the country picnics in Sherwood forest on Fridays are generally nice enough, depending on the weather. So if it's raining we generally choose to stay in. We also try to get out to at least one gig on Saturdays (yeah right), and rest on the Sundays as is proper for that proper day. Ha-ha. I'm not mad just mentally deranged (said the mad hatter to the giant frog on his way to church). 'What do you do?' He asked to the giant toad sitting in his way.

'Sometimes I fart and sometimes I burp' replied the frog sheepishly 'but I'm always Bonnie and Blythe and Happy and Gay!'

Please don't forget that I have been here before. She is a scoundrel this Mare. Fast when she gets going and something of an animal too. I think that she thinks that she likes to be a stallion when the mood overcomes her. But that is wishful thinking. And in fact I wouldn't trade her for the world. Now what's your offer?

I have been here before and don't plan on coming back again. I'm actually going to leave the country. In some-ways my life bears certain resemblances to dancing the Tango. One step forwards and two steps back. Like when I am given fifteen minutes unescorted leave for good behaviour, and then have it taken away again for making sexually inappropriate comments towards staff. Whoops.

Or when I get one hour section seventeen (that's unescorted leave from the ward and hospital itself). But this time there is going to be no looking back. At least not if I can help it. So big deal, it's not my fault if they can't hack it. They have to resort to medical intervention and or group suffocation whereas all I was doing was playing the game. Or a game rather perhaps I should say. And what a gay game it was. :-) But I am still a hacker and still (desperately perhaps) trying to find a portal in, to find a way out (of this dump).

'Do you know what?' Joseph asked of his friend, Shadow, one day.

'I like playing games of pretty much any sort or description. But especially what I consider to be good computer games. And that means RPGs or at least KOEI ones of the Samurai/Dynasty Warriors variety. Don't worry if all of this is going over your head like a Boeing 747. I suppose only but a few of the younger techno-freak generation will have any idea what I am talking about there. But suffice to say that there is nothing sweeter than taking out a whole army of ninjas with just one general and her trusty horse!

Also with regards to playing chess, my old favourite pastime, I like winning the games, or even winning the games I lose. Which is when I have had some influence on the course of events on the battlefield if not totally determining/dictating the outcome.'

'What do you mean by all this?' Shadow inquired, bemused if not intrigued by the other's apparently mindless outburst.

'Well..' Joseph continued, 'You have locked me up here for some three to four months now. I lose track of the exact time. I am even beginning to lose track of my grammar. Okay so I have never been very good at that, like an aficionado, but that's not the point. The point is the longer you keep me here what do you want me to do, just go away or something? But I did it before! I know the ropes this time round. I know that I am not supposed to do certain things and that by betraying the hospital's trust in my trust of the trust's rules I am pushing it. But the whole point is that betraying me they have broken my trust, and that by breaking it I have no intention of going back to where I was before. Absolutely none.'

'You may take that as no indicator of me being of sound of mind, but no difference. I am not here for you, rather myself, and if the two coincide then so be it. Let the Doctors experiment with me their little rat; we are approaching the right (Chinese) year after all. And so let the tools fall where they may lie.'

'If you crumble a fortune cookie the rats are bound to come a sniffing around the pieces. Let them. Out of the woodwork and into the fire I say. Eager for a bite to eat. What's more is that rats, like Trolls, can't cook. So let them come I say. I want to see how many I can slice and dice before the exhaustion finally gets the better of me! They are scavengers, vermin and best left unfed.'

'So what do I plan to do about the present predicament that I find myself in then you may ask?' Joseph asked his friend, whereas the Shadow just stood there quiet and quietly shaking his head. Feeling more then just a little bit disheartened at his once best friend's now apparent inability to, if not respond to, then at least acknowledge his questions which he had, if not been firing, then at least posing. But as if poisoned by some incurable root venom, his best pal would only occasionally shake his head and frown. So Joseph continued undeterred.

'Absolutely nothing,' Joseph fired back. 'As I said already I have a plan. And you may, or most probably may not be a part of it. Seeing as you have had nothing to do with me in my critical time of need, I can't be bothered to invite you into mine when the dust finally settles around me.'

Lying here in the middle of the night. All I can hear is the quiet breathing of my own shadow. His strength alarms me and without my comrades I think I will slip further into this pit of now which I have just dug.

As he aggressively bustles his way through the world I trail him. Anticipating his every move just as he has predicted mine.

He wants a fight and I want to give him one. But from where, thin air? Still we are both men, then again let me stress, under duress even the best can stoop so low as to think what no man should know. And go where no man should be, quite easily.

I know for a fact that I can't fight, but then do I really have to? Sleep, like peace, is a great healer; it soothes all wounds and creates bridges where once there were none. Can you imagine a world without it? What it would be like? Bleary eyed and runny nosed, the insomniacs would run from appointment to appointment, crashing into each other on the way and never getting anywhere on time. That is chaos and this is insanity.

Fortunately our world is not like that. By and large for each hour spent awake we try to spend another safely wrapped up at home in the warm comforts of our own pads. Padded up to sleep. So it is and so it should be.

This is the healing mechanism which mends the bridges, hearts and lives of a thousand needless deaths and wars. Without it the blood grows cold and the mind and body shuts down. Don't I know it and don't you forget it.

To the unbelievers and sceptics I say to you this:

'Do not falter to make your purpose known. Keep tomorrow in the present and you shall get your just rewards, whatever they may be!'

I'd like to address another demon for a moment if I may. This one of anger being a fierce beast, like a black dragon and closely aligned to his brother, hatred.

Anger can motivate people to do all sorts of evil acts. From punching another man, to whacking the living daylights out of a virgin, to exterminating them, and actually taking out not just his entire family, but even his whole street, neighbourhood, city and country as well. Look at what they've done to Iraq and specifically Fallujah if you want a concrete example of this clause in operation. And it was my enemy who tried this outcome so that he could try to get to me. But I'm still fighting.

Much like how the Irish Republican Guard (IRA) blew up the city centre of Manchester a few years back. I wonder if he (my enemy/ies) had anything to do with that. Or perhaps it was a Vietcong (the North-Vietnamese Guerrilla Army of the war in the mid seventies who won a war they fought out-manned, out-gunned and out-of-luck) style display of strength and resistance. Fortunately Northern Ireland is now at peace, and this is in no small part thanks to the efforts of Bill Clinton former president of the USA, who despite his shortfalls, can at least be said to have done one great thing in his life time. Which as I just said, was to call talks and broker a peace between the warring factions of Northern Ireland. Now how many of you can be said to have done that?

To achieve the kind of hatred which mass-destruction implies, requires more than just a single insult or verbal barrage. It requires a virtual offensive spanning the media, TV, radio and tabloids to capture and coerce the general public's opinion. It is true that everybody will have their own opinion with regards to this or that. But no-one is stronger then God, not even Allah, and just as the liars and ignorants will get their comeuppances on Judgement day, so too the heavens will open and the Lord our saviour will return.

When the heavens finally open and Jesus returns to the land so it has been written and so God will destroy the world in order that he might create a new one. World War Three takes place at every level, from the TV shows, to the DVD music and the sexual predators (male AND female). Who will win? That's for you to decide.

If the voices can get to me then they can get to you too. No-one is invincible. Not even Him. Not even me. Not even you.

I have tried hiding in the shadows and they jump out of the night to get me. I immerse myself in my books, games and DVDs and I find myself being lied to and surrounded by the seven deadly assassins. Perversion, sorcery, rapists, murderers, idolatry, liars and adulterers. They have me surrounded and trapped.   And there are no exits.

43

Whatever country I run to I find myself trapped and cornered. But I am a fighter and alone in this world. That has a whole lot of weaknesses but a strength or two as well. Such as I can act where no other man would dare to act.

Or hold back when everyone else dives in head first, like lemmings. Please listen to what I am telling you. Let us stand together, despite our differences, and fight side by side, to defeat these enemies with a four million mile punch. Why four? Because it is the gross product of two, which itself stands for man and wife, which is the root of the family. Higher level Maths? I should coco.

That is all I can manage today (metaphorically speaking), but tomorrow I'm aiming to flex my muscles and go for a two lap run. Starting with a walk. To town.

Trust in the lord and we can only hope to be given our dues. Let the thirsty come and he whom-so-ever wishes to accept the water of life drink it as a gift.

One last thing:

Do not be afraid of death, only once it is upon you there will be no turning back. And each mile we tread is another mile down that slippery road to our graces (graves). Then you fall and then you will have to face Him in all of His glory alone. For now we see dimly as in a mirror, but a poor reflection of our inner selves. But then we shall know even as we are known, warts and all, face to face.

Here we go again. I am taking my medication and co-operating with the doctors just as I have been ordered to. But with God as my witness I will bow down to no man. With only my shadows for company. The dead of the night in the dead of the night, but deadly never-the-less.

This is when ninjas like to work. Silent and deadly assassins, unseen and unknown. But they fill your vision and your knowledge if only you but knew it. Pulling the strings from just about every major election victory, to the little things in life like the way a polar bear moves.

Be aware of the colours because they will tan your hide if you are not careful. They will. But love beats all things and world war three will be not so much a nuclear war as a nuclear one. Guns versus love. A man and wife versus two men and two women. So then have to ask you the question which is stronger the number two or four. They are both factors of the other, and one is definitely smaller, but is large necessarily better? I doubt it.

The shadow is a clever beast. It will mirror your thoughts, assuming you are brave enough to stand by them, and then it will pounce. Consuming your every desire and ducking out of the way when you try to fight back. So how do you fight it? Have strength in your convictions. Go on the run; go under-cover. Play it at its own game. Even try to make your own rules, or discover what the proper rules are. Trial and experimentation go a long way towards realising the truth.

Just as rhythm and rhyme are critical to a successful song, so also are lyrics and lyricist. I have no doubt that there is only one light, but you can only see this with the curtains open. That means a wife and babies if you are lucky enough to be blessed with these gifts. And if you are not, don't worry. God isn't picky, and there is a place for everyone in heaven if only you would dare to walk through those pearly gates.

The minute they think that I am winning the fight, I find that they have tricked me. Hostilities then become apparent and manifest. I do not mean to be a threatening person, but I can sense my enemy crushing my heart with his every move. And he has got me where he wants me. I feel a little better now that I have had a cigarette. I feel freed. Don't start smoking – it kills you. Christ sacrificed his life on the cross for our sins. I am still fighting.

So the question we have to ask ourselves now is this:

Who exactly is this enemy whom we are fighting? Is he really the devil himself? Standing seven feet tall with a red horn protruding from his forehead, ten metres long, and a fiery pitchfork grasped in both hands, desperately looking for an enemy to attack.

If she goes I go, simple as. That's not so much a threat as a promise. And you think I couldn't do it? Perhaps that's why they hide the railway lines out of sight and under bridges.

But public transport does wonderful things. And Zimbabwe was such a nice place in the summer. Hopefully he will let me have this one baby. This one ray of light in a pitch black and frosty night. It's cold outside, and as the darkness closes in it really hurts me. The ignorant mother-damn**s are fighting us and presumably will continue to until the gates of hell close.

Then the proud soldiers soldier on. I'm not crying so much for the loss of my love, although I do cry for her. But I am crying for the loss of my love. And I wouldn't be a man if I didn't. It's not a coward's thing to cry. Rather a human one.

Here we go again; it's getting dark and, as the frost closes in, I can hear voices. Worse than that my memory is failing. I can't well remember names but the choices available to my palate are simplifying. Currently I'm looking at chalk and cheese. One used unto the other to eat. Not much of a life-style is it? But everyone has to write once in a while.

Today I reconciled or should that be remonstrated with some of my better friends, sharing complex and happy conversations on the top floor of a burning house. It's not that I don't like playing the game. I'm as addicted as the next man. Still somehow, and quite frequently recently, for a matter of fact, I have been feeling tired. So tired, in-fact, that yesterday I couldn't even dare lift pen to paper. Call me a mouse but I rather think of myself as a cat. It's like the great shadow once said, whereas foxes are predators and cunning, they are in fact just a hybrid between the loyal dog and the independent cat.

But a fox is a predator; they are out for the meat and quick and quiet. Compared to a fox I'm more like a lumberjack 'Timber!'

Fatherhood provides a range of responsibilities and priority. Firstly to the baby, secondly to the mother and thirdly to myself. Making sure that I get better, get well and get out of here.

I love my family; they are the most important thing to me in the entire world. I have faith and hope and charity to guide me through these turbulent waters and I very much suspect that the outcome of this battle with me (will be) a testimony to the holy spiritual compassion of the world at large. Here's looking at you, kid.

Let us speculate for a minute on extraterrestrial life. I know what the text-books say: that there is no more beyond the planet earth. Nothing more past this rock of sea and sand and fish. That life beyond one is impossible.

And what does modern science tell us also? That this is impossible: a mere figment of the imagination of the science fiction boffins who have nothing better to do than to spend their time twiddling their thumbs. But what I ask you gives these supposedly 'all powerful' and 'all knowing' scientists reach and realm over anyone else in particular, especially those creative individuals who dare to dream and those exciting ones who dare to do so also.

Time is often considered in years, measured largely from the birth of thirst two millennium back. Then what about the future and, perhaps more importantly, the present. For all the concern about what goals we have yet to achieve or the mistakes we have already committed, it is often forgotten the achievements or losses of today. I am not saying that everyone forgets all of the time. Far from it, in fact. Most people seem to remember for some of the time. But I'll be honest with you; I have only ever had a few close friends who I have known who appreciate life for what it is when it is, precisely now. Then more's the pity that they have, or at least some of them have been snatched from this land of plenty, at ages premature and immature. Let us hold their memories peacefully.

It's a bit early for me to be up, but I want to chat to you for a while. When I say early I don't mean that we are together now. I mean we aren't. Dawn is on the horizon. I can smell it, and sense it through the bird song and as the blackbirds rear their ugly heads. Dawn is just beginning to break. I have even heard a sparrow tweet today and that is definitely a good start to the day.

I think that some people can disguise the faith far too easily much like a magician spins his cards or a gambler calls his hands (and shuffles the deck), I realise also that certain shadow ninjas have this ability down to a fine par, but not the ninjas of the light. They are far more concerned with telling the truth and doing good and honest actions for the well-being of mankind instead of the interests of any particular shadowy individual masters or   organisations.

Yesterday I was granted an honorary white belt in Ninjitsu. This is quite an achievement for some-body born in the wrong country, to the wrong school, at the wrong time. But as well as a player I am (learning to be) a fighter. And I will buy the suit and wear the badge with pride.

Whether I reach my target of human emancipation in this species, as a father, remains to be seen. But I treasure the love of my life like the best thing that has ever happened to me, which it is, and so I will make this work touch wood.

I'm sorry that so many people have had to die. But I really would be happier if they just stopped fighting now. I don't know how we can put an end to World War three. I appreciate that if I fell dead it would solve all of someone's problems. But it wouldn't solve mine, and it certainly wouldn't simply end the war. Rather than a coward's retreat as in the exit from Vietnam has virtually destroyed that country.

I think what we need now is peace and reconciliation. And multi-faith dialogue. If I can study other religions such as Hinduism, Islam and Christianity I don't see why the soldiers on the front lines can't do the same. And I bet that if they were to learn a little bit more about the grunts whom they are suckering it would go a long way towards solving the world's problems. But oh yeah, sorry I forgot this is war and when someone taps out rather than releasing, you apply more pressure until they die. So what are you telling me? That the mortars continue to fall? Oh, but you have won this war, the last scream of a dying fox hardly requires kicking it in the face, does it?

Whose master is the master of all the grand-masters in the world? Not Bruce Lee, not even Jackie Chan or even elephant-man. Look with your eyes and hear with your ears, feel with your heart and cry with your tears. The bad men surround me again and I have no way out. They drug me up to the eye-balls. Try to confine me, anticipate my footsteps, and stab me in the back. But I have no more time for their lies. I have seen the light and the closer I get to its warmth I find it entices me and drags me in.

I cannot escape the love of God now. I am caught in his net. I struggle and fight but only find myself drowning further in the sea of compassion. A funny (use of) metaphor but true none-the-less.

'How can I write when my hands are tied and my tongue is dirty?' Joe pleaded to the shadow one day after a particularly hard session at it (smoking). I appreciate what happens to me is of my own undoing, that the underworld is a dirty place and prison sentences have time and reason.

I am lucky in as much as I have sense and reason and have seen the moon through the clouds on this dark and foreboding night. So like a mummy I lie in this sarcophagus and bide my time. And this time when I get out there will be no turning back. Mercy not asked (so) none given. And I am a man and I am a fighter and I have striven for the much sought after but seldom realised ideal of gentleman. And today I stopped smoking to the credit of my fiancée and unborn baby.

Today my dad agreed to increase and start a regular payment to her, on a monthly basis which is more than just nice but actually a critical movement in a largely paralyzed and insensitive world. At least that's what it feels like to be in here!

Today I smoked a spliff. When I say smoked a spliff I really mean that I smoked a cigarette like it was a spliff. And when I say like it was a spliff I mean that I inhaled it deeply to the root of my gut, and when I say to the root of my gut I mean the bones in my arms. And when I say the bones in my arms I mean the sinecure holding my bones to my arms and my arms to my wrists and my shoulders and my waist and my trousers. And when I say smoked a joint, I mean smoked some dirty crack mixed with brown sugar.

Crack is naturally white but looks a dirty colour after it has been cut. And when I say cut I mean cut with a knife or a razor. And when I say crack I mean heroin. And when I said heroin I mean I had sex. And when I say I had dirty sex I mean I used a condom. And when I say I had dirty sex I mean my girlfriend didn't enjoy it. And when I say my girlfriend didn't enjoy it I mean to say I had a w*. And when I say I had a w* I mean I injected dirty crack. And when I say the crack I mean I had a w* as even without cigarettes I need something, and my body by itself is weak and fragile and subject to chemical abuse and misuse!

Hi everyone.

My name is Joseph and today I would like to share with you all a little more about the martial art which I am studying. This is Ninjitsu and that is life. My first great teachers were the late and great Teenage Mutant Ninja Turtles. You know the ones: firstly Raphael (good with technology), Leonardo (good with Nunchuckas), Donatello (wise guy) and Mikey (laugh a minute). At least I think Leonardo had the Nunchuckas, but knowing my memory I may well have got that little detail mistaken.

Anyway with Splinter the Rat as their mentor, these aquatic mutants were also bound for greatness. Plus they team up with a human called Shredder who is sometimes good sometimes bad, kind of like a martial schizophrenic you might say. Also April the intellectual woman is on their side. And they are up against firstly Kerrang a giant Brain beast, although in terms of the TV series he actually died years ago.

I also know that they have to fight their own shadow in a certain episode, in as much as they have to fight each other. Some refuse to do so and some kick-ass. I think Mikey won the fight of the four on account of his honesty allied with awesome strength and weapon stuff.

But I wouldn't recommend on trusting honesty alone to win the war. The demons have twisted and manipulated people's minds to such an extent that finding an honest working man in this day and age, with honour and pride seems to be a hard thing to do (for me anyway).

'Where are the safest places for my most valued treasures?'
The blue ninja thought to himself one day whilst out walking
down the hill. 'If I hold my valuable treasures on me then they
may well be dropped if I am so clumsy as to do this. And even
if I do not then someone could rob them off me. So common
sense would tell me to put them in a bag. But even in a bag
they might get nicked, especially if one of my enemies has
inside information.

But even if he does not, the problem still remains that
he may notice from my body language and posture that I am
carrying something and hence decide to steal them on the
moment as it seizes him, so to speak. Then I am forced to
stash the goods in a safe place. Which can again be robbed. Or
an electronic bank which can be hacked. Probably a steel and
stone bank remains the safest place. Without this the goods
burn and don't I know it. I am no longer trying to own that
which is not mine. Only now that which is.

Face to face I square off with my enemy. He refuses
to look at me otherwise with a demeaning sneer. And I just
stare at his awesomeness with a pleasing aura and an unhealthy
stare. But am I bothered? I am learning the weapons, learning
the looks, learning the rules of the game and the health of the
fight. So when people kill I call foul play. Stop it, get a grip,
and control that unhealthy appetite if you don't want it cutting
off. Your tongue see. Even I am a barbarian. Even I have
manners.

Grief courses through my body like a rat on fire. Running blindly out of the sewers screaming a high pitched tone and flailing madly in all directions as it goes. A thick black fog descends over my eyelids as my third eye disappears and I am left with the large brown stain where once it was. But my skin looks and feels yellow.

I have been felled like the mighty oak which has had a chop cut out of it for time after time over all these years. Until nothing is left but a raccoon stiletto and a lumberjack's cry of 'Timber!'

The bees have left the hive, or rather I am like a solitary bee, or just the red sting throbbing after the injection: red, sore and unlit. Over the past few days I have seen the whole of life flash before my eyes. Happy times and friendship, love warmth and compassion. But yesterday I was over again left feeling cold and (also) alone.

Not a pleasant feeling, especially given there is so much at stake. But I am still fighting; to be quite honest with you, I consider that my green belt. I am now in the middle of earning my orange. I am sorry to translate everything into martial terms for you, but stuck in this prison hospital as I have been, sometimes that is the only way I know how.

I appreciate I have been very poorly over the past month or so. This has been, whilst of my own doing, also out of my control. I am rather like a leaf then in the wind. A little bit to do, a little bit of sky.

'What else can we talk about Joe?' asked Ren.

'Let's discuss the merits of the garden,' replied Joe.

'And what exactly are they?' inquired Ren.

'They are the flowers and the birds. The sunshine and the vegetables. The power and the faith. How is it that the shadow can sense my every move, anticipate my every weakness and beat me at my own game. I have to play fair and try and be a good dad.

I love my baby just as I love my fiancée; I love the flowers much as I love the mountains. Even as my friends desert me I can see clearly. But the pain only befuddles my vision and confuses it.

I'm not a loner but I have lost more fights than anyone I know. It's only when I am losing, however, that I can see with really clear vision.

Even my eyes betray a faltering heart which stutters and trembles at each and every last distraction. My writing seems to have a cooling and reflective process. Much as my species provides an outlet for my emotions. But my pain is palpable and my disgust universal. I cannot write any more.

Now I am swimming again. Plumes of smoke surround and embrace me, and carry me ever higher on a fairytale trip to the stars. In this wonderful hot air balloon.

James was an old teacher with a penchant for drinking cups of whisky. Joe was his young friend who one day went up to him to inquire what all the fuss was about.

'Look sonny,' James replied. 'It's simple; either you've got it or you ain't. And if you've got it the fortune cookies crumble your way.'

'Teacher,' Joe asked. 'You must help me.'

'How can I help you if you cannot even help yourself?' James scolded him. 'Even all the great artists of the modern world would do nothing to help a case like yours. You're a basket case – do you know that and all of your efforts have been in vain? Look at me; I'm the man. I can control my emotions and reap the rewards of my emotional output. Look at you; you are nothing, a mere bubble gum wrapper on the side of my shoe, ready to be kicked off and down the gutter when-so-ever I feel like it.

Your friends are retards and drug-addicts. They have about as much punch between them as a cowboy from the stars, flying through the night at half mast and crashing into a wide variety of comets and meteors along the way.

How many women have you slept with? One? Bah, I have nailed thousands, tens of thousands, and still I am hungry for more. Like a used fag end you have been raped and discarded. I hate you, not so much for what you have done but for what you are. A loser!'

Ancient Greek history is a great thing which most people in today's fast paced and hectic schedule seem to know little about. And no, I doubt that it's all about big men and small women. Even I love sex and I'm sure they did do, but I don't believe for one minute the lies that have been spread around their gay orgies or parasitical dithyrambs. Far from it. I think it was a place of soul and character. I'm sure the men back then were eventually conquered by the barbarians. But I am sure, if not certain even, that they put up a big fight and didn't take it lying down.

Sorry if my mind is somewhat befuddled at the moment, but that's what comes of being drugged up, stressed to the max and on lockdown.

All we have left down to us through antiquity is their tales of great adventure and godly epics. From Homer to Euripides, Socrates to Plato, the great Greeks sure left their stamp on the world of philosophy and religion among other things. Which isn't surprising given that they were very clever as I think I have already mentioned.

So yeah a few incomplete plays and nonsensical sayings about some men who ran up a mountain besotted by women, to 'I think and therefore I am'. What that hell is that supposed to mean anyway? I appreciate the importance of thought in existence, like we need to think to stay alive, to hunt for food and even grow vegetables to eat for instance. We need to think to dig up carrots and plants and then pick, chop and cook in a pan with hot oil, leek roots for another. But to annihilate the physical sensitivity as well as the spiritual one is much like digging yourself into a hole which becomes increasingly deeper and even harder to escape from. I also think we should remember here that history is written by the writers, and some glories of knowledge can only ever be seen deep in the universal heart, at risk of sounding fake and audacious.

Weakness is a metaphor which neither of us needs and none of us wants. The sides of my temple throb like my head is on fire. My backside canes. As does the little soldier. My neck hurts. My ears ache (probably another ear infection). My heart flutters. Where are my strengths then? My baby number one, my fiancée number two and myself number three. Four and five do exist but I'm going to keep stumm about em for the time being for the simple privacy of confidence, should be a fine thing. But the point remains. Seems like the odds are stacked against me, but this is my game as much it is his and hence I play to win. Trying to drown me, electrocute me, suffocate me, wipe me out, extinguish me, pollute me, poly-extricate me, grass on me and annoy me. I hate a grass. But I love grass. Joke.

A great man once said that history repeats itself. He sure got that right. Sitting here in seclusion yet again they have nailed me. In a small room about ten foot by eight, I turn left with nothing save for three cold beakers of water, a urine jug, a bed with a low pillow. And a ward full of enemies. There are some allies and even a couple of good friends in here. But my confidence is sapped by their every attack. Why can't the world just be a happy place, where mothers love their children? And men are kind and generous, supportive of their sons and not afraid to fight?

The world was supposed to become a much smaller place with the advent of the internet and the world-wide-web. But this is only for those lucky few who access to a sewer. For the rest of us we have to look forward to a microcosm of the martial arts, or rather a mini-adventure within the frame of a much larger one. I cannot possibly hope to win the fight on my own. The only way to do that would be with my allies.

I shall not name them for you now because I know that you are reading my every word and are eager to pounce on my mistakes. But if I say The East and The Middle East, perhaps that will give you some idea of where I am fighting from.

I cannot expect to win the fight on my own. But fight alone I must. And as the evil joker beseeches his wicked last laugh, Jack Windsor takes the piss with electrodes and even a laboratory. I don't think they did that to me. At least I hope they didn't. Also I will read you tomorrow too my love. I am fighting him.

'Hiya love do you think I'm not playing the game?' I'm playing the game like the rest of them.

The smoke soothes and cools my aching heart. I fall into a whirl-pool of colours and myriad of images. Each one transcending the first and each love surpassing the next. Until I have found my one. And I have found her. So what if she was raped and paraded across the front cover of my local daily rag, all in the name of commerce. Love is between kindred spirits and together we are stronger then the sum of our separate parts.

I love her and that is finite. That is final. And despite whatever he may do to me, he hasn't made her fall in love with him. Far from it.

Today, this morning I called her. And then I told her off. I told her off for sleeping with bad men and I told her to close her legs. And I shouted at her each step of the way. But how do you expect me to feel. Happy? Glad? Or angry and resentful. So that is why I hate him. But we kissed over eight thousand miles at the end of the conversation, and love like sleep, is a great healer.

The fight is nearly over. I can see the finish line in sight. My line of sight reveals a pot of gold at the end of the rainbow. Or a beautiful sunset hidden behind the dark stormy clouds. I'm not there yet but today I had a glimpse of something special, magical and something which I am not easily going to let go of. Even me, even her, even us. There are more ways than one to skin a cat. Make love not war. And little baby steps will make you a man my son. Our family has been torn asunder, but I have every intention of getting them back!

I think I need to add a short epilogue to this parable. Which is that I don't think that thieves are the worst kind of scoundrels. They are only doing their job which is basically attempting to wrest control over something which was taken from them a long time ago. They are only playing the game and cannot necessarily see the stars for the satellites in the dark navy blue sky. Even I was a thief once. I stole clothes, money, favour, friends, school work and sleep from God. But I am still fighting and loving and I am committed (to the pay-back).

A close friend once told me a very nice thing today. He said, 'You're born, you go to Heaven.' I think what he meant by that is that once we, as human beings, become good and honest people through and through, the need to play the sex game disappears.

Also I talked to another close friend this afternoon who told me that making a baby is the greatest thing two parents can ever hope to achieve. There is great wisdom in these words and I would be wise to heed them. Also yesterday I saw a lady for a kiss in the middle of the night, and today as well as seeing the Red Arrows in the sky I was born again and also saw the sun behind the clouds and also talked to the love of my life. She will save me where no-one else can.

5: Time Waits for No Man

The control is out of my hands. They call me a baby and laugh in my face. They steal my baby and steal my wives. They are trying to break me in two. They are my shadow. They are too dark for my eyes.

I try to retain order and stability. I try to sleep and heal. He kills me at my every turn. All because I once keyed his woman. But I am stronger now. I feel more ready for a fight.

One is for the babies. Two is for the family. Three is for love. Four is for charity and five is for companionship.

That is the truth and that is the way. So it has been said and so it must be written. And don't let any of those deceitful and lying back-stabbers fool you into one of their traps.

Don't let the evil men steal away your families and break your heart. Don't let them kill you.

'Ungh!' Joseph screamed as he was hit in the stomach. 'I will do you for that!' he roared, bleeding heavily internally.

'You frying pan,' his enemy responded with a sneer over his shoulder.

'Why when I catch hold of you–' big Joe tried again.

'You and whose army – a plumber's?' Brian called back.

'When I catch hold of you…' Joseph tried again, feeling desperate.

'Accept it; it's over!' his enemy triumphantly bellowed.

'Can I have some Weetabix?' Joseph tried again, this time somewhat sheepishly.

'Enough,' Brian snarled as he was walking away.

'Fill me up then, you service man.' Joe tried again. But Brian was too far away in the distance to hear him. And when he called out again he was long gone, busy with his own life, doing important things, meeting important people.

'A trial by Jury!' Joseph cried, before the racist jurors closed in on him, surrounded him and attempted to smother him. Stop it! he cried out in desperation, feebly struggling against the immense load. And it is only by the good grace of God and perhaps a pinch of good luck and a sprinkle of human realising-compassion that he prevailed against the load. Then, pulling himself to his knees, he tried again,

'I will hunt you down to the ends of the Earth, you dirty beast. This fight ain't even nearly over yet!' But as I think I have said already, his enemy wasn't even listening. World War three is a nuclear one, or it will be!

I need to make some more friends, Joseph thought to himself one day. With his friend, Shadow, long since departed he was now looking decidedly short on the ground in that department. And so he went out into the street and up to the nearest young person.

'Hello young person!' he said. 'What's your name?'

'Ninja?' the young person sheepishly replied, before Joe laughed and bellowed out loud.

'God? Dog spelt backwards! I don't believe in you or any of your false prophets. I have just witnessed my entire family, street, city, nation wiped out by your army, so don't talk to me about babies or nourishment being sent from heaven. Don't tell me of holy bandage to cover my cut. How can your bandage mend my broken heart?'

'Before we were as but children. We behaved as them, thought as them and were them in all means ways and to extent. But now I am an adult, I leave behind my childish things. That is as true and valid an exclamation I have made and I will stand by it, on threat not so much of death but of life.'

'For with the baby came responsibility, and the incoming parenthood requires a change of perspectives from certainly my part even if these others around me refuse to see it. They will over time.'

'Really?' The kid asked somewhat befuddled by what had just taken place before him, but still somewhat impressed never-the-less.

I'm feeling a little bit better today, Joseph thought to himself one late day, whilst quietly sitting down and listening to some tunes and quietly chewing a Nicorette.

Nothing much has happened to me, only the police were supposed to be paying a call to interview me under caution with regards to stealing a flame-thrower and using it to kill a man. Only joking – I didn't hurt a fly, only burnt a small gauge of flesh out of my arm. That didn't really hurt.

It's just the waiting. I actually packed my bags ready to leave for prison at one point, expecting the worst. But because I have been here before, like when I smoked a reefer on the Intensive Care Unit hospital at Kingsway, and the police actually paid a visit to investigate me then, except nothing was pressed. So I think there is a good chance that nothing will come of it this time. Except the heroes die futile battles fighting invisible beasties and knackered the deadly warriors into stone.

The time still awaits when these bronze mandarin Samurai will once again raise their heads above the parapet and lead us into battle again. So now I am waiting…

I look across to my side and see my two tiger generals standing steadfast and proud. Behind me my camp has been attacked. The houses are dying and inside the women and children are crying. This is Dynasty warriors and that is war.

Around me grunts line up. But at the first sign of rifle fire half of them tremble and the other half desert or, worse still, convert. Without my wife I am castrated. And I can hear my enemy laughing in the distance. To him it is all just a big game. Even you.

So what am I supposed to do? Retreat, never! Co-operate, okay to a point. But I will bow down to no man. End of.

6: Interpretation of Corinthians 1:13 from the Bible

Although I speak with voices and grunts, without energy and love I am but a hissing kettle or a dripping tap.

And although I can speak to others and believe in myself, without friendship and self belief I am but a liar and a fool.

And although I might have absolute power and perfect insight without friends I have no-one.

And while I can help the children and the elderly, if I cannot help the poor and psychotic I cannot help myself.

There are men to fear out there but if you are of a honest and decent persuasion you have nothing to fear of me. Only fear itself and rather the demons within.

Charity knows no boundaries, fears no men and helps no evil.

It never fails, and where there are lies they will fail. Liars will eventually sting and unravel as their treads become undone. But where there is love it will never fail.

The books may well be burnt just as the liars will grow fat. But then the thin ones will run faster and the decent men will survive. A hero runs fast and a martyr runs even faster.

For now we know in part and see as through tainted glass. But in the future we will see clearly even as we are ourselves seen purely as face to face.

Judgement is upon us and our fate rests in our own hands.

So I say to you this, the choice is now yours.

Time ticks by so slowly but time waits for no man. Without it we would lose our way, but with it we lose our minds. I am bored of waiting but we must wait. Time suffocates and surrounds me; I feel a strange sense of peace descending on my subtle corpse. I struggle to see but as it gets darker my eyes switch to red and then the enemy emerges with his gun blazing. How do I deal with these shadows? With stealth or strength? Strategy or secrecy?

An old friend of mine Arjun once told me that; 'the key to success is fighting with all your arms. How many do you have?'

I told him that he was half right. 'We need our left for shaking hands with, and our right for punching. Assuming our course you're not South-paw. In which case the situation is reversed. Without the soul the mind is but a blowing candle, and without the spirit the soul is meaningless. World war three was coming. I felt it. And this time the bomb was dropped!'

Though I speak with the tongue of prophecy if I have not love I have nothing.

Though I love with the heart of a lover if I have not charity it bequeath me nothing

And though I fight the demons of time if I have not strength I am weak.

Strength never fails but where there are fighters they will fail. Where there are statues they will fall. And where there is God I think that he is sleeping.

For whereas we once knew in part Now we know nothing. Where is this holy life which has been done away with?

Sacrifices to the lambs? Or to the demons more like it.

When I was a child I behaved as a child, spoke as a child and thought like a child.

Now I am a man I throw away these childish things.

As an adult I am my own master and I will bow down to no man. I will lead my own army into the world and hope to escape with minimum casualties. Triumphant.

The herald bearer carries a silver banner with his blue crosses hand painted on it in golden blue acrylics. Then we saw through a mirror but dimly and quietly. Now we will see truly even as we will be seen face to face on judgement day.

Santa eating pies. Xmas trees.

Green leaf tree, we've listened to Green Day

A present of the past that makes us so so so GLAD.

Happy Xmas for you boyz and girls

This is Ward 32 and we've got to celebrate.

HAPPY XMAS Derbyshire ward.

Don't be bored

Be glad don't be sad, we'll eat drink chit chat. Smoke on the Hour.

Blessing at Xmas, give peace all day

watch and listen for Santa's sleigh

You've pulled 2gether 2 make a good day.

Happy Christmas Ward 32

—McReble Man (my mate the shadow boxer, Dean, on a poster for a Christmas decoration which also coincidentally our ward won.)

7: To Where We Go

Shaking his head and rolling his eyes, our as yet unnamed patient rolled around on the floor of the room he found himself in. It was unlike anywhere he had ever set foot in before. Cold and alone. The walls stank of cobwebs and the doors creaked like the rusty hinges on which they had been hung God knows how many years before.

This place was not fit for rats much less the men and seldom women who were captured there within it, patient thought. But still he vowed to himself, even more determinedly now than ever before, that should he ever again see the light of day from outside of these cool cold prison walls, he would flee from this place so far away that even the shadows could not catch him.

He would travel to a different land, where they speak and think in a different language, drink a different wine, eat different foods, shake different hands, kiss different lips and emerge as a different man. This was his dream and God help any man who tried to wrest it from him. But God did they try.

I'm not going to bore you with the details of which they went to interrogate our prisoner. The sufferings and abuse they put this poor lad through in an attempt to break his spirit. And did it work? Well to learn the answer to that you're just going to have to carry on reading to find out.

You know, trapped in a cage, man learns a lot about himself. Such as the feelings of loneliness. What it means to have nothing, and what you have – the real value of any thing given to you. The treasure of a song in the Chapel when the outside world of Christians in a Christian country seem to have forgotten their very soul. And as they want you kept in here, or so it seems, you want to be out.

So you sing the hymns on the Sunday when you can remember to attend the service, and assuming you don't sleep in. And just as the patients come and go, so you get weaker and more desperate. I've not finished talking about this time.

I hear voices in my head. All the time sure I do. I think that the difference between me and most people, is that whereas I listen to the voices, others don't. Does that make me more dangerous than other people? I don't see why it should. Assuming that I keep control of my more evil tendencies and the harmful ones, then I don't see why it should.

I don't like being ignored, to be made to feel worthless and inconsequential. I don't suppose anyone does. One of the worst things, me and pretty much anyone who has been trapped in one of those places (psychiatric hospitals) for any great period of time will testify to, I would wager, is that you become a figure. A number for the government's NHS to crunch. And the outside world does look down on you. You can notice it in the looks cast your way when outside those perimeter boundaries. I'm not saying that everyone looks at you in that way. Sure they don't, but you should believe me that a great many do.

That's the second stint I have done in a psych ward, and the third in hospital altogether. The first being a three monther, and then two sevens respectively. If you must know, if you want to know my CV details.

Anyhow, another point I might add is that outsiders when admitted to the ward/hospital, clearly don't want to become a part of the system. God knows I vowed never to let it trap me in its greasy jaws again after being digested by it the first time. I even went so far as to write a book to challenge the legitimacy of the imprisonment, passed a college course, and still it got me. But now I'm out. Some things remain the same, such as I am writing another book. Some things remain similar. Such as my relationship with the majority of my friends and family, and my absolute refusal to learn to drive, not that they would let me, and some things are completely different. Such as my future plans for the next two years say.

It is lonely being in hospital. It's like a wedge is driven between you and the world around you and only the very strongest, or fondest of relationships remain.

Time can be a great healer for the wounds of the personality, of that I am sure. But time also creates echoes, and the waves erode the sullen rock face into dust. That is the reason why we must keep on walking and breathing, and talking. Friends will change, so will emotions, and people will age. Humanity does evolve, there are different cultures, and differences between cultures. Some wars will not be resolved in my lifetime, but we can but try.

My dad is a keen environmentalist. He stresses the need for collective action for change, and has picketed the local council to set up targets for the reduction in harmful emissions to help slow down the warpath humanity has seemingly set itself on. But I think that individuals' efforts need to be recognised, as not only does genius stem from ordinary people, but also everybody is unique and has a part to play. So it is important not to smudge them all together in such a way.

Let's get back to the case in hand. I think that I was talking about the hospital. Oh yeah, before I get back to that, I want to put up an argument for something else which my mum said to me today. She said that, 'The world isn't all just fantasy.' I appreciate this. I think we managed to talk about what I thought without arguing at least too much, and finished on a reasonably amicable note, actually on a different topic altogether.

I do certainly appreciate the time which she has spent visiting me when inside that 'prison', and she did see me frequently this time around. Having visits by loved ones means the world to us patients, and just in case you ever find yourself in the position of considering whether to while away a spare hour or two with a friend in a similar situation, regardless of the details or circumstances, I think that you should. Whether or not they show their appreciation for the visit is another matter; perhaps they are unable to; perhaps they are too ill. But assuming they do get through it, which I suppose the great majority will. Well they will remember that you were there for them in their harshest hour, of that I have no doubt.

So yeah, I was saying that I have seen a great number of people enter those four walls, still desperately trying to cling onto the ego and personality they had on the outside. But I haven't seen one, not one, that hasn't left drastically changed and warped even. Some get better. Some don't. But who am I to be the judge of that? Everybody is different. If there is one thing that you as a patient learn on the inside, and that is that how to impress a Doctor. As I have said already, some of us try to hang on for longer than others. Some of us have studied drama and so know all about personality impressions, and the whatnot. Some of the kids caught in the trap think it's a game, or a hotel even, and try to cruise along that way.

The lucky few don't have to change one iota and are taken favourably by their particular consultants and gone within two weeks. Some do two months, you know I think that that was probably the average time for a stay at the unit in the time I was there. Then two of us did seven months and a guy who I got friendly with before he got let out, did nine. His name is Luca, and I used to enjoy a drink with this Italian man, and a laugh.

You've got to try and make friends in there because they will help you through the difficult times, and also protect you from your enemies, of which you will also have. Especially if you appear as an 'independent' as having a mind of your own, or stand up for yourself in any given circumstance.

Relationships are strictly not allowed in the hospital I was staying at, at the time I was there. That's not to say that we didn't have them. Anything from a peck on the cheek, to a snog, to full blown sex does go on there I know that for a fact. But if it's caught out, even suspected by the nurses then you can expect to be split to separate wings of the hospital, with the resumption of contact only on the both of your discharges. By which point, either or both of the offending parties will have lost interest and gone off for greener pastures, or so the establishment – in this case the ward sisters – would hope. Sometimes that happens, and sometimes it doesn't. Mistakes are made in hospital, and this is probably the reason for the hospital policy. I mean I was accused of taking advantage of this one lass, even though a kiss is give and take. And even though they tried to split us, we still caught glances of each other when we could.

Of course it couldn't last. In my case. I was already engaged, and so there was no future in this hospital fling. But I have no regrets of anything that we did in there, and I hope neither does she. There are moments in life when you just need somebody.

I'm sorry if I'm making this sound a little melodramatic for you, but not only is that just my writing, and speaking style, but this is the honest way I felt events happened at that time.

This book is both a chance for me to get some thoughts off my chest, as well as to explore ideas with you, my reader, which I may not have had, and you probably haven't either, ever before.

One thing that strikes me as funny straightaway is that since being released from that trap, and I use this choice of words in no uncertain terms, is that the capacity for my work-output and by that I mean the quantity of writing I can produce in a single sitting, has gone up dramatically. Perhaps it has something to do with me being well. I am in no doubt that the fact that my meds have been chopped, gives me better concentration and clarity of thought. This must also affect it.

You may also notice that my confidence in my own written speech, and choice of words, has likewise increased. This is something which I have developed with the experience of writing one book already, not to mention having completed my college certificate. And is also affected by my general confidence in life, as attained by the resumption of a couple of old friendships, and when I say resumption I mean resuming, as a sane and out of hospital citizen, the strength of which they were before. Sure I may sometimes use words considered by some of you to be inapt and odd for the circumstance. I suspect that my grammar may sometimes be considered equally dubious, and likewise the content of this book. I mean what is it? Not fiction, not 'fact'. Its more just a personal log of events and feelings, of writings and expression. Creative writing, but with a purpose. I don't expect you to understand all of what I am saying, all of the time. Every reader is a different person. I do however hope to speak to most of you personally through reading this, and I hope that you can at least learn from my experiences if not my thoughts.

There are some things which I do consider it inappropriate to put. This may surprise some of you given my freedom of expression, and all. But certain people's feelings close to me, whom I respect, I will only try to honour by writing about and not abuse. Likewise I have chosen to go places which few writers dare to, I might suggest. I do this by facing reality by seizing it by the horns and squaring up to it one on one.

I have previously discussed major political world issues, not to mention rewriting a good selection of my earlier work, in an attempt to do it once the way it should be done. But I try not to copy other people, and hope to be as original as I can be forthright.

I was telling you about the time I spent in hospital. Okay. Well no, actually it wasn't, but I am out now. What's more, a couple of gals who I have been visiting have been, or are on their way to soon being, discharged, and the sooner I can leave those bad man walls the better.

It was funny how a good friend of mine commented, on the last time I visited the place with him, how everybody now knew me by name, or at least most of the people we seemed to meet in there seemed to anyway. Sure that was nice, to be remembered by these nice hospital staff, with a friendly word and a smile. But there were certainly times when I got more frowns in there than smiles. When I felt rejected, and not suicidal because I am past that stage of my life, but very low none-the-less. When no-one was listening to me, much less my parents or the Doctors. It is at times like these that it helps having other patients around you, with whom you can share your woes. It is true, I was changed wards thrice, between two main wards. So I saw quite a lot of new faces, not to mention that as people came and went, there I was staying the same. And when you are in there you make plans like to get out by Christmas. Well I got out in May, from October entry. You see what I mean?

I don't consider myself unlucky for what I have been through. I actually consider myself lucky for having the friends I have had, and many of which continue to have. I am blessed for having a loving and supportive wife, sorry fiancée, whom I am hoping to move in with soon. And for these reasons I think everything is now A-okay.

As I think I have already told you, despite being unpopular in all my classes at school, I was at least thrilled by drama, and considered myself something of a dab hand at it anyway. This and reading both plays, from Shakespeare to Stanislavsky has given me something of a theatrical pedigree.

Another of my loves is, and always has been, computer games. From the early BBC micro my dad used to own, to his PCs, to the play stations one and two, to the now towering heights of the Xbox360, I have probably spent more hours of my life blasting away at those things as you have had drinking hot tea. But I don't regret a single minute of it. Cause despite what they say about screen time causing brain damage and the what not, I also think that you can actually learn a lot from these things. Certainly my preferable ones (Role-Playing-Games) are often more akin to reading a book than doing anything mindless, and a good one at that. And whereas a book is generally written by one, or two, persons, a game can be designed and programmed by a team of anywhere up to a hundred dedicated people. Which assuming they get it right, which of course they don't always do, but when they do, then the finished product really is a work of art as much as anything else.

I appreciate that games are frequently looked down upon by some of the older, and perhaps less computer savvy generations. Sure many people just see them a waste of time and money, and they are expensive and many of us kids/young adults/adults do play many hours on them. But they do stimulate our imaginations, and I personally have learnt a lot about the games reviewers own prejudices and particulars, from reading them from the now free and online games website at IGN. Not to mention that particular site allows for us gamers to post, read, and so discuss amongst ourselves about the pros and cons of any particular given game. Thus it becomes evident that there are various camps of opinion (the most striking now being the differences between the Play station 3ers and the Xbox360ers), just as there seems to have been general points of consensus from the site's users, such as a love of gaming and entertainment in general, not to mention use of the internet and freedom of expression (i.e. to state your pet groans) etc. One thing is for certain, gaming is evolving. What many of these new-timers who jump in and throw 10s (that's a ten out of ten score) to some of these games, don't see is that what makes a game great is not just savvy graphics or even what other people/sites are saying about it. To understand that is really needed a comprehensive grasp of both what the machine, and mediums are capable of, and one of the best ways of learning this is through experience of them.

For all the difficulties and dislikes a player may or may not have with a particular game, at least they have this one thing over the older, pc and earlier counterparts. They have no bugs. I mean not the kind which stop the console from even loading up, or throw you out after the first thirty seconds play, which was sadly the case in the earlier generations, and hence a good reason why I am never going back.

8: Hope in Prayer

Enough about computers. As I was saying, in hospital I found a certain hope in the small chapel which opens twice a week. I tried to attend the Sunday service when I could, when I was able to pray and sing. This was like an eye in the storm for me, and I always felt refreshed and empowered after leaving the services. I think a large problem with today's society (especially here in the West), is that people are Godless. This country seems to have been built on the foundations of a bickering government, with no respect for mutual consent much less the Holy Spirit. My faith is not under question. It never was any time I attended the services in this hospital. Belief in God is a personal thing I suppose. It is also a shared thing. Much the same as love, or laughter, or discussion, or eating, is better shared.

People who attended the services changed, likewise I felt changes inside. I was very poorly after being admitted. My breathing was terrible for one thing. I think that this was mainly caused by my medication, but also not helped by my smoking. Which I gave up as soon as I could having left hospital, I might stress here. So I attended Holy Communion and there found time. I also worried quite a lot about my fiancée who gave birth during my stay in hospital. I had hoped to be there for her at that most difficult time in a woman's life. But we are planning to get together soon, and this time for life.

I think that the Bible is a book written by men. Inspired by God, but written by human hands, and a long time ago at that. It has since undergone numerous translations and revisions, and I fear that echoes of its message have been lost over the years and these processes. It is the Christian's main anchor, in literary form. So Jesus speaks to his disciples and miracles are performed. But I think that Jesus was a philosopher above all. And it was/is his philosophy which challenges men and women to look beyond their meagre existence to the source of all life, and love, as we know it. He says in one of Mark's books, that 'Which is it harder to do? For a man to renounce sin, or a cripple to walk again?' In this way he provides an answer by asking a question. This may sound contradictory, but much of the great ancient Buddhist scriptures (or koans) which I have also studied, are also posed as questions or unanswerable riddles. Here the power of Jesus is asking the reader to think into the matter. Some might say that sin is easier to renounce, physical disabilities are often genetic/inherited and apparently incurable. Surely anyone can enter their local church or temple of their faith and renounce sin to the altar. But I think that some people don't even recognise that they do sin. They don't accept the notion of a fraternity of believers, much less of mankind, and reject the importance of repentance. In this way it is not simply enough to go to your local church once, or perhaps when you feel like it, to renounce your sins and be saved. The idea of 'born again' would well suggest that to find the Lord, it is only necessary to do away with your old sinful self and enter the life of a Christian to cure all of your problems.

Believe me this just won't cut it. Not to mention the fact that a great many of our problems are shared, so our sins are shared too. And we as people live in a communal society. There are things going on out of our control, but I think that if we do take control of our own lives then there is a great deal more open to us than most of us imagined. Back to the quote. I think more than just challenging the reader to think for themselves, the Bible is also asking us to examine the nature of sin and, in this way, also look at our own participation in it and in so doing, how we can change the world.

It would be a cosy fantasy to imagine that we live in a world with borders and walls beyond our control. Indeed, once erected, a concrete wall certainly seems immovable to the prisoner caged behind it. I can vouch that from personal experience as you will probably appreciate having read this far. Yet isolated we are alone, and fragile and weak. Stripped of his clothes man is cold. Stripped of his food, hungry, without books and games he gets bored, without companionship lonely. This is the fact of life and not open for debate. Certainly some people think they have 'got it made'. They do not fear the challenges isolation presents when it invariably does. They think that they will live for ever. And so in this way they are unafraid to go pillaging and raping virgin rainforests, native continents and countries, be it for oil or Titanium.

But equally as the weaknesses of the individual become apparent in the dazzling glare of the approaching car headlights, so the strength of men united is made much greater than the ability of them apart. A survey, or expedition may be put together to include specialists from different fields in order to get a job done. I know that from Star-trek, where Kirk would select a few to beam down with him who had the necessary expertise. Likewise an orchestra needs the percussion, wind, strings and piano generally, to play a complete symphony. We can also appreciate that a Rally, whilst not operating along a strictly delineated or defined structure, is made real by the spirit of the damn thing. The old socialist marching phrase, 'The workers united, will never be defeated' and 'united we stand divided we fall', seems to conjure up the sentiment of the expression I am seeking here perfectly.

Back to the question of sin. Well, I made the point that the trapped individual has no means of escape. I am not challenging this premise. Flesh cannot break through concrete, or perhaps Bruce Lee might be able to smash his way out, but most of us ordinary civilians certainly couldn't. And they will try to break you. By keeping you in for all that time it is almost as if they are trying to drill into your brain – not just that you have erred, but that you are a lesser person than they are and always have been.

You need to take meds because of your biological deficiency. But I thought God created his children perfectly? I hear the good man cry. Not for you, the Doctor scorns. You were built Imperfectly. A mistake. Clearly he took his eye off the instructions, and thus you are doomed to a life of a zombie-like stare, walking into lampposts, always feeling sleepy but not being able to get to sleep, always feeling bored but not being able to sit and concentrate on anything for more than a minute at a time. This is what you are and this is what you will continue to be.

Well I chose something else. I chose not to submit to their will, their machine. I never intended to get caught, then when I escaped, I mean for the second time, I didn't look back. I have made some good friends on the inside. Most of them I will never see again. That doesn't mean that they weren't good friends. I think that I have probably made some of the best friends I have ever had in that relatively short time I was in hospital. It just means that things move on. They will remain with me in my memories, and my ID for a good while yet. Perhaps 'til the end of my days.

My friends teach me to be loving and kind, to share and to smile, to look forward to getting up in the morning and not to be afraid of going to bed at night. They each teach me something new. They are like colours which enliven my painting.

But in hospital each and every patient is fighting his or her own personal struggle. With the system, with themselves. Perhaps with the medication, perhaps with the police on the outside, perhaps with their family, their neighbours, their mind. Although I can quite honestly say that in hospital I have never met a more decent and sane bunch of people than ever before. One thing is that the friends you make in hospital stay in hospital. I think that this is a sad but perhaps inevitable truth. Which is that we all had our own lives upon being admitted, with which the cosy worlds we lived in were suddenly and horribly snatched away from us. And we all leave, or most of us do, scarred from our stays. Sure we learn things, such as better communication skills and an honesty to live, to face unknown strangers kindly and give them the benefit of the doubt. Certainly I think that the patients from our hospital by and large turned out this way. With an honest to goodness approach to things and other people in general. What was I saying?

Oh yeah, we all have our own battles. And we make associates and friends along the way. Last time I was in intensive psych care I said that, 'No friends in this place, only associates,' and I think I was right, to a point. Perhaps I was too ill to have known the difference. And the whole set up over there seems to be a bit different, a bit more like lockdown than at this other lower grade hospital. But they were both secure, and they were both difficult. If anything being 'inside' only makes me more determined to get things right when I get let out, which I was sure I would. Now I find this network of friends invisible if not disappeared completely. That's not to say that I feel like I don't have any. Far from it. I am fortunate to live in an area of the city where people are friendly and there are things to do with my spare time. Not to mention I have got my Xbox360 (the latest games console) working, which has given me and I hope will give me many more hundreds of hours of entertainment still to come in the near future.

It's just that on discharge, people, most people, try to get on with rebuilding their lives. Away from the hospital. Perhaps with family, perhaps with their jobs. Most people are lucky to get visitors, which help tremendously to break up the monotony of the week. Realizing the value of this, not to mention that of the friends I still had on the inside, and that I didn't have anything better to do with my time on the most part, I have actively tried to get back to the place to visit some of my friends there, when I can. Now though it seems that they are all moving on, and so should I. But as I get older I am starting to value my memories more. And as the pain of my childhood recedes into the darkness of oblivion, so the light of my future guides me on my way. I don't think that there is anything wrong with remembering the good times we had together. And I am hoping that there will be many more to come. For both of us, with new friends and old ones too.

Yeah, so I think that a wall can be knocked down if enough people want it done. And Jesus was a friend before he was anything else. What was the point I was trying to make? My Doctor told me off the last time I saw him, for rambling, like I have just been doing now I suppose. But there was a point, just like I told him. Let me remember. Okay, earlier I was saying that together we sin. And I think that these sins are often group help prejudices, such as propagated by the trashy newspapers and BBC. Like how they hijack an article or item and subject it to their own western analysis and persuasion. Then expect the mass public to believe them because unfortunately a great many of them will because they know nothing better. And in this way wars are fought, and lives lost. This is sin, and that is reality. But not my reality. I don't believe everything they tell us. I have studied the press long enough to appreciate their bias and distortion. But I could go on forever about this aspect of life and that is not my intention right now. What I will do instead is go back to what I first was talking about when I started writing today.

Oh yeah, I was talking about visiting the chapel. I also remember walking around the outside of the building and looking at it. Seeing that it had an upstairs (behind the congregation spot) and wondering what went on up there. This is a memory. I think unlike the first book I created, which will be remembered for its mistakes as much as its original style of rehashing old legends, and organic artwork, I want this one to retain a sense of organic writing but to carry on with more of the self reflective and philosophical side of my work. My writing will have evolved as indeed my thoughts of myself and the world around me have changed as I have met new people and undergone the various life experiences which have made me who I am today.

Such as being a new first time father. Albeit across the sea, to a family which isn't even my own. The love is however. And as I write, and my confidence over my ability in the use of the English language improves, I am not afraid of speaking in a way in which I would not (speak). Which is to say that I can churn this stuff out, without fear of the consequent blasts and incrimination from some disgruntled teacher or lecturer, questioning my spelling or grammar. I write like I speak. Or at least I don't write like I speak; the written word is a different medium altogether. With different purposes. But when I am writing my books, it is for an unquantifiable audience. Certainly the first one was. In this way I required myself to tone down some of the more sophisticated poetical excesses and imagination. But on the second, while still given the freedom of expression, and still determined to explore certain thoughts and areas of my life previously untouched, here I can narrow the focus. Here I am no longer forced to cater for the younger elements of the population simply from the knowledge that out of the first print run I don't think that one kid bought a copy of my book. I still write like I speak. Thoughtful, carefully measured. But speech I mean when we speak it is generally for a one on one. When we write a book it is for the world.

I think that fatherhood, much as leaving hospital (again), much as resuming a good relationship with my mum, and continuing a strong one with my girlfriend are all important life stages, which perhaps looking unavoidable on paper, actually have been very important medals in my life. And I wear the medals.

Please don't be thrown back by the way I speak, the way I write. I think that the creative imagination should be allowed to explore the wonders of adventure and the human spirit. These are not just words as I have been thrown by my dad on more than one occasion (as he clearly does not appreciate the experiences to which I am relating) but more a gateway into a heartfelt expression and personal journey of discovery. I do think that I am important. When I play my computer games I can rule the world, so to speak. And I rule my world, by creating and attempting to hold onto relationships and things around me. I try to keep in control of my own destiny. There certainly seem to be elements which challenge this cosy sense of well being which I attempt to surround myself with. And my dad's not the only one.

Ah I have forgotten what I was going to say. Okay, so with language and its use, we as people can go beyond the expected. There is a known approach to intelligence called IQ (which stands for Intelligence Quotient), and is the perquisite for the membership to Mensa. This is tested for by some cruddy generally mathematical like paper based tests and is supposed to determine something about you, like, well how clever you are. There is also another little known intelligence called Emotional Intelligence on which I have also read a book, which involves a completely different area of the mind and cannot be tested for. I think that lots of people who would do terribly at the IQ tests would come out as champions on EQ. Not that there is a test for EQ. Clearly there is not; this is something like what a mother feels for her baby, or a friend for his friend. All I am saying is that there is often more than meets the eye to many of the people you meet out there on the street. People generally are good, and should be given the benefit of the doubt. Even convicted criminals should be listened to and by and large helped back into normality. I want people who read this to come away with not just a sense of empowerment, freedom and hope, but also the idea, the conviction, that they are able to achieve the dreams to which they have set out to aspire in their lives, however many years they have left in front of them.

I was once described as something of a dreamer in an online discussion site: a dreamer, a prodigy even. I think that the guy who posted that was referring to my debate on some current political hotspot of the time. But for him to come out with that description of me made me feel happy and proud. I think that it is a generous compliment, which he didn't have to say, especially considering that he started on an opposing side of the fence in this given debate. And I am not saying that he has forgiven me for all of my sins, if he could even do that anyway. Just that he recognised some of the things that I had told him such as how I was, and am still, trying to help one of my good friends from hospital return home, and in this way share an expression of faith. I'm going to leave it there because I have been rattling on for some time now. But I am sure that if you make efforts in your life, to communicate to others and defeat your own personal demons, then I am hopeful you will indeed be able to do these things.

9: Fuzzy Logic

Perhaps you think that I am too fuzzy in my appraisal of things. Perhaps my writings strike you as too off the beaten road, too imprecise, too loose in getting to the point. Perhaps my style of work comes across as confused, that I don't know what I am saying or thinking about myself. Or maybe you disagree with some of the evidence/theories I use to compile some of the conclusions I reach. I suppose you could question what I have done with my life, without examining or appreciating how I have got to where I have today. I appreciate that few other writers use such a scrubby and wavy approach to determine what results to be as not just powerful but concrete and very sharp decisions. Yet this is the way I work. People couldn't criticise me for my honesty no matter what you think of my outcomes. And I think a lot of people will be able to relate to my thought processes as I faithfully replicate what I am thinking to the written page as per se. There is no difference between this loose thought and my thoughts. I appreciate that most people seem not to think like this. Blame it on my head injury, my mental illnesses, an erratic and at times eccentric personality, a personality disorder or whatever. I would prefer that you attribute it to a fertile imagination combined with a fuzzy grasp of logic as argued for by a combination of the chaos theory, theology and my right to exist as a human being combined. This does not make me who I am so much as explains my way of tackling certain arguments. So I do not believe in a 'right' way of doing things, much as an engineer or soldier would, and towards which most teachers would teach. After all in school there is only one correct answer to the sum two plus two equals four, isn't there? This is actually not the case, as I discussed with my philosophy teacher at college. Or not so much, it isn't the case, so much as it doesn't have to be. Sure for all intents and purposes, for the soldier in the field the orders are clear just as are the requirements of the task in hand. Likewise for the engineer, if the sums don't add up the building will fall over. But for the theologian, or the philosopher working at a high level in today's rich and diverse political and cultural economy, a basic mathematical deconstruction to problems only provides one possible solution to the quantums being asked of them. Such as does god exist, or what is the colour of the soul? These challenges can be addressed in a formal environment, I suppose it will only enhance the cause by subjecting them to a precise and calculated examination required of the teaching professions/schools. But still that does not mean that an unorthodox or even free-radical cannot approach the subject and possibly emerge with some startling and hitherto unforeseen insights. I suppose it's like the question of how did the pyramids be built without modern design and technology. I suppose any such insight coming from without the university hierarchy will be sniffed at and ignored quicker than you could blink your eyes. But was not Van Gogh a certified madman, his great paintings only recognised once he was dead. I think quite a few geniuses of the past were not appreciated in this way during their lifetimes alone, and so I suppose too, were there great men (and women) who died taking their knowledge with   them to the grave.

But I also think that we would be mistaken to judge a person by their visible creations/constructions. Jesus Christ was not famous for any physical monuments or such like. It is the legacy of freedom and compassion which he left behind, which inspires men and women to pray in his name to this very day.

The challenge presented before each of us is to lead a good life, a law abiding one, perhaps raise a family, perhaps get a job, and so doing become an ordinary and decent member of the community. Whatever your colour or creed.

So as I was saying, in primary school Maths, secondary school and indeed much of the other curriculums, at indeed any level, the requirements for the exam will, in our society, stipulate that the right answers are provided for the questions. Or the right style, and content sought. This is not to challenge the whole of the education faculty, although I do. It seems to be geared up especially for rich 6th formers who watch the right programs and know how to provide what the markers are looking for. Basically it's a con. When providing higher level work, the choice of words made by a free thinking egalitarian will not necessarily meet the requirements for the rigid and strictly static question marker. So for instance, if the student is answering a question by asking another, as a means of approach the marker may well not be able to do this, and so will provide at best a question mark, which denotes as much. And does not provide the all important tick. Then having lost the thread of the discussion, it is highly unlikely that they will ever pick it up again, as a good essay should build from one point to the next, in its journey towards completion. So the student who actually surpasses the boundaries required for this given subject area will find himself penalised and failing as a result. Then it is down to him or her, to conjure up some other white rabbit from his box of tricks, such as making an appeal against the grade, before being doomed to resit or drop-out. And yeah this has happened to me.

But for the student of life working for no-one but themselves, and beyond the constraints of the straightjacket which is another's institution, the only off button is on the switch on the lamp at the side of your bed. Meaning that you can continue learning right the way through life, both from what you read, the discussions you have and the people you meet. There is no right and wrong way to go about many things in this life. New parents will love their babies no matter what. So there is no right or wrong way to love. Sure sometimes infatuation and love can have blurry boundaries. But that is generally one of the good things in life, although it doesn't always seem that way. It is better to have loved and lost then not to have loved at all, is one of the mottoes I swear by and will continue to do so until my dying day.

I am not saying that my 'fuzzy' approach to things is the only way of doing it. Far from it, the more conventional straight and fast approach certainly does have its benefits in any given situation. Yet people generally stick to what they know, and specialise in this. Then when they are required to step beyond the realms of their expertise they are found at a loss. Now they resort to deeper instincts and gut impressions.

I am not trying to slag people off. But another thing I have tried to do in all of these years of inaction, is trace my own, and those around me, fears and mass feelings. So I have followed mass emotions, be they fears, or thoughts, leading to wars or elections. This is initially quite a thankless task, and on occasions I have been criticised for my thoughts. I especially had this problem at school, when I remember sticking up for the Vietcong outside of class one day, as just one example. I'm not going to explain that here, just say that I am used to struggling against the tide from an early age, and find that it is only now as an adult, when I am attempting to spread my wings, that I am able to do so.

Having left home I can actually talk to and see other 'freedom fighters' who are not afraid of sharing my points of view and finding that it is okay to be different. Maybe one day there will be enough of us differents, to actually be considered normal. And I don't think that that day is far off at all.

So we keep on struggling and keep on arguing. I do hold a good sense of morals I would say. Sure I am a sinner, and I can't always keep to my word. Yet I don't lie purposely. And never to my wife. In this way I do consider myself a good person trying his best in the world, and I hope that if you read this you can appreciate what I mean. Thanks a lot.

The skies this morning were blue, and that promoted me to wear my shorts and t-shirt and sandals. Suddenly I am on the beach again, the sun beating down upon my back and the waves lapping at my heels. I can see the little baby crabs scuttling about from one dune to the next, always in search for something to eat or a plaything to occupy its time. I can see the dozen or so fishing boats out at sea, the African boys kicking a pigskin about the beach, the hotels up over the ridge where they are safe from the ever encroaching pain of the sea. And I feel happy, with my loved one on my arm, or holding my hand at least. This is not paradise, it is the real human world. But actually for me it is paradise. An escape from the rat-run of my old life. The always busy chase from one job to the next, from one street to the next, from one industry to world domination. But here in Africa, I can be my own master and not somebody else's slave.

Sure I still like playing on my xbox360. I am after all a cyber kid, brought up into the cyber age and electronic world of master and domination. But I am truly excited by this exotic culture of new sounds and tastes, of new music and new emotions. Who would have thought that the other side of the world actually tasted this good? That it actually was like a completely different planet. I have had access to a new phenomena, a new experience.

Not just is the Kenyan way of life a new way of living, but something which changes me, makes me stronger and endears me to it. Of course I travel, not as a journalist, or a backpacker, or a tourist. But as someone who wants to escape from the pain of his past. From the monotony of England and the greed and selfish self-centredness of it all. I have earned the right to live there. Having suffered as I have since my accident, having suffered going through college after college, always seeking to meet the right one. Until eventually I found her.

So now I commit to her. I give her everything I can. Not everything I have got, but at least half of it. That does not seem unreal to me, but actually fashioned in the way marriages were designed. Were meant to be. This is not about love but a lifelong commitment. It is more than love. I hope that every-one reading this has been in love sometime or other in their lives. I dare say you all will have been. I imagine it is, after all, part of the human condition. Something which gives us our soul and the strength to say that I am. That's sweet.

My missus gives me something else. She gives me support when I have no-one else. She is my best friend and my most valuable critic. She is my lover. She is my everything. Who would have thought that I would have been blessed to meet her. In this respect I am very lucky. And I am damned if I am going to let the evil ogres of the country steal her away from me, ever again.

That is why there are none of my family invited to my wedding. Just leave it at that. If I do so choose to have a reception back in good old Blighty at some point in the future, well so be it. But not this time, not now. I plan to marry in Kenya, to a special person. That's my decision, right? No one can take that away from me.

What else shall I talk about today? Well I saw my sister yesterday. It was good to see her. I don't get to very often, now that she is going to university in Manchester, she has her own life and I am proud of her for having done it. She has her own friends and relationships. The past is in the past and thank God for that. But whereas I don't see eye to eye with my dad on a great deal of things, with little sis I am able to talk openly and expressively about the things which are important to me. Like how I was buggered at college by a mass paedophile, so to speak, or helped out greatly by another of my teachers. These are things that I remember, struggles I have been through, moments of difficulty, but I persevered and got the certificate in that case. There have been many more times before when I did not.

I often struggle. I often do. This is not something I like. I think that overcoming difficulties makes one a stronger character inside. But constantly battling back the hatred can pose a difficult time of your mental equilibrium. Finding solace from pain is not easy and difficult at the best of times. We have to try and support each other wherever we can in this turbulent world.

I don't think that there is one person who owns all our money or deals the cards. More like we are each dealt a hand and have to play it as best we can in life. I'm not saying that things are equal; clearly they are not. Some people seem to have a lot more power than others. But it is actually the organisations and institutions which run the show, on a large part at least. So the media controls the perceptions of those who don't know better, certainly it affects them, whether they believe the lies or not. Trust me. I have studied the facts, of the Vietnam war, of Iraq and to a lesser extent Afghanistan. And I do talk to people. Not to mention I study language and have learnt a great deal about the way the populous thinks.

So in this way, yeah I do consider myself just and able to stand by any and all my convictions. On particular facts I may make slight mistakes, the occasional errors in judgement and whatever. But my insight into the operations of the machine, be it media, the government, and the learning of years of careful study of the workings of the heart, do give me credit and ability where others have none. Most people are so concerned with the workings of their own lives, the details of their own business to want anything to do with me. That's okay, as long as they don't kick me in the teeth. Or try and hurt me.

Perhaps I deserve what I have suffered. I suppose I do to an extent. I think I have put enough back into the world however to think of myself and my family now. I mean my immediate family. I don't propose to flee the country, rather take a graceful exit. This is my right as a free citizen, which I am now once again, having left hospital and been taken off section once again (thank God), and one I fully intend to endorse. The old motto goes; 'you don't realise what you've got until its gone' and damn that's true. But now that I have got most of it back, there will be no turning back. Not this time.

No more putting up with the bull-trouble from the liars and transvestites. No more suffering the pain of others through a world of hell and hell-fire. To live beneath the pavements of the supposed heaven dwellers and hence being clear up their trouble after them, is not my idea of paradise, and belongs to no Jesus I intend on worshipping. I don't want to confuse the issue too much here, nor to offend people who are sensitive to this topic. But the more atheists I see, dumping on the civil liberties of the past, the more I remember. And remember when I escape this prison, there will be no turning back. There will be no forgetting.

The good people should receive their just rewards and the bad can rot in hell for all I am concerned. After what they have done to me and my (spiritual) family. You bad men.

I am very sorry if today's writings at least thus far, have given you the reader the impression of a personal struggle in my head, between me and a number of demons. This may or may not be true. I mean, I believe what I say, and when I feel up to it, I feel that I have the confidence to say it. Some times it takes a young(ish) person to say these challenging ideas, to take the beast by the horns so to speak. No one else'll dare to. Yet still I have other times when I feel low, and I hope that in this book, this time, that I am creating something that I can be proud of. That I will be able to look back on and hand down to my children as a part of who I want to be and like a good piece of music, executed well. Do you understand?

Sometimes in order to appreciate the meaning of what I am saying I suppose it will be necessary to read the text slowly and carefully. If you are one of those types who jumps to conclusions, who skips to the last pages of a book in order to summarise the middle, who thinks they know everything I have to say before I have even said it, well I suppose you will have already made your mind up by now and may as well not even bother reading any more at all. Or go ahead and do what you were going to, read the last page and then put this away. You know, I think that firstly you are doing neither me nor yourself any great favours. Well, I hope that many more people will enjoy reading this, and right the way through. Will give me the time to listen to what I have to say and the way I am saying it. Will try and picture the images I conjure up perhaps from their memories and imagination. That is not so difficult, is it? I enjoy writing sure. I like reading good books, but have reached a point in my life whereby I think I do have enough good comments and stuff to say about the world and am taking this opportunity to do so. And despite the times when I feel that I don't, I suppose that I have been blessed with a group of good friends, mostly about my age, but not all, who God has given to me in His wisdom. This lets me find freedom.

My friends have a great effect of influencing and creating me. These little relationships with other active spirits, help us all on our journeys through life, and that's just great. Then please try and listen out for wisdom when you can hear it. Whether or not you believe in the Holy Spirit, well that is your personal choice. Surely that is crucial and critical. A basic human right, although there would be those who seek to deprive us of them, knowingly or otherwise. Still we all need friends, and happiness. For our moments alone and with others in good company. For when we are doing good work, and when our hands are tied. I suppose I'm gonna finish with a poem, or a line of poetic verse. Which is; The road we have travelled has been a long one, and we're not there yet. But keep up the faith and your pride in who we are, and let us hope that we will make it safely through to the morning.

Okay I appreciate that some of you may think that this book is somewhat an attempt to receive attention and thereby be a case of self commiseration. While I accept this to be true, to an extent, I also see this as a chance to correct the mistakes of my last book (Jojo's Amazing Adventure). That book was very much a collection of short stories, as well as other mostly creative writing. Which could, and was very much expected, to be read as the reader saw fit. So it could be read as a whole, or in pieces, much like the bible. On the other hand, for A Patient in Time, I am attempting to write it with the minimum amount of outside interference. And I am specifically intending for it to be read from start to finish.

That is the only way students of my work will be able to gather a full understanding of what I am trying to say in my writings. I do not mean that excerpts can't be taken and analysed separate from the whole. Certainly this is a valid means of study, when used to back up a certain point which another author/writer may be trying to make. Yet all I am asking is that, for the reader to try as best they might, to finish the book once they have   started it.

Obviously I do not mean anyone to rush through, I actually think that to be fully appreciated, this as any other literary project, is best read slowly and carefully in a non-rushed manner which could threaten to glaze over any subtleties that the author could place in that project. I also do try to write in an easy going manner, which very much does replicate the way I speak. So there is an element of the oral tradition in there as well.

I actually had something of a big row with my mum earlier today regarding the significance of spelling mistakes/typos in literature, or specifically this book. Her argument seemed to be that a certain amount of time needs to be spent proof reading a work in order to obliterate these. By contrast my argument was that 'over' proof reading/editing actually led to errors being inserted into the book, especially when the additional work is being done by person/s who do not fully understand the writing methods used and thereby are liable to mistake unusual, but intended spellings of words for mistakes.

I guess not a lot of people realise, but I actually began and largely finished work on another small book in-between my first printed one and this. In that one I paid especial attention to the use of language and words, and also included something of a comic element into some of the chapters. I had previously heard how people like to laugh, and felt quite happy at the time, and so was able to, I think, put that happiness onto the page. Whether it would have had the desired effect, I mean whether it would have actually got people laughing now I guess I will never know. Cos I destroyed that document with my second 'invitation' into the psychiatric wards. Okay.

What was I trying to say? About spelling not being critical to the effect of a book's output? Something like that, if you can even understand what that means. To expand this idea, it is not a case like in school where the GCSE teachers will mark you down for so many spelling mistakes, etc. I am writing for an educated audience, who I don't expect to understand every word which I use (or grammatical order in which I phrase them). Not because I have used an 'invalid' use of the English language (if ever there was such a thing), but simply because in the case of spellings, they may not have encountered that word before, or grammar, they simply haven't spent long enough to understand what I might mean.

I do have a knowledge of language, built up from my French studies at school, and subsequently looking at both Arabic, Chinese (written Mandarin specifically), and Swahili in some detail. I am not saying that I am fluent in any of these, most certainly I am not. But my studies of language have taught me that the first most import thing to be multi-lingual is to be a good listener. Ultimately the use of particular vocabulary, and its precise spelling, falls far short of the carry of meaning to the listener or in this case the reader. So If you are in a foreign country and cannot so much as order a loaf of bread in a shop because of your poor communication skills, what good is that?

Likewise I am able to watch foreign TV, in languages which I don't understand, and still laugh at the jokes. Maybe I wouldn't understand them fully, but as I am trying to express, I think that there is actually a lot more to communication then just the way it is written.

I am also a musician I might add, and the element of music should remind us that things like rhythm and harmony are also important. This may at first look odd and incompatible with the written word on the paper page. But as alliteration and onomatopoeia use the words to achieve granted effects, so also the ease of writing and clarity of expression also achieve something else. I suppose what I am trying to say is that one of the features of my work is an attempt to speak to the reader directly and face to face as it were. I am sure that you can picture me speaking this stuff in front of you, in this way.

Certainly I imagine you are probably able to do this with most modern fiction, which is now generally written in an easy to read, and enjoyable style. But unlike other fiction, I endeavour to be honest. I do not make up make-believe characters and place them in imagined settings facing fantastical personalities and undergoing purely mythical adventures. I deal with the here and now. With what's happening to me. And I don't lie. Certainly that is one of my sticking points, one of my virtues which I am proud of and I think that is a strength as well.

That is not to say that I do not write creatively. Far from it. I have tried to explore my emotions and imagination both in the preceding pages and will continue to do so, with a power which I hope supersedes any of the grim sticking points which the reader may themselves face in my work with their journey though it. And in this way I am able to produce a unique but none-the-less effective BOOK.

Ah. It seems like I have spent the last two pages at least justifying myself to the world with self reflection and the what-not. But where's the fun in that? Well it is something that I felt I needed to do, both on the back of a fierce (if infrequent) argument with my mum, and through a personal inclination and intent as well.

I remember at primary school, I was criticised by the Royal-School-of-Pianoforte music examiner for hammering down the notes too hard when I played through my grade two set pieces and thus only managing a pass for them, even though I had hoped for more. Then perhaps I was treating that instrument more like a drum than a piano. But in fact I actually think that this is just me. I mean this is just the way I am. I seem to be more bothered that the right notes are played in the right order, than the delicacy with which they are hit. And I do tend to be slow to learn new things, and even perhaps pick up on certain emotions. Yet I don't so much as blame this on anything internal.

Nah, I am happy with who I am, and now as an adult I do have a small circle of adult friends who I get along with just fine. And if there are others out there who don't like this, well they can just go and shoot themselves for all I care.

As adults people should respect one another, and share things and just be good people. Not doing so, and living in the past is both ignorant and childlike. I will stand up for my rights and those of my friends, just as I would have appreciated for someone else to do so on my behalf when there was no-one else. But that is the past and this is the present/future. It is important to be self-empowered, but if you are one of those well paid people with a good job somewhere doing whatever you may be doing.

Don't think that that gives you the right to look down on someone who doesn't have a job, who can't do what you do, who doesn't think what you think. There are too many ignorant people in Britain, who get paid a lot of money, and never have found themselves on the wrong end of the law and so are happy to laugh in the face of those less successful/fortunate than themselves. By all means, many people will lead happy lives, and never have any problems with the authorities and or the general 'public opinion', so by going to their graves in this way.

But if you have never stood up for the oppressed, for those at the bottom of society who don't have it as good as you, can you really understand their plight? If you have never spoken to, let alone related with the 'other side' how can you claim to know them? Let alone know them well enough to kill them. I don't mean to relate everything to war, but it does seem as if a lot of the hatred in this country, certainly on behalf of the whites, is generated and fostered by this fact. But if you knew what I know I guarantee that you wouldn't be so coy in toeing the party line. Not that I'm even going to begin to attempt to tell you any of those details, and provide even half of a description of this. Let's just leave that subject now as best we can.

I was hoping to talk to you a little bit more about metaphysics before I leave you today. That is a realm philosophy which attempts to understand and explain the reasons and causes of things, beyond a simple theoretical platform. To attempt to delve beneath the covers and pull up the roots. To collect and appreciate the human significance of the study of thought as being essential before separating and exploring these ideas and facts whatever they may be.

This probably all sounds a bit puzzling to you, especially if you don't know about the structure of philosophy let alone any levels deeper. Well it is difficult to explain, not least because I studied it at college a while ago now, and despite remembering the feelings and emotions of tackling some of the challenges presented by the studies at the time, I am struggling to remember the specific details. Suffice to say that there are currents, I am certain, beyond the evident easy to use and accessible surface layer, of the sciences, and various other schools of thought as well.

Meta-philosophy must be studied in first hand, to be grasped. It is like what makes a man from a boy? That is not just the physical age, but the mental one as well. There are a great many so called men who actually wouldn't know how to be a real man, if it was written down for them in a book, it is my opinion. So you have to study the workings of things, that is philosophy, and then after a while hopefully you can begin to go that stage further. As I have said already, I find it very difficult to describe this experience, and these emotions. To the cold piece of paper. I realise that you may have no idea what I am talking about. It is certainly a deep thing, and its complexity will be beyond some people. But I hope that I helped some others to be promoted to attempt to access the hidden meanings behind these words and phrases, and in so doing open the door to discovering a new realm of interaction with the present world. I cannot say any more than that on the matter and so will leave this there.

10: The Importance of Writing

So writing this book has been for me both an uplifting and reflective experience. The first part has given me yet another chance to dabble with the art of fiction, which I do think holds certain merits over other forms of writing. But just as my mum has criticized me for being too fantasy-like in my earlier work, well so too there are certain things which you can only say in non-fiction writing. So hence the second part of the book is written in a straight talking, no messing about way.

Okay, earlier I mentioned singing, and used that idea to draw a parallel, a metaphor, between it and the art of writing. Sorry, I actually was talking about music, and said that just as music has rhythm and harmony, well so too can language encompass a lot more than just the bland and mundane assumption that the dreary and prescribed of state endorsed 'freedom' is all any of us have to look forward to. I am also hoping to demonstrate by both my writing styles and content, that this is possible and indeed advisable, and to demonstrate that how easy it is to write with an open tongue and look with an open mind, so to thereby discovering a world restricted to previous pain and congestion.

But I would now like to spend a while thinking about the art of music in and as of itself. As I may have already told you, and you may remember, I was previously a musician. Not that that kind of thing ever dies. It doesn't. Just I haven't been able to get going again much with the guitar since my first stint inside, much less   this second.

Still my love for music remains with me forever. I remember going to visit the hospital one day since my release, and stumbling across a duet of guitarists, happily plucking away to some complicated sheet music. Well I didn't stay and listen to them, being on my way to the ward for the visit, and primarily focused on getting that particular job in hand done. But my good friend, Tabith, insisted that after having our nice chat, for us to go back and hear the music, which she had been looking forward to. So indeed we went back and listened. And it was good. The melodies were splendid and performed with a skill which was really quite special. I don't suppose if any one else listening was a guitarist themselves, and so they wouldn't have known the feats or the physical difficulties and technicalities which the men were reaching in their show. But that won't have taken away from the audio pleasure, I mean at least I hope that it will not have. So we heard some great music from say two hundred years ago. With my memory being as dreadful as it is, I cannot remember for the life of me the names of the composers. Just that they were special. And I did know them at the time. Oh I think that one of Chopin's pieces were played, specially adapted for the guitar. That should give you a sense of the quality of music being performed, assuming you even know who he is/was. That's not to say that there weren't mistakes. Certainly I noticed at least two, perhaps three slip ups on the fret-board and again another time where the two musicians got slightly out of synch. But they soon pulled it together, and carried on playing unfazed, to complete their set to a tumultuous round of applause. This is a great example of music, and hopefully you can get some sense of the courage and emotions that being there actually inspired, just from this description.

I do think that there is so much more to music than simply listening to a CD. The same as watching live theatre tends to beat recorded shows on TV hands down every time. Both formats have their advantages, but I don't think that one can ever completely provide what the other does, and it will be a sad day if ever theatre does go the way of Betamax.

Back to the music. The reason why I have started again on this idea was promoted to me by watching a TV show last night on a group of South African kid singers from Johannesburg in South Africa (The Children of Agape), who produced a CD called We Are Together. Now all of the children on that show are orphans, and together they sang really wonderful songs. The TV show also saw me cry a couple of times as we witnessed one of the young men from the orphanage be diagnosed with HIV, which is another word for AIDS. Then he didn't even have the strength to walk back from the hospital track to their house; he had to be carried on the back of one of the gals. He was able to help correct a singing mistake one of the girls made in her rendition of a song. Singing himself, albeit difficultly, to what the song should be. And he told the baby not to cry so that her mum wouldn't cry, but they both cried. He also asked them not to cry when he was gone. Poor guy. Without parents and now without life. I saw the bundle of pills in little plastic bags which he had been given from the hospital. She (his sister) said that they might take away the pain. So then he died, and they held a small funeral and burial to pass this brave warrior onto the next life. What a sad loss.

The singing in this show was great, and also reminded me of another of my good friends from hospital, another gal called Lindi, who was another great singer. This friend is from Zambia and I am hoping to stay in touch with her when I go over there.

My singing isn't that great. I have difficulty breathing you see, and that creates like a wheezy noise when I have to struggle to deeply intake a breath. It's not that I can't breathe, I can, just it's different. And the hospital has never got to the bottom of either what's wrong with me, or how to fix it. But I don't think that the human body should be treated like a machine, like a robot, with everything fixable. So they have wanted to operate, to cut a hole through my throat on the inside with a laser, to see if that would make any difference. And I have opposed them.

It has sometimes been difficult for me, arguing with these senior Doctors, sometimes, more than one of them, sometimes a whole roomful, to stem the flow of the general medical opinion tide. But I did it. I got out of hospital with my soul intact. And now out, not only do I not intend going back, not only do I not intend to continue with their bad man medication which has only worn me down and held me back since I went in there, but I plan to leave the country, to help another good friend do the same, and do everything I have ever dreamed myself capable of.

In hospital my dad commented that he thought I saw everything as a fight, a struggle, and that I needn't. That they were only trying to help. But actually they weren't. Truth be told those bad men nearly killed me from my time in there. With all of those drugs I was on, a once formerly clever and relatively sharp lad turned into something of a zombie. The very blob of which I have also previously been described. With little or no control over the events over my own life.

Trust me this is not a pleasant situation to find oneself in. I hated it. I hated the bullies in there, the food, the items of mine going missing, and the way people looked down on you when I finally got out for some leave outside. That wasn't me, and well I am angry for having been put through that. I also now have an affinity towards other patients/ex patients, and I do think that I have learnt and developed a certain confidence and conviction of strength, to carry on with my struggle, in my future and wherever it may lead me.

Time is like an alibi; it always moves on and changes, but always stays the same. On the inside, time dragged. Trust me on this one. The visits I had were important to me, and provided a certain amount of release from the steam pressure cooker which is the institutional hospital. But it is a bad place, and needs to be shut. I don't agree with the general perception that mentally ill people are somehow different from the rest of us. We all have problems. Some of us mental, some stress related.

However, to come up with these catch all diagnoses such as paranoid-schizophrenic, manic depressive psychotic and 'organic personality disorder' seems to me not just feigned and artificial but condescending and actually harmfully destructive. Who would have thought that the very Doctors, nurses and hospitals themselves would actually turn into the instruments generating the very symptoms which they were set up to alleviate?

Sitting down and writing helps me chill out. I can find space here with my thoughts which helps me escape from the voices and troubles of the hectic everyday world. Even today, here on the way to this internet café, I think I heard someone call out, or mutter under their breath 'queer', as I walked by. See that's the kind of stuff which I have to put up with and, well you can probably imagine, it didn't help. I try to create a space within myself and around me, perhaps to the people who I talk to and spend my life with.

A personal space of peace and tranquillity, where problems are solved and people are happy and constructive. Yet there are other times when I feel that others, perhaps through misinformed intentions, or for whatever reasons they care to invent, upset my personal well-being. I nowadays find that I can comfortably watch TV WITHOUT this happening. All apart from the news which for most of the time, I sense is largely invented by a pack of not always well-intentioned liars. Yet TV is by and large okay.

People are, by and large, decent folk. Except like yesterday when sitting here I noticed a fire-engine hurtle past with a guy giving me a one-fingered salute from its window. Well that upset me. As it did when some people in the supermarket, near to my hostel, when they refused to join the new queue behind me which I started when a helpful shop assistant started it for me. These are by and large little things, but they can have a big impact on my somewhat fragile state of mind at the time.

I find that a sleep, or a period engrossed in computer games, helps me to forget about whatever it was that upset me. And also my partner helps sooth out my emotional chaos when it is rocky, greatly. But I think you can probably understand now, how much I want to get away from the crooks in this country and start afresh somewhere else.

I think that there are definitely certain benefits in standing out from the crowd. Besides just giving me a larger perspective, it helps me empathise with others away from my physical soul. So in this way it helps broaden my horizon and empower my reach. Hence what my meagre frame may lack in muscle strength or endurance, it sure as hell makes up for with insight and clarity. My problems now seem to stem largely from the way others treat me, and I need to join with Margaret to be able to present a united front. Together a loving couple are so much stronger than the sum of their individual parts. Yet another adage which I have found to be true after I have now experienced it in my later stage, (age) sorry. And perhaps the most important of them all.

Something else which I vowed to write about today was something that I and a close friend who lives in my hostel were talking about on TV this morning. It was the Jeremy Kyle chat show, hosted by some outside agent, who I recognised vaguely, but wasn't Jeremy and in my opinion wasn't half as good as him. Because despite having a reasonable rapport with his guests and the audience, took sides in the debates which I didn't like. The actual 'hot topic' being presented at the time, which I disagreed with, was about the question of Creationism, and whether it should be taught in schools alongside Evolution. These are two THEORIES about the creation of mankind. However, the host was keen to point out that evolution is actually 'fact', and thereby had a place in the science classes. As opposed to creationism, or the six day advent creation, which the host had apparently already spent 'some time looking at' and presumably considered himself an expert in. Expert enough to dismiss out of hand.

This reminds me of a situation which I was in at college some years back, when I met a teacher who came out with some statements about biology and evolution which I took disagreement with. I can't remember what the exact issue we discussed was, just that I made the point that his assertion of evolution as being fact, was incorrect, false, despite perhaps the majority of modern (Western) biologists subscribing to it at the very least.

My argument was that, a few old fossils was the only concrete evidence we have that certain older species existed, and that it is just an assumption to say that we evolved from them. Sure it seems unlikely that the world was made in seven days. But it is just as ridiculous to state that we all evolved from fish.

Being quite a spiritual person myself, which you may or may not have gathered from my writings, I am fondly proud of the truths of the Bible for one. And to not appreciate that it is a book written by men, is to misunderstand the whole question. Nobody for a minute has suggested that the Bible is written by God. Just that it has been INSPIRED by God. These are two completely separate things.

What's more an understanding of God is not given to men and women at birth, but has to be evolved over time, in the duration of their sentient life times. This is real evolution. So this apparent knowledge of evolution in the face of creationism, actually seems to stem from the presumption of a knowledge about the divine and indeed an actual complete ignorance about this very thing. I accept that a complete literal interpretation of the Bible does throw up mistakes and seeming contradictions.

As a Western mathematical text book it would receive a big cross, from any teacher here I am sure. I actually think that that reveals more about the limits of Western Math, than it does of the holy Christian book. Such as often the Maths question being asked will implicitly if not predict the exact answer, then at least the bounds of one, within the initial cause itself. This is the way it works. Anything without, or beyond those bounds would not be picked up on by definition and hence be discarded out of hand, despite whatever truth they may have. This is not a point I will care to give an example for here.

I suppose if you have come this far and either don't understand or disagree with what I am saying, despite the efforts I have taken to both prove and illustrate both my arguments and ways of reaching them to this point, that proving yet another example will do nothing to cure YOUR mental block.

Anyway I was talking about something else. The Bible, it's not a standard book, written from start to finish by a single author, even in a single lifetime. But actually a collection of books written over many lifetimes, by several people. And perhaps more important still, the God, or Jehovah, which can be appreciated, and felt by Christians reading it, is not a big White Guy, who sits up in the clouds somewhere throwing down thunderbolts to all who disobey him.

Everybody is entitled to their own belief in God. This is something that Richard Dawkins, that eminent but thoroughly inadequate scientist fails to appreciate. Everybody has a right to believe in what they will. Modern science concerning the creation of the world, has comprehensively build up a popular picture of other world religions, and then effectively dismantled them (or disproved them), brick by brick and plank by plank. Yet this doesn't prove anything, or only at most that what they think they believe is wrong.

No wonder as a child I grew up being from a family of socialists who thoroughly didn't believe in a god. So I have had to learn about him as an adult, without the help of my parents, by myself. And if anything as a child all of those years I have spent criticising and arguing with my Christian friend, has only served to ultimately demonstrate to me the limits of the atheistic persuasions. God is not this or that. I do not even think that He is a he.

Well, the old Egyptian ideas of Ra the god of the Sun, now is long discarded as outdated and false. But as I was talking about earlier, I think we have to be careful not to include the answer to the question we are asking in the clause to the question itself. So, if we say does God exist? Do we mean by God, an all powerful universal conscience which punishes misdemeanours according to the testaments exclusively, sometimes with thunderbolts or whatever, or do what do we mean?

Well of course these Atheists, like R. Dawkins, or the Oxfordites who have attended his lectures and sucked his c!! (metaphorically speaking), think that God is that. But they don't know he is, they assume it. Probably looked it up in their dictionaries, and confident in their dominance over the English language and knowledge base altogether, can proudly assert such rubbish.

This in the face of others who do believe in god. Not as this or that, but well something special. Magic, long since forgotten and discarded by many Westerners in general. The almighty who does deserve respect and adoration, whoever you are.

There are clearly in this day and age, a number of pressing issues on the international scene which would seemingly demonstrate that 'God' or religion, is the cause of all wars. With the current hidden war of the West against Islam, this is unsurprising, that you get this impression I mean. And I really can't go into this now. If anything the war seems to be driven by atheists driven by their desire to conclusively 'prove' that they, and not 'God', are masters over the world one way or another.

So how much a pity that they haven't studied the true meaning of God, which can only be appreciated with an open and giving heart. And what a shame that they haven't helped others who have been in need, given whenever they could, and demonstrated to him that they are worthy as human beings. John Lennon was right. There are no such things as borders, as religions or possessions. These are all just figments of our imaginations. And so much happier would we be if we recognised this. To share everything we owned, and our love.

Without war, without prejudice. I wonder if he fully knew the significance of what he was signing? Sure he knew the tune, as I expect most of my readers do. But I don't think that it would have been possible to write such a great song without a faith in the absolute. So thereby he was singing Irony. But no irony which our English teachers at school ever taught us about. Rather he was asking us to think, and thereby challenge the assumptions of the world as many of us know it.

Then he, like other great men – Kennedy for one, was shot, and the alleged killers were caught and brought to justice. Convenient – hey that the establishment had nothing to do with it, either of their murders, even though here is one of their most apt and powerful critics.

But I want to return to Sun-Ra for a minute. I see no contradiction between the Sun, that great and universal power that brings us light in the mornings and puts us to bed once again at night. Who warms our hearts and our seas too, and provides light all around. This and the miracle of God.

Because that is, in my sincere and true opinion, what God is. A miracle. The miracle of love, of light, of strength and happiness. All of these things. Of the answers to questions of which you haven't even thought of yet, and certainly Richard Dawkins and his ilk never will. The hope which leads from the end of wars, and the peace which is built on the foundation of international unity.

Some of these things we can greet in the morning, every morning; some take years and some I fear we never will. Not in our lifetimes at least. I do think that humanity as a whole moves in directions, not always progression, sometimes forwards, sometimes back. But I have hope and faith, and hopefully one day our dreams will be realised.

Hi. I was hoping to do some writing every day on this book and so I will make the effort to do so now. I did have some 'critical' things to talk to you about, but I have kind of forgotten what they were. Or rather I am feeling a bit tired, a bit worn out from all of this in depth study and consequential conclusion, and so I think that I would like to just chill out for a while.

Some people are kind. They have it inbuilt into their nature. I would like to say that everybody is, but I am getting away from this country because of a lifetime's worth of misery. Still there are certainly a lot of good people kicking about, and we meet them now and again. Complete strangers, or people who we know quite well and just seem like strangers because we haven't talked to them for a while. Or people who we know but only by face. They may smile at us, or shake our hand, or just be kind and this helps us work our way through the days. How about it helps me work my way through my days?

You know I try to be a good person. I try to help those worse off than me when I can, either by money donations (perhaps buying them cigarettes or maybe providing them with company), so that they can return to getting control over their own lives and returning to a state of self-empowerment which I hope is every adult's birthright. Then this helps the world go round.

I like playing on my computer games. For me this provides a little bit of distraction, a little bit of points based entertainment. I am nowadays quite picky about which games

I play. That's not to say that I don't try to give them the chance, given the amount of time and effort which goes into their making. But I generally prefer the Role-Playing-Games, because they generally provide a story, characters and characterisation, and ask for thinking to accompany particular movements of whatever the circumstances may be.

Also I try to complete the games I am playing if I possibly can. In the past I normally wasn't able to do this, for a number of possible reasons. Such as the game (first person shooters especially) was just too hard, or on some of the older titles (such as PC games) too bugged (hence kept on crashing). Still I enjoy getting into a game and whiling away the hours playing it when I have nothing better to do.

I can see the argument for saying that this is a waste of time. A waste of my life and so forth. But I don't think that it is. I enjoy it and it keeps me company. Trust me I am careful over which games I pick and so have something of a distinguished taste for these. And given the number of years I have been playing them (about two dozen now), I can appreciate things which maybe other gamers would skim over. Such as a well rendered sky-line, or semi-independent and intellectual members of a fighting horde: that kind of thing.

But let's not talk just about games. I want to mention that I am hoping to buy a new CD in a few days time as well. A poppy/dance track which I hope will provide me with some more entertainment and chill out time.

I also saw my mum and sister yesterday, which was nice. We had lunch at a Chinese restaurant in town, which mum paid for. Plus it is the first time the three of us have sat down together for a meal in a number of years, since I left home about seven years ago, and Cathy maybe two. We didn't argue, just talked about things. Mum is getting older, Cathy (my sister) is doing well, and I moaned but that was all good. Hopefully I will be able to see them again next week, assuming they both are happy about this.

As I think I mentioned at the start of today's writing, I'm really not jumping to talk about anything today. It's not that I don't like talking to you, it's just that there are times when I could argue the world to shreds, and times when I just want to relax. I am feeling okay, and that is one of the most important things (to me). There was something else which has been bugging my mind for the past couple of days, something that I have thought about, realised and or discovered. However it is not the type of information which I care to disclose to you at this time, because it's private.

Personal information, sometimes I will and have discussed with you the general public, and at other times chose to hold back. Let us say out of respect for people who I am not even going to name or anything else. I only chose to mention it because I felt like it, and sometimes, that is reason enough.

I am looking forward to going on holiday to match up again with my partner overseas. I hope that I don't have a plane crash. I realise that this probably won't happen, but it still is quite scary you know. Anyone who isn't at least a little bit nervous on touchdown is either braver or more stupid than me. Either way let's hope that I can go, and as soon as possible. I'm gonna leave it there, 'cause I am feeling quite tired and I want to browse the internet. Thanks for listening and 'til next time...

Hi. So what are we going to talk about today? Well firstly I saw a little red fox this morning on the way to town and my vegetarian brunch. It wasn't at all scared but was just seemingly meandering about, over the road and off to the back of the supermarket. I had tried to get a picture, but by the time I had my camera ready it was away. Breakfast was nice you know. It's payday tomorrow, but I wanted a treat and the small café I go to do nice proper traditional English ones. So I had today, like I have had before, eggs, tomatoes, toast, beans and mushrooms not to mention three potato wedges.

They offer on the menu veggie sausages, but seeing as they have a pink interior and actually taste like meat, I asked her to give me extra wedges instead. Well after that I just sat down and enjoyed the rays in Derby city centre for a bit.

On a slightly different note, yesterday something happened to me which made me both happy and proud. After I called up my girlfriend in Africa, her little baby Michelle said 'Dada' as soon as she answered the phone. She was talking to me, and this was a special time for me. I don't have to stress what they both mean to me; I think you should have worked that out by now for yourself. Just to say that I really feel that we are a family now and that is a real blessing. I hope I can get over there again, and soon!

What else? I am feeling quite in control of my own life nowadays. I have not been talking to my dad for the past week or so. You might think that is being a bit harsh, but seeing as ultimately it was a large part his fault getting me admitted last time. So that's seven months taken off my life. I feel I don't need that any more; you know I want to be an adult now and no longer feel the compulsion to talk to him every day.

Not to mention the mess he made of my last book, and all the years of rows I have had with him, I am quite happy having nothing to do with him for the time being at least. Sure, he won't like it but I have to think about number one now, as the saying goes.

Yeah, so I am feeling quite happy; it is another nice day which is another blessing. I am getting on well with Sunjeev (another of my close friends), and even the other people in my house. Sure we have ups and downs; I have had in the past the occasional dispute with one or two of them, and no doubt we will see more to come. But between eating and cooking my meals there, watching TV, playing on the computer and chatting to Martin (another resident), everything is looking okay.

Oh yeah, I also went in to see my local bank manager today to go over a couple of things, not to mention get the money out for this computer time which I am using now, and he was nice to me which was good as well. I may even give him a copy of this book, seeing if I ever get to actually printing it, just as a thank you present you know. I actually hope to give everyone I can copies. Like all of my friends and family, for example, and a few people whom I don't even know as well. Call it a gesture of goodwill or something. Plus it is free advertising and getting my voice out there, which is good publicity as well.

I got up quite early this morning. Too early for The Hits on TV, so I just watched normal TV with Martin, who was already up. And when I say early I mean about half past six. But after about half an hour or so the 24 hour news seems to loop, plus they seem to cover many of the same stories on the other breakfast shows/news channels, so I eventually got bored with that. Even after The Hits did come on, I can only watch that for so long at one time.

Then I went upstairs to give my 360 its regular pounding for another few hours or so; went to town and here I find myself now in the internet café. So the routine of my life goes on. But as you well know, if you have paid attention so far, I thoroughly intend to go to Africa in order to fulfil my dreams and hopefully my destiny. So I do have something to look forward to in the long run.

133

As a kid I used to dream of going to outer space. To be floating amongst the stars and chasing away the Aliens even. My mum even wrote off to NASA and we received back from them a bumper information pack on NASA's space centres in the US, I think. No free tickets though. You can probably imagine I was gutted. Then it dawned on me how much training goes into becoming a space pilot.

Only the very best of the normal pilots make it, and many of them had had military training. And how about the risks of going up there at all? I mean, if I get scared flying on a jumbo jet, what would it be like to go up in a rocket? You could break up in-orbit, take-off or re-entry, not to mention have a fuel explosion, and that's not to mention the aliens. Nah, I think it's best left to those people who actually want to put a lifelong dedication into it, which isn't me.

Instead I am happy working away at my books, spending time talking to, and hopefully staying with, my family. Talking to different people, playing on the computer and watching TV and eating food. Simple and effective. Sometimes I feel tired, then I sleep. Sometimes I feel sad, and sometimes I cry. That is all okay. Sweet-dreams.

Hi again. Now I have just had some woman be rude to me over the phone. Two women in fact. And I don't have to put up with it. The book gives me a chance to express my feelings. Gives me a friend to talk to when I am feeling down. Kind-of like a diary really.

Yeah, the first woman (one of my solicitors) returned my call seeing as I had been calling her office this morning trying to speak to her boss. It has to be her boss, because she isn't capable of addressing my concerns. Concerns to do with going to Africa. It is her boss who I need to address this, by speaking to my Doctor one to one, so to speak, in order to make this happen. She is insisting that they need a medical report before letting me go. But given that they didn't receive this last time, and that my Doctor has already said to me that he thinks that I do have the capacity to decide for myself about going to Africa, then I don't see the need.

I have told Ian, my solicitor, this exactly, but he did not give me an exact reply. Or if he did it was to leave me with the impression that he was going to try to call my Doctor to sort it out as requested when he could. Instead we now have the situation where I am forced to wait for some medical report which is never going to happen, because me and the Doctor don't see the need.

Instead I am now seriously considering just flying over there and being done with it. Damn the lot of them. I don't have to put up with being treated like that. Previously, the only thing holding me back from going was that I intended to pay for Tabby's ticket to Africa. But I really have to put myself first when it comes to life-changing decisions such as these. And then there was dad in the background, constantly throwing his two cents in, and quipping that I shouldn't go without the 'general consensus'. But as I think that I have amply demonstrated, his opinion does not suffice, or represent how I feel for one thing. I need to try and stand on my own two feet. Anyway after a short conversation with Jo (the female junior solicitor who called me this morn), well she said what she had to say because she just did, and then I started to reply, explaining what I thought (about the need for a phone call between Ian and my Doctor), and she just hung up on me! Now how rude is that!

Then I called my mum to try and find someone to talk-to about it, and mum said that 'maybe I had been going on at her, like I did her'. Well, I said, or shouted, something that I won't repeat over the page, and hung up. She tried twice more to speak to me, but I'm not putting up with that. And given the way things are going, I think that I am flying at the next possible opportunity. Flying out there, and not in any hurry to come back.

Tabby will have to wait and understand that I need to put myself first now. I am still intent on helping her if possible, but me and my family comes first which I am sure that she will understand. The other issues, such as the intent on my part to get a medical report written in order to have me taken out of the court of protection, again I hope to get this done. Although I don't think that my present Doctor is prepared to write it and in which case I am going to have to ask my new one to do it. But even this falls by the wayside in terms of priorities right now.

Right now my number one concern is that I might move to Africa to be with my missus. I want to get away from all of these trouble-heads and liars and back-stabbers. You know, the kind of people who put me in this financial halo and intend to keep me there. Well I have got a family now. I have got a project to work on, and I have even got a sister. I don't need this kind of trouble, and I have no intention of putting up with it any longer.

Going over there for a long stay will demonstrate a number of things. Not least that we have a family now which is very strong. And built to last. But also that I am well enough to act in the capacity of a responsible, and mentally fit, adult. And that I am sincere in my love for my wife, Margaret. These are the kind of things that can't be damned with my meddling good-for-nothings whom-so-ever they may be. This is Duracell power, built to last.

Sorry if that seemed like a rant, but now you can probably see how my mood is reflected strongly in my writing. So when I get hurt or worked up it makes me write a bit more passionately than if not. And sorry about some of my language. But when I am feeling emotional, I think that I am justified to let off a bit of steam. It's not like I swear all the time. Only when these pratts niggle my wig. That will do for now, cheers.

This book is really turning out to be something of an auto-biographical/day by day account of my life. I didn't really intend for it to turn out like this, but then being my own editor I don't suppose I had any good preconceptions over what the result was going to be.

One thing that I have learnt from my earlier writings, is that the very art of writing itself can help to change history dramatically. Or not history but the present and moreover the future. So for instance I did write a little funny (and as yet unpublished) book before going to Africa, with one of the sole intentions being that of going. In it I made clear the expression of love for my fiancée, and it did the job. Even without anyone else so much as laying eyes on the manuscript, it was read by God's eyes and he listened to me and carried me over there, for one of the best holidays of my life, if not indeed actually the very best.

Now yet again there are forces at work which are blocking my efforts to visit and marry the love of my life. My mum for one, today actually said that she didn't want me to marry Margaret, and that she had tried to block it. And my dad also has called it out of the question that I consider flying out there by myself, without the court's knowledge or consent.

But the fact of the matter is that that is exactly what I did last time, all with the small exception of paying for the holiday. Which I did eventually get funds for from them at the very last minute. But as I said then, I wasn't prepared to go through that again, having them leave it 'til the last minute, and then having to bend over backwards in order to get it done, which also ultimately resulted in my being sectioned on my return. How much better would it have been if we had just left it that little bit longer, and I saved up for the trip myself to go then, and it would have saved me from seven months of hell.

But that is in the past now. Still with yet again Irwin Mitchell damning me about, and failing to call my consultant when that is needed, instead insisting that he write some report on my mental health which he has already refused to do, again I am forced to make a decision which I know not all of the concerned parties are going to be happy about.

My mum doesn't want me to marry my lover because she doesn't trust her and has even told me so. My dad thinks that I am going against everybody else's wishes by acting on my own decisions, and perhaps doesn't appreciate that I take into account other's wishes when making these big choices. And Irwin Mitchell clearly believes that they are acting in my best interest by having ultimate control over my finances, where I can attribute their wasting literally thousands of pounds on Vicky Baker, not to mention getting me a negative credit rating which I can't get out of, and making me see an incompetent doctor who can mock me with his false claims and assertions as well as other things.

So hence there are very good reasons for me to no longer be in the court's control, and when I fly back from Africa a married man, I fully intend to proceed to attempt to be rid of them once and for all.

It is my decision and right to fly over there and get married. This is the first step. I very much hope to later go over there for good. That is to commit the rest of my life to the woman of my dreams. Let us hope that I am successful in my endeavour. There are sacrifices which have had to be made, and more yet will have to be I am sure if I am going to realise my ambition.

Money, while no longer desperate, is for the time being at least, reasonably tight, and something which I am and will have to continue to, keep a close eye on. I suppose this is how it is for most normal people, and that I have had it a little too good for too long. Not that I feel guilty about any of that. Just that, unlike those rich lawyers and Doctors, who have put me here, and must be getting ten times what I do, this is yet another step in my life's journey which I must overcome or else yet fall down.

Hi again. I have needed a break from writing for the past few days owing to family problems. I don't intend to give you the whole nitty-gritty of my internal businesses, but suffice to say that they are private and influential to me. I think that perhaps a great deal of these problems have been self imagined, perhaps greatly influenced by my reduction and cessation of the prescription which I am supposed to be taking. But I have stopped this for good reasons, specifically that I want to gain or regain as much control over my life as possible. And this is best presently achieved by not being in a drug induced state all of the time.

Despite suffering last minute butterflies, the holiday is still planned for Africa, and a subsequent wedding, is also planned. My wedding with my girlfriend of many years. It is something which I am really looking forward to, and I just hope that the weather is as good then as it is today. I love it when the sun shines brightly through a warm blue sky. Especially in the summer months, like it is supposed to do.

I do still have some stresses in my life. Undergoing major life changes such as we have been, and are anticipating, is when long awaited plans can be put into execution, and further plans need to be made. And I like planning. I'll also be damned if I'm not good at it. Being in a coma for so many weeks of my life was a time for me which, despite what anyone else may say, and despite what anyone else may have experienced, this was a time for me when I could think and plan and listen and imagine.

Only physical movement was impossible. And the other months (over a year) in which I have spent in medium to high security hospital wards, also has taught me the importance of planning. You certainly get plenty of time to do this when inside. Time to think and reflect, and communicate with those closest to you, be it physically or emotionally.

God has helped me a lot through my time inside. I daresay he has helped me through life in general. I now wear my cross with pride, and the understanding that I love Him just as he loves me. But I am not just a Christian. This isn't to say that I am not one, just that I am also a Buddhist and also a Muslim, although albeit to a lesser extent. I don't want to do too much preaching to you now. Because everybody should have the right to decide for themselves.

I understand the plight of one of my friends (Nick), who said that he had lost faith in God since his second before last girlfriend dumped him. And this is his right. But I don't like these well-to-do Atheists who wear their disbelief as a badge. Not knowing the meaning of what religion stands for does not give you the right to condemn it and dismiss it at all.

I understand that there are a-lot of different beliefs even within the same strict religion 'boxes'. And I will confess to taking definite problems with certain 'believers' from within Christianity for one. Such as the armies of so called Christian nations, who have devastated first Vietnam and then later Iraq all in the name of 'freedom' or 'democracy' or whatever.

Yeah, I understand that not all soldiers are bad people. But I am now reading yet another book written by one man's experience in the army, and it is thus becoming clear to me how brutal and ruthless the training regimes the soldiers are put through in order to instil into them the ultimate fitness and conviction. Yet we can't all be super-fit. And whilst these men may be lethal killing machines, they are also robots to my mind. Only carrying out orders and hence not in complete control of their own destiny.

Not able to deviate from the norm, or disagree with their commanding officers whatever they should wish to do. Of course my own personal experience with the armed services is limited to what I see on the press, and such like.

But as a living breathing human being, I am quite entitled to think, and this is what I do. We live in a collective world of individuals.

Everyone has his or her own dreams and imaginations and fantasies only. People have expectations both of the state and his friends and family. People sometimes assume that they can judge another on the colour of his or her skin, or the content of their character, and at other times assume that they 'know' history based on what they have read or have been told.

In order to question some, if not several, of these preconceptions, it has been necessary for me to delve deep down into the roots of people's prejudices. Both into group consciousness and media broadcasting. I likewise have taken an active participation in the evolution of history. Starting with my own (we are after all our own personal deities, or at least we should have that power over ourselves when we are in complete control of our own lives), and moving on to those around me, primarily my friends and family, and then even further afield as when I take the decisions to commit to engaging with particular topics, perhaps via the internet or personal engagement (such as working in a charity shop, or drinking in a cafe), whenever that choice should present itself to me.

I am not a bad character, and do have certain theatrical skills which have been long honed and developed and which I fully intend to put back into the field of drama teaching one day. So we are all cogs in the wheel of life. I remember one day when, near her death bed, my Italian granny asked me over the phone what the point of life was. I am not sure that these were her exact words, but she said something to that effect to the best of my memory. And what I think she was actually saying was that 'can you help me John find meaning in this world of madness?'

So I chatted to her for a bit. We discussed the terrorism in Italy which had taken place there not long ago, and I explained to her my outlook on living. These are the kind of things I remember talking to her about, and I hope that it comforted her somewhat having this friendly chat with her now nearly fully grown grandson, just as it helped me to talk to her. Sometimes it is not just what we say to our loved ones, but the fact that we are talking to them in the first place. I think that I was also trying to share with her a piece of my spirit, which for all of the bad things I've done, is still intact and living to this day. Which is more than I can say for my dear old gran.

11: Congregation

Hi everyone. I think that you have to be careful when discussing the Bible without actually having read it. And no I don't claim to have read the whole thing (which in case any of you hadn't realised is a collection of many books), just page for page Genesis, Exodus and other selected bits.

Belief in God is something every grown adult must make his or her mind up about at some point in life. I think it is folly to exterminate all hope of faith by a rational and deterministic outlook, based on a collection of assumed half-truths and collective fallacies.

They once believed the world to be flat, and god-damn-it the world is flat. Only from outer space it's round. I think that Christianity is about Jesus Christ. I don't have any proof that he died for our sins. I don't know for sure that he was ever alive.

Yet when you read the Bible you shouldn't assume that everything in it is either wrong or 'right'. Clearly it is a book written by men. I think that it was written over a considerable period of time, and there have been addendums and extractions. So what? Are you really telling me that most modern records were all recorded in one go, with no editing and on one mike?

And I even recognise that there are discrepancies, or apparent discrepancies in the text. But I don't think that we should spend all of this time dwelling on these minor issues. In my mind the Bible is a special book because of what it promises. It promises hope and salvation, which nobody else will care about because they are all too busy fussing with their own business to save you, while you can still be saved.

That is what the Bible says. It is about hope and freedom and salvation and spirit. In this war-torn and selfish world of the present it is difficult frequently to find a way through the mess. Wars have been committed in the name of religion, whether this be officially recognised or not. So there has been a-lot of suffering.

One of the standard arguments against God is how could he permit such pain and strife in the world whilst he sits on high up there with his angels and lightning, sipping fresh grape-juice and colouring in the rainbows? Yet I don't think of God as an entity so much as he is everywhere. He is in everything.

Read 1 Corinthians v 13 (earlier transcribed) if you want to see how my words are justified in the Bible itself. Clearly a-lot of it has been written to a prescription of an all powerful deity godhead figure. But in that little book, written by Paul I think, it says that God is love. Not God is loving, not anything else. Just God is love. This would appear to contradict the outside meaning of the whole of the rest of the book. Suddenly Jesus is a concept, accessible to all of us in the present day, right here. Suddenly all of the pomp and rigmarole of ceremony and custom is left standing alien and possibly stranded from the hearts of the cruel and selfish men who re-enact them.

Because I am not saying that we are a bad lot. But it is a cruel and selfish world. Not that 'God' made it that way. Just man did. Men, or women as well, would rather see you starving on the streets or dying of thirst than lend a quid, or a helping hand.

As I have said already I don't think that everybody is like this. And honestly we all do need to place ourselves first at some times in our life. But when things are stable for you, when things are going alright and you have everything that you need, why not take a chance? This could be helping some-one less fortunate than you, could be questioning somebody near to yours' prejudices or bullying, which you notice and they think that they can get away with. It could even be questioning some of your own fears or long held mistrusts. Whatever. To do these things it takes a certain amount of commitment. And it also needs you to have a head on your shoulders, a sense of ethical responsibility, of Karmic trust. It doesn't require you to believe in him, whoever he may be.

Sorry if I've been going on for some time, but as you have probably gathered this is something which I feel quite strongly about and I wanted to have my say. So God, whoever He may be, is not something you have to believe in. I would argue that He is out there to be discovered. And I am saying this as a Christian, a Buddhist and a sinner.

I want us to all take some more responsibility over the actions we make in our own lives. With regards to the Bible, read it if it helps you. There is a-lot of hidden meaning in it, beneath the surface if you spend some time thinking and exploring the ideas therein.

One such story is from the book of Mark. Jesus came across a disabled man who was in clear need of some help. He asked him, which would it be easier for you: to get up and walk again, or repent all of your sin. Lo and behold the man got up and walked off.

You can say, as generally is discerned I would imagine, that this is a record of Jesus's healing powers. But also I want you to see it as a question to the reader, asking you to think about your own sins, or bad deeds in the past. And thereby start to live life with a sense of responsibility and ability rather than just stumbling from one fated encounter to the next, never truly in control of your destiny much less those of your children. Think about it.

Hi, sorry if I haven't been exactly working on the book for the last couple of days but I have been doing other things, like trying to change the world! Above you will just have read a post I made on the official Koei website about God really, and my interpretation of it. This post was made under a heading 'the holy bible', and was actually a response to about a couple of dozen or so earlier comments about the bible, and faith in general. However if you had read them I think that you will find that they were not half as charismatic or either forthcoming as mine was. That is to say that the majority of others who had contributed to that site were sceptical, some Agnostic, some Atheistic, perhaps one Christian, but none as eloquent or all encompassing as mine. I'm not blowing my own trumpet, just describing it the way it is.

So why did I go on about God the way I have, you might be wondering? Well in answering that question let me first take us a step back and look a bit at the history of the situation, specifically my dealings with Koei.com in the past. Okay, I have been a great fan of many of their earlier console games. Firstly with the likes of the Kessen and Dynasty Warriors series on the Play station 2, and then more recently with Samurai Warriors 2, Bladestorm and Oroichi Warriors on the Xbox360. These are all great games, and indeed before I even got around to talking about my faith I did make a couple of contributions elsewhere on the site, more specifically game related and so demonstrating that I am a fan of their work. But just under a year ago I was actually banned from that site in question. Something to do with me 'breaking the rules', which amounted to speaking personally (dropping one of my [imagined] enemies' names for instance), and also posting all of my messages in the 'introduce yourself here/welcome back' section of the site, instead of the relevant area.

So yeah I got a warning and then was banned. That means that if I try and log on from any computer, it will just come up with the error message that access is not available. And in the spirit of the thing I have left the site alone now for a good period of time, just so that things could be given the chance to settle down a bit. The thing is that I have now been able to get back on by using a different email address, and logging on under a different name. Also I have been forced to make no reference to my identity, for fear of getting banned once they realize that it's me. In fact this doesn't bother me. If anything, one of the beauties of the net is that it enables this kind of double identity, if you know what you're doing. I was reasonably happy until today. I am quite happy today.

So I wanted to talk about God to these guys. I thought that it was nice that I had the opportunity to do so. All under a section of the site entitled 'Literature'. It's not every day that we are given the chance to preach/spout off about our beliefs, much less on a tightly guarded/maintained computer game forum. But why not? Games players are on the by and large clever sods like myself, I imagine. Hopefully at least a few of them will read my comments, and perhaps I will even get a reply, which I intend to checkout shortly.

The other thing which I have been doing over the last couple of days is trying to make head or tail out of this business that is happening in Georgia right now. Russia seems to have endangered the peace with their heavy handed actions, but I imagine that it is quite difficult for them to go from a super-power to a small 'normal' country with just the stroke of some other diplomat's pen. And whether Georgia actually started the whole thing off, by offending/attacking South Ossetia before Russia stepped in is another possibility again. We have to try and be as broad minded as possible when studying this conflict. I have actually been busy reading some intelligent posts on a BBC website, by different members of the public, all engaging and contributing their perceptions as to the events unfolding before us. It is clear that there is no love lost between the two sides. But I would also propose that it is clear also that there is quite a bit more going on behind the scenes than meets the eye, at least on first appraisal. After all both the Russians and the Georgians are acting as if they are in the right. Each side presumes the air of honesty in their statements to the press. All be it with Russia coming across that much more determinedly, perhaps having learnt to stand on its own two feet.

Compare this to Georgia which appears weak and leaning almost totally on promises of support from the US and Europe, which may or may not be forthcoming. Whether the US will or will not dare to take an active engagement with this war, all on the basis of 'upholding world democracies' comes across a bit weak seeing as what they have done now to Iraq and are in the process of doing to Afghanistan. Sure those two countries weren't democratic before they were invaded, but never-the-less a lot of innocent people have lost their lives over there and am I the only one to be concerned about this?

The other thing which I have been reading about is 9/11. I know that the Bush US administration used these attacks to justify its war on terror for both of the aforementioned invasions in the middle east, but the amount of evidence which is being unveiled to counter the official line of events is really turning out to be quite remarkable. From questions over how the towers collapsed (in the manner of controlled demolitions), to a pre-warning the BBC received prior to the collapse of a third World Trade Tower which wasn't hit by a plane, to the cover up after these events all took place.

I don't really have the time to go into it all now; suffice to say that I smell a rat, and suspected one right from the outset. Things are rarely as they seem given many man-made disasters, and given the right amount of attention to detail and questioning of facts and sources, it is often possible to gleam more into these events than is apparent from the outset. I am not saying that the US or British Special Forces is responsible for the attacks on the World Trade Towers, but that is what I suspect. In fact I wouldn't be surprised if it was the British who did 9/11, and then in retaliation the US responded with 7/7. Although clearly they have covered their tracks well, but what do you expect? They are after all among the best trained and skilled military units in the world. Maybe they planted the bombs on the suspects, or whatever, I really cannot say. And I suppose we will never know for sure the true causes of both of those terrible events. I just have my suspicions and I'm not the only one.

Hiya everyone. I am feeling reasonably happy and content today so I am sitting down to write. Yesterday I was watching a concert on Channel 4 Music the new music channel which has replaced the hits on our cable box. So there was a concert being shown us from some place else in the UK, some festival being headlined by the Kaiser Chiefs. Despite not initially liking them I have grown to that band, and now am a fan really. It was quite scary watching the lead singer climb up a scaffold by the side of the stage all the whilst singing one of his songs. Now the crowd, a predominantly white British group, looked as if they had a real attitude problem, but I tell you what, if most of the festivals are like that then I am pleased that I have never been to one. I did go on some of the London stop the war demonstrations and – you know what – they were as good as any festival in my opinion.

There have been a couple of other things happen to me over the past few days. Take when I sat down on a park bench and a friendly squirrel decided to venture quite close to me to say hello. Well I vowed that if it tried it again that I would get it. Not hurt it you understand, just pat it on its head to say hello. Well you'd never believe it but a minute later and it did come back. Maybe it was a girl squirrel but I don't know. Anyway it came back rested its little foot on my left big toe and well I think it wanted something to eat. I didn't have anything to give it, was rubbing my thumb and index finger together to coax it in. Then after saying hello to it, it ran away again.

Also on that day I saw something on TV about a gorilla held in a German zoo who had recently lost her baby son. That was quite upsetting. And she was holding onto the dead baby boy as if it was still alive. You know we were told by the news show that she had previously last year given birth to a baby girl which the wardens had taken off her, and so I imagine that she didn't want to let her new one go, even though it was dead. After all she didn't know that the girl was doing well in her new home. It must be very upsetting and quite lonely to live as a caged animal in one of those zoos. Living from day to day as best you can. I understand some of that from my own time in captivity. And yeah I do think that animals are intelligent like humans. Obviously they are not quite the same as people, but they still have hearts and emotions which anyone who has ever had a pet should be able to vouch for.

Also yesterday I was sitting in the park reading my book on the navy seals when some pigeons decided to come and say hello to me. A whole flock of them in fact. They were sitting all around me, I was seriously covered on all sides. One of the cheeky buggers even decided to come up to me and peck my foot. Which I yelped at because as I'm sure that you will be able to imagine was slightly off putting. But it didn't do any harm, and thinking back I suppose that is the only way they can communicate, by pecking. They were also a burly group of lads sitting some way behind me and drinking. They were also shouting quite a bit and putting me off my book. There was also a lass with them. I eventually decided that I had had enough and so made my way back to my home over the road. Walking by that group through they didn't make any rude comments and a few of them even got up themselves at that point, so I wasn't bothered by that.

12: Georgia: Post

I want to show for you some more work which I have been doing on the internet. This is from the BBC news website blogosphere and pertains to the conflict in Georgia which we have just witnessed. Note I am waqqar2054, that is my handle here, and here is part of the discussion posted so far:

<Sorry it appears that the BBC have wiped the forum which our discussion was taking place in! Well here's what I have posted somewhere else right now, in response to that..>

At 10:51am on 22 Aug 2008, waqqar2054 wrote:

Yada yada yada. Not that any of you will know this but we were all having a strong and heated debate on this very matter over on the BBC's the editors forum separating fact from fiction. Now the BBC seems to have closed this site down not because people weren't talking but rather because they didn't like the way the argument was headed, specifically the case was being put that the UK media are wrong in their portrayal of this war, and basically cowards. There were a few bloggers posting in support of the status quo, but not many, and the argument was being won. Obviously the BBC didn't like the way things were headed and shut the whole thing down. Or when I say the BBC what I really mean is certain people within your organisation. I appreciate that it was probably a joint decision, but that still doesn't make it right. We the public should be allowed to speak freely on the internet to discuss these contemporary matters, amongst educated adults, and without fear of censorship. Big Brother was a concept George Orwell invented to mimic the Soviet power over everyday people in his work of fiction 1984. How much sadder then that we can see certain elements of this control taking place now today. Okay think about it…

…It seems as if the BBC has had a change of heart, perhaps because of me, and restored all of our comments on Georgia back to their site. Without any further ado I will replicate these for you here to give a taste of what we have been discussing.

At 10:32am on 21 Aug 2008, Nikolay3 wrote:

I was greatly disappointed to find the article? Uncovering truth about Georgia conflict? by Stephanie Holmes, to be a clear example of propaganda, not information. The content is in sharp contrast to the title, and any serious reader can see this. Here are some of my reasons:

1. There are 2 photos (Picture 1? Residential buildings were hit during the conflict?; Picture 2? Russian forces have been accused of using cluster bombs?), and both lack information about the towns/villages, where those terrible devastations took place. Only an outright anti-Russian bias can explain

this, since both photos were apparently taken in Tskhinvali and depict results of the Georgian assault (I saw practically the same in Russian reports, or on Reuters). So, having no matching signs of war devastations from the ? Georgia proper?, the BBC simply hide as the true and full information.

2. The phrase: Russian prosecutors have announced they are opening criminal cases into the deaths of 133 civilians who they say were killed by Georgian forces. Initially, however, Russia suggested more than 1,500 people had died in the conflict. It makes the reader think that there are (or at least there are already found) only 133 civilians dead in South Ossetia, instead of the announced 1,500 killed. But in the same short piece of information from the Russian authorities it was also said that those 133 dead were already formerly buried by relatives, while yet unknown, but many dead civilians were still temporarily buried in the gardens and off the streets of Tskhinvali, and the latter could be counted only after formal procedures of establishing their personalities and reburials take place. Again a clear sign of biased propaganda, aimed at strengthening anti-Russian feelings among less attentive readers. I can only say that this article, thank God, is a rare case of openly biased and unprofessional reporting on the BBC site.

At 12:17pm on 21 Aug 2008, punctdevedere wrote:

Russia launched into this war on the basis of a preposterous accusation – the 'genocide' of 1,600 South Ossetian civilians

158

in Tskhnivali. Now even the Russians are admitting that they are only able to document 134 deaths in all of S. Ossetia. At these levels, any military activity outside the confines of S. Ossetia was completely unjustified. If the Russian government has any honour, then:

1. It should immediately withdraw all of its military personnel and hardware from Georgia. Not tomorrow. Today. There was no excuse for the invasion and there is no excuse for continuing occupation.

2. Russia should commit to paying reparations for all the unnecessary damage it has caused to Georgian infrastructure (e.g. the sinking of coastguard ships at anchor in Poti).

3. The President or Prime Minister of Russia should make a formal televised apology to his citizens for the Government's dishonesty. The damage that the initial propaganda did to Russian attitudes needs to be unwound.

4. International investigators should be given free access to all of Georgia so that the truth can be established once and for all. Russian, Georgian and separatist administrations need to cooperate and hand over any commanders or leaders who have a criminal case to answer.

5. International peacekeeping forces should be put in place in S. Ossetia and Abkhazia so that Georgians can return to their homes in those regions whilst ensuring the protection of Ossetians and Abkhazians.

At 1:04pm on 21 Aug 2008, waqqar2054 wrote:

Hey punctdevedere;

It is clear that you don't know what you are talking about.
Georgia started this damned conflict by invading and attacking
the South Ossetians first. Russia responded by sending in
peace keeping troops to secure the area. Now everyone is
blaming the Russians for the damage and telling them to get
out, where the villagers in South Ossetia have made it clear
that the Russian soldiers were civilized in their passing, and
that it has been the armed militias who have done the killings.

Next time you want to post I suggest that you get your facts
straight!

At 2:54pm on 21 Aug 2008, S D Porter wrote:

I am amazed by the US application of double standards
between this dispute and that of Kosovo. I am also stunned by
the US regime's blind support for Stalinist policies. After all
both Abkhazia and Ossetia were subsumed into Georgia as a
result of a policy directed by Stalin and enacted by Lavrenti
Beria in the 30s.

So it's kind of ironic that the government of "The Land of the
Free" should so unthinkingly follow the path set out by that
murderous pair. What's really tragic is that the US
administration would not accept or understand their
contradictory stance.

At 3:09pm on 21 Aug 2008, S D Porter wrote:

I'm also fed up with reading articles and posts by people who want to characterise the Russian position as that of a Soviet state. Russia is without doubt probably the most capitalist state in the world. The Russian government's protectionist policies; if they can be called that, are concerned with the correct management of the country's resources. I think it's absolutely right the Russia government wants to control the extraction of these resources.

Pretty much of the rest of the economy is a "Free for all". The point is that it's flabby thinking to state that it's just the clock being turned back. The people who do this I believe have no real experience of modern Russia, of the people and of conducting business there.

At 5:14pm on 21 Aug 2008, stanhj wrote:

#198 "1. It should immediately withdraw all of its military personnel and hardware from Georgia. Not tomorrow. Today. There was no excuse for the invasion and there is no excuse for continuing occupation."

Russian will withdraw eventually. I don't see any viable case they would want to stay in 'ethnic Georgia' region. But as any responsible country with honour they should ensure that withdrawal is orderly and that Georgian police will take control over the area. There is so much ammunition left behind so guess what will happen if this gets to the hands of people bent on revenge. I read interesting news headline: 'S. Ossetian villagers captured 2 Georgian soldiers with tank.' The headline is ambiguous in detail who had the tank, if it was Georgians or the villagers, but anyway the tank already was or is in hands of those villagers.....

"2. Russia should commit to paying reparations for all the unnecessary damage it has caused to Georgian infrastructure (e.g. the sinking of coastguard ships at anchor in Poti)"

Right, maybe there was no direct threat posed by the coastguard ships, but if you do this strong claim, should not you also call on the US to commit the same way to restore the infrastructure not only in area inhabited by ethnic Georgians but also in S. Ossetia? The damage to Tskhinvali was also absolutely unnecessary. I wonder how the international aid delivered there is distributed and if it all lands in Tbilisi airport, how much will get to S. Ossetia

"3. The President or Prime Minister of Russia should make a formal televised apology to his citizens for the Government's dishonesty. The damage that the initial propaganda did to Russian attitudes needs to be unwound."

Judging from the Russian language news available online, Russian people are best informed of the facts from all sides of the conflict, and have had a long time to make up their minds. Don't forget the conflict is now nearly 20 years old and there has been —all reported about it, with many people questioning the events. I see here return to old Cold-war-style propaganda on both sides, but Western side is leading by many points in this regard. It is only Russians who have enough access and independent news media to provide balanced coverage.

"4. International investigators should be given free access to all of Georgia so that the truth can be established once and for all. Russian, Georgian and separatist administrations need to cooperate and hand over any commanders or leaders who have a criminal case to answer."

Indeed. However, hold on to your anger. War is dirty business, and when you point finger on someone, there are usually 3 fingers pointing back onto you. I wonder what they would find? Border skirmishes were well documented already from before. Use of heavy artillery to shell Tshinkvali as reported by human right organizations? Georgians are also alleged to finish-off wounded Russian soldiers. I believe there may be a few Russian families who would want to have this allegation investigated too.

"5. International peacekeeping forces should be put in place in S. Ossetia and Abkhazia so that Georgians can return to their homes in those regions whilst ensuring the protection of Ossetians and Abkhazians."

International UN backed peacekeepers have been there, but they were reported to be leaving in hurry just few hours before the first attack. Only Russian part of peacekeepers stayed to do what they were meant to do: protect S. Ossetians against Georgian attack. Don't you have a better suggestion? read post #188

13: Zimbabwe: post

These are posted freely by members of the general public in discussion with one another and so I see no reason why the BBC should hold copyright over them. Hence I think I am okay to replicate them here. Reading the above points and taking part in the discussion proves both informative and interesting, and I think that all of us who take an active role in these group discussions learn quite a lot from having done so.

Another web-discussion which I have been involved in revolves around the troubles in Zimbabwe they have been having there recently. Well I don't plan on showing you all of this; now the main thing seems to have settled down that is the outcome I was working towards certainly. There are still problems over there by all means, and not just the inflation. There still seems to be a definite amount of antagonism between the three main ruling parties, the MDC the Zanu-PF and the break-away group led by Morgan Tsvangiri. They have all come out of talks and I am hoping will settle down to form some kind of government to rule their country. Also there still seems to be a certain amount of lies and 'righteous intervention' led by outside interfering bodies such as the West and the UK in particular, spurned on by blatant lies in the media (I will give one example of a duped piece of 'filming' for channel 4 and the Guardian, which was actually no more then a bunch of actors reading out a pre-prepared script to blurry video images of people talking. This is no more evidence of mass torture than a bloody fairy-tale. What it actually is is propaganda, instigated by the UK, or certain agencies within for some uncertain agenda.)

I am not saying that there hasn't been torture and killing on both sides, like there always is in any war. Just that the way the UK media and government has jumped on the bandwagon to crucify Mugabe is plainly wrong in my opinion and this is a considered judgement, also weighed by years of fighting the status quo, firstly South Africa's Apartheid, then researching Vietnam through reading, then more recently Iraq and Afghanistan. So don't you tell me that I don't know what I am talking about. I have also spent time arguing my case in college, most recently with a Sociology lecturer who plainly didn't like my politics and failed me on account of this (under the apparent guise of my essays not meeting the standard), and then also with another lecturer who I had the pleasure to listen to, and he listened to me, and taught me about religion and philosophy, and it was thanks to him that I passed the course. This is something about my past. In the future I am planning to move in with and spend the rest of my life with my long time girl-friend. I am blessed to know her and hope that our marriage will be a fruitful one. I mean this in terms of love. Then we are planning to return to Britain together at some-point and hopefully both be accepted onto a Drama degree at university together.

Drama was the one subject that I loved and excelled at in school. Despite having a couple of rather miserable attempts to restart it at sixth form, then two different colleges, I am a firm believer that it will go better at university. Obviously this is going to take a certain amount of preparation for the audition pieces, not least that I am going to have to help my partner prepare her piece as well. But I am confident that we will both do well at this. Drama is after all a 'living' art, meaning that it breathes with the actors who instil it with life. And it is also dynamic so that in a group show, or even a duo-log as we are hoping to perform, it is very much about the amount of spirit and creative potential the two performers can instil in each other when reading their lines. Don't think that I haven't thought long and hard about this eulogy of mine in all of the years when I have been away from the stage. It's not just about performing up there, although that is the end product, but also about the process you have to go through in order to reach this stage. That is why rehearsals should be missed at your peril. And indeed the last college play I was in (a hastily directed and pulled together mess called 'The Night Before Christmas', where I played an elf!) was such a disaster, in as much I forgot all of my lines and got an E for it. Not that the audience could tell the difference, they seemed to enjoy it and we got a good clap at the end. But my point is that by cutting down the rehearsals to practically nothing, and not even doing a proper dress rehearsal, we were setting ourselves up to fail.

I actually blame our drama teacher of the day, who seemed quite happy for us to screw it up. She didn't actually seem to know much about what she was doing anyway, even congratulating us on doing quite well after the event, even though we clearly hadn't. And get this neither of my parents showed up to watch it, even though I think they both were in Derby in time and should have made the effort! I was however lucky enough to have a good adult friend, Janet, watch it and that meant a lot to me.

So when just before the performance we were supposed to be rehearsing, what they instead did was a quick run through the 'best bits' which didn't include my lines. No wonder I screwed it up. Never mind. It was also quite difficult for me given that I was quite a lot older than the rest of the group. Indeed the class had dwindled from thirty odd, to just the four of us by that last show, and the guy who had started teaching us for it was replaced by this time after the first term and a half because he clearly didn't know what he was doing. So even for the last exam we seriously had no help whatsoever, and I got a C in it simply because I am good at exams from my GCSE days, swotted up on what was being asked from us for the correct syllabus on the internet, and this lifted my overall grade up to an E. Which now you can probably see why I am still quite proud of. Compare our dismal play to the other (all girl) groups, from the year above. They practised theirs over and over until their eyes were watering. You know we even had to sacrifice a lesson or two of our class time just to sit through their dress rehearsal. And I don't think that we realised at that point that we were sitting in the same performance! Let alone that we hadn't even chosen our play yet! Oh my God. So no wonder they did theirs perfect. Here's a hint for all of you budding Thespians: the key to good drama is in good preparation. Something that I've learnt the hard way.

Something else that I learnt, actually after the show but before our final exam, was that the teacher assigned to us to take that

A-level drama class from the start used to be in the army. Which something explains maybe why he had us doing push-ups and sit-ups in the warm ups, and very little actually acting or even discussing drama. And I question his claims to having a drama degree under his belt given the way he led us. But it was a learning experience, and despite an anger I felt for the whole thing at the time, I don't regret having done it.

I spent some quality time with some good students over that year we studied drama together, and despite not achieving the grades for which we might have hoped, we did learn both about live performance and textual matters in the time we worked together. This was only, and I stress only, down to the work we put in amongst ourselves and nothing to do with the teachers at all. But set to study and act excerpts out of Oscar Wilde's The Importance Of Being Earnest and Chekhov's The Three Sisters, we were required to study them, engage with the plays, try to eke out the playwright's meaning from them, and then capture this and display it to the audience in brief renditions. I've actually learned to love both of these radically different works, great in their own ways, in ways that I never thought I could. Earnest is full of witty rapport and critical comment on pretty much everything, which must have been well ahead of his time. And the Sisters is actually a biting piece of love and tragic drama which is emotionally beautiful and crushing.

You do have to spend a certain amount of time reading them though, and perhaps re-reading them if you don't get the language. But after they are appreciated then I am of the opinion that both of those works can stand as equals to Shakespeare's protégés and that is great.

There is also another of Chekov's works which I now remember reading after completing my college class, largely as something to do in my spare time. Perhaps it was A Doll's House. Yeah, I think it was, and it was that one which actually moved me the most of all. Despite only acting out the drama in my head, on reading it, I remember that it is the story of a doomed marriage between a young and beautiful Russian seamstress and her well-to-do accountant husband. I won't spoil it for you by telling you the ending, but suffice to say that it is a tragedy and an emotional masterpiece at that. It came to me at a time when I was myself undergoing certain definite rigours of having a long-term long-distance relationship away from home. And forced me to ask questions of my own love, and look at our love again perhaps also deciding what the most important things were in my life, and the order of their importance. Yeah A Doll's House is a powerful and great piece of drama, and it's not set outdoors in case you were wondering!

The only other thing that I wanted to do today was now show you some of the conversation we have been having on this yahoo Zimbabwe forum. This is not really about the pressing issues at hand, to do with Mugabe and his cronies. Rather it is about one man's ignorance and my responding to that. See what you think..

The Evil Scotsman,

Should have stayed with white rulers __12-Aug-08 03:52 PM__

This country should have kept the white people in charge; it was the breadbasket of Africa and the people were happy. They were not hungry and had clothes, houses and money; instead it was used in the "cold war" by soviet Russia giving the small band of rebels weapons. People keep banging on about the Iran, Iraq, Georgia things and how people have been treated badly; you should find out what happened to young white girls by these communist backed animals. Go back to Rhodesia and kill every one of these animals and chase the rest back into the jungle where they belong.

Bern,

Hey Evil S, you are trying to live up to your name I see. Yes there are many who think as you do. Even though you may think these Black African people are not humans, you are wrong. From the way you speak, I would say that there are many who are more human than you. I think that you need a renewal of your soul. You are just causing more racial prejudice from all sides, yet we need to bring peace, which is possible, if people would just stop thinking only of themselves. My brother was murdered by these people, and my wife and I shot at by them, but that does not give me the right to think as you do. You really do need help.

The Evil Scotsman,

Well maybe its because of gutless people like you these things are happening; stand your ground for your kin and country. The weak don't deserve to rule.

john2054 (me),

After all we have been through and you have the cheek to insult this community with posts like that. It is because of ignorant $%^&s like yourself that wars are started in the first place, and you really ought to be put out of your misery in my opinion. Either that or piss off back up north.

Stephen Berns,

Who is being a racist and bigot now "piss off back up north"? What made you think I was in the bloody south and do you have a complex against people from Scotland or the north of England you racist?

john2054,

Hey Stephen, I wasn't talking to you but the poster b4 you. He is an evil T w o t. And I've got to say that for fear of abusing the Yahoo moderator's sensibilities. Look from what you've said you've seen the rough times and should be commended for that. It is the bloody hooligans and terrorists on this site, who think that they can hijack the discussions with their racist and prejudicial polemic that I want to have beef with.

You may or may not realise that I have a couple of good African friends who I am close to. I also like the British, by and large. God I am one! But as I said already, some people think they can hijack this place with their bloody ignorant noses, and I hope you will agree with me that they are not welcome here. This is for intelligent adults to discuss important world-wide events. On the subject of which, I hope that you will agree with me that it is a good thing that things over in Zimbabwe seemed to have settled down a bit now, with the major parties in talks and hopefully going towards a peaceful option.

Stephen Berns,

Hey John, you sure got him riled. I agree with Your sentiments. I must say though, I think that if we cannot take people banging us on our corns then we should not be on this site or an other. For you will get people doing that, they just lack a little between the ears, that is all. In fact, there are a lot of reasons why people have a go at each other, but one fact is sure, if one cannot talk calmly about something, one has a problem, and should not make it other people's problems. If you catch my drift.

Mike E,

Hi I totally agree if you go back to the mid 60s to early 70s
and how the black and whites lived in comparative harmony
until the now uncle Bob and his communist buddies
hoodwinked the black population, not all I say, but dangerous
few, decided that the white man had no place in Africa. I was
Born there along with my two sisters, as were my parents and
theirs before. So WHO IS AFRICAN! In the world today
where racism is not politically correct, the white-man of
Africa has to be the most discriminated against group of
people in the world. It is TIME FOR US TO STAND UP
AND STAND TALL: GIVE RHODESIA BACK TO THE
WHITE AND LET US GET IT BACK ON TRACK.

Hi every-one another day another dollar huh?

Well the past couple of days have been kind of rough for me
again. Yesterday I found out that someone had been into my
room, I think in the early hours of the morning when I was
having a bath, and taken forty quid out of my bedside cabinet.

This made me mad, understandably. I even know who did it
and I think that I would be quite justified in knocking him for
six. But I have other responsibilities now as my girlfriend has
rightfully reminded to me, chatting to her on the phone, and
so I need to just pay my rent, ignore the little bad man and

focus on getting over to Africa. This is what I have done this morning.

Also this morning two incompetent staff from my house accosted me for the rent which I have not paid in like three weeks. Or I approached them about it. Either way I paid them a double-whammy and they had to give me just under four-pounds change. Well I suggested paying them a pound and then taking a fiver off them. Actually going as far as to doing this. But then they queried the Math. Like I tried to explain it to them 5 minus one is four, but they insisted on having the note back and giving me the change when they had it. Well this is just taking the piss. It's bad enough that I had to suffer the indignity of having my cash robbed from under my nose in that hostel, but now for the staff to piss about with giving me change? So what if they can't do basic Maths. I sure as hell didn't do Maths GCSE to an A star standard for nothing. Bloody hell this is basic subtraction. Anyway I just walked out with the note, promising that I would pay the eight pence difference late on. You know the main woman staff member who was making most of the noise about this incident is the same woman who yesterday said to me in the morning when I came down distressed about discovering that my money had gone missing, that she wasn't listening to any more of my nonsense. This is no way to speak to me like then or any other time of the day. And quite honestly I am looking forward to leaving behind that place and the rest of the UK when I fly away in about a couple of weeks now.

The actual reason why I wanted to start talking to you today was regarding a cute message I found on a Christian web board. They were in the midst of discussing God, and specifically the differences between the sexes in relation to him. See what you think:

Re: BANG for women

Whether in the Jewish or Christian beliefs, then yes women can have a relationship with God, but why do you not think that God has an order?
And why do you think that someone as a leader and someone as a helper aren't equal in the eyes of God? Do you feel only the more power on earth one has the more of a relationship they have with Him? But yes if you are faithful in small things He gives you more. And do not look at those in leadership today. They could have been given that power by Satan. This is what I say with some in our very own churches.

<This is actually quite a precious moment and I think you should read it slowly perhaps re-read it to give it its full due. Okay I have just made my own contribution to the comments, which I will copy for you to see now.>

Hiya every1. I have been following this thread quite carefully and I'd like to make a few comments of my own. First of all the faith you army of one, have shown towards our God is commendable. In the face of adversity you have persevered and stayed true to what you know is right in your heart. If only many others in this calamitous world showed the same strength and humanity in the face of terror then I think we wouldn't have half as many problems as we do today.

Secondly what you all in here have to try and realize is that the Bible was a book written by MEN. Inspired by God, but written by human hands. And it has been edited and changed over the years from translations to different languages for example. Not to mention the document we have at home is missing large chunks: take the dead sea scrolls as found in the east not long ago. There some of the writings are the same and yet there are many new ones which have not been included.

Belief in God is something which we each have to look for in our own hearts. Some of us will find him, some of us never will. And I for one don't say of Him like, God is in the rainbow. That was His proof to us that He exists. Have you ever looked up at one, I mean really looked? It says so in the Bible. I think that some people take too much of what it says in there as concrete fact and lose the meaning of its spiritual value.

We all are educated adults and so please try not to argue about it, especially given that it is clear that most of you haven't even attempted to read it.

I'm gonna finish with a story of my own. Well when I was in hospital a few months back and went to the local hospital Chapel of Holy Congregation, I was then accompanied by a good friend, Tabith, or Tabitha as I used to call her. She is a precious person who has been through hard times and is making good progress now, I do still keep in touch with her even though she has moved away. Anyhow the story in question being taught us that day was about how Jesus came across a sick and dying woman in a house and I think he healed her. Anyway you will never guess what her name was? That's right Tabith. Right there in the Bible itself. I don't know if this is a miracle or co-incidence, but surely remarkable.

Take it easy y'all.

Oh yeah and just one more thing. Yesterday when I was sitting on the park bench feeling miserable and sorry for myself, that little squirrel I saw before, at least I think it was the same one, came up on the bench and said hello to me again. Well he held my hand in his little paws if I remember correctly and just kinda let me know that every-thing is going to be alright. Also the pigeons gathered around me at that time as well and that was a touching moment really. I'm going to buy some brown bread and go back today to see if I can find them again to feed them.

OK I'm going to talk to you for another little bit of time right now. I am quite happy with the way this book is progressing. It seems to be developing into a diary which also chronicles my adventures in cyberspace as accounted for by posts on various different web-sites. Likewise there are personal events and thoughts which I go through and have which I have been able to express and explore with you, the reader, here.

Well I don't remember if I have told you this, but recently I have signed up to a martial arts forum at martialartstalk.net They don't just take anybody I think. It's kind-of like you have to prove yourself to be accepted as a member in there. Well around Christmas time when I was in hospital, I tried to join another similar site. It certainly appears that they are a lot of beefed up black-belts as a part of both of them. But seeing as I am interested in MA I wanted to join. Last time I got booted out after about one hour's membership, if that! I think it was something to do with the fact that I said that I had trained in 'Monkey' style. That was a joke, but maybe they didn't see the funny side. Either that or my comment that 'All these American kick boxers can do is kick!'

Ha-ha. I realise that if they aren't American themselves, then they do have a good number of members who are. Clearly this went down like a ton of bricks. And you know when you get banned, it just means you type in your user-name and password and it comes up with a message such as 'username not recognised', or something such-with.

I have been banned from quite a few sites before in the past, and I want to give you a concrete example of what is shown when the moderators finally decide that they have had enough of my rantings and ban me. This is from Koei dot com, a rather strictly monitored site run by the official Koei company. At least they pay for it and the registered Moderators run it. How you actually become a 'mod' is another story. I suppose each site has its different policies for getting them. I think that they are mostly unpaid, and just do it as a hobby in their free time.

An Error Has Occurred! Sorry Guest, you are banned from using this forum! He kept spamming even after being warned by a Moderator. He posted back to back.

Okay, and I have been banned a second time from them more recently. With a more simple 'you have been banned' message this time. This time around after logging in under a completely different user name and email address, and never revealing my true identity to them, although I did in the end drop a hint, and I think they may have remembered me from my way of being blunt. Still I had a difficulty making friends, or cyber-friends on there, and in the end ended up going head to head with one of the moderators on a Christianity discussion. Which I think I have already copied for you in one of the above posts. Or even if it wasn't exactly the same as that, it was at least very similar. Written in a preaching kind of tone, and assuming the confidence of someone who has spent a lot of time studying and or arguing about God over the years, from either side of the fence I might add.

But you know what? They didn't even ban me over that. Instead I think they did it right at the end, when I had started talking about other more inconsequential issues, and I threw into the fire the remark that I thought that their head administrator 'evilruler' was a tyrant. I was already on my final straw at that point and clearly he blew his top with me and struck me off without another word.

Luckily on my brief foray into their realm I discovered the name of a new, breakaway site for fans of Koei games. Which lots of the old members had been jumping ship for, and joining. Well near the end of my time there I also made a real sarky remark that if they kept the faith and held their heads up high, I was sure that things would work out in the end. Actually this isn't what I think at all. Theirs is a top heavy website, with too much interference from the administrators. They will censor posts for swear words, this I understand, it's usual policy, for vague or rambling thread titles, or even if they don't like the cut of someone's jib. Not okay. I'm now going to show for you the entrance post I threw at this new break-away games forum in an attempt to get in there:

Hi mate. I've just been banned AGAIN from Koei dot com! And I swear I didn't break any of the rules, not this time! Look I promise to be on my best behaviour here and hopefully we can have a long and fruitful relationship together & eviladministrator is a NOOB. And here is his reply:

Account Validated.
This message is to inform you that your account has been approved by admin and you now have full account privileges on the forum. These include but are not limited to ability to reply and start topics throughout the forum, and access Member Only Downloads.
We do however ask that you read over KW Forum Rules before doing anything on the site, once you have an understanding of them feel welcome to use your new account, set-up your profile etc. and introduce yourself to the community, if you encounter any problems or wish to provide the forum feedback please do so in the Support/Feedback forum.
I don't know whatever happened with KOEI.com, but I hope

180

you enjoy the KOEI Warriors Forum!
Best Regards,
KOEI Warriors

Funny huh? Well I think so anyway.

14: Martial Madness

So back to what I was saying, I have recently been able to subscribe to a <new> martial arts site. I have always fancied myself as something of a freedom fighter, and so wanted to try my luck with some of these hot-blooded animals to see how I might fare.

One of the first replies I got was not promising:

Re:Hi guys - 2008/08/23 17:59

I have read these messages several times now. I have searched for coding, enciphering, and complex letter placements. I have run each word through a scanner and fed them into machines whose purpose even I'm not cleared to know, and I invented them. I burned the paper these words were written on to see if flame could in turn transcribe their true meaning into smoke and thus learn the glorious meaning of all things. Alas, all I could achieve in this period was the Question to Life, the Universe, and Everything.

That question is: huh?

He's basically taking the piss. And notice his 'filthy hippy alert' thread at the bottom. This I think is referring to me, and it doesn't look promising. Okay, so what if I've got a hygiene problem sometimes? I know sometimes I do smell, and sometimes despite washing it just won't seem to go away. But it still doesn't warrant his being rude to me now, does it?

Anyway, undeterred I kept on posting, about various topics from my belief in the spirit and how this relates to fighting, to my involvement with the secret service and things like that. This was in response to someone else's almost mythical comment of a scuffle he'd had with the triads, some time ago now. I didn't know what to make of what he said, I was just suspicious that he might have been making it up shall we say. But I know for a fact that what I've been through is real. Although I don't propose to go over all the evidence for what I'm talking about now.

Instead I will continue with the line which follows my story from entering this site. Well I think that a lot of them took me as something of a novelty. Someone who clearly doesn't have the physical skills that they possess, yet still has the audacity to square up to each and every one of them and take them at their own game as it were. Well you know I have been playing this game for much too long to even pretend not to be good at it. I am prepared to challenge the injustices of this world, and hope to prevail in the long run. See what you think of the thread I started for myself, entitled 'Philosophy'.

Don't dismiss philosophy, or religion, so readily when it is clear that none of you have studied them. It is possible to fight with your ideas, but the presumption that martial-arts reigns supreme is both false and misguided.

<OspreyTKD>

I think you've been reading all the wrong posts mate, not a lot of us think that here, just a minority.

<pennmartkd>
I am very curious about this thread, but also a good bit confused. Could you please elaborate a bit more on what you're poking at? Thanks.

<john2054>
OK I'm no MA but I am a fighter. I have fought for my family and will continue to do so. I also try to stand up for my friends and principles, such as truth. Just lend a helping hand and I am vulnerable to being stabbed myself. So I got robbed of 40 quid 2day 4 example. Cheers

<osrkd_101>

OK. I'm confused again.

<ProfessorPain>
What are you trying to say? That philosophy is important? Lots of people here know plenty about philosophy. I minored in it at college. It might help you avoid a fight, but once fists start flying being able to construct a valid deductive argument doesn't really do much for you.

<Rajah>

Martial arts aren't just physical; they have heavy philosophy
and I'm pretty sure all of us know that martial arts aren't all
powerful. I have studied Religion for many years so don't
assume that all of us are the same.

<john2054>
Hi Professor and Rajah,

I'm glad that at least two of you appreciate some things about
what I am saying. Look I fought with my parents to get
Nelson Mandela and the others released from Robben Island
and to overthrow the South African Apartheid regime back in
the day. This is a fight that we won. I've fought to stay alive
after getting hit and put in a coma for about 3 weeks I think,
back in '97. I have also fought for my sanity and dignity after
being held in secure hospitals against my will twice each time
for seven months, and certainly the second time through no
fault of my own. I have fought to retain the love of my
sweetheart who is the other side of the world and has been
separate from me for about eight years now. I argued her case
when no one else believed me and they all told me to forget
about her. Some turn-around that has been. And I argue for
the truth to be told, in the Iraq war, via college studies and
demonstrations in London, and in the press such as now with
Georgia on the BBC blogosphere website and earlier about
Zimbabwe on the yahoo forum. So please don't tell me about

fighting. These are big struggles, much bigger than who could win a fisticuff fight.

Also the true meaning of philosophy comes from not just the study of what these scholars from Oxbridge universities and wherever, have to say, but also learning how to implement the knowledge you have learned to craft your everyday life and change the world around you, preferably for the better of mankind. This is something that you won't have learned at uni, and is what I call higher knowledge/philosophy. It is to do with the power of the human mind and soul and expansion of this power. It is hard to talk to you guys about it if you are so busy beating up bricks or showing off your kira and whatever. That's what I think anyway.

<pennmartkd>

Philosophy - 2008/08/24 15:47 You have some absolutely solid points. For me it's summed up in one word. "Character." That's what gives you the wherewithal to stand for something that you know is right regardless of the tide, persist through tough situations even when you feel like quitting, and letting your actions reflect your beliefs instead of it all being just lip service.
It sounds like you have a kind of one-sided view of what the martial arts are all about. There are certainly some threads on here as of late that have the emphasis of the combative facet of the arts, but often interwoven are some comments about a philosophy of avoiding it if you can.

Any true martial artist, I believe, is going to have the higher point of character development behind their training and teaching. I think John Rhee said something to the effect that martial arts without philosophy is just street-fighting.

If you want to get things going more along these lines, I'd suggest starting more threads like this. I think you might be surprised at the posts you'll get.

<john2054>

Hiya everyone again,

OK this is really starting to p*ss me off. This is gonna be the third time that I am posting this message (seeing as both the other times it got deleted probably by admin, or a hacker!). I've gotta try and remember what I was saying.

One of the points had to do with my musical past. I played piano at school and then the guitar as an adult. I have never taken any grades at the guitar but that doesn't mean that I wasn't good at it. I think that I was, and so did the people who fed me money on the days I went busking in reasonable weather.

Next I met a guy in the park when I was feeding the pigeons today. I told him where to go in no uncertain terms (that is editing [and also probably why this message got deleted before]). Sorry, he told me to quit feeding them because they're vermin, and I said that, and he was like 'I'll knock your head off', and I was like come on then. But then he wandered off and peace and harmony reigned supreme once more in my local park. Enabling me to feed them and a couple of squirrels too.

The thing about the music is that despite not getting any formal grades didn't mean that I wasn't any good. Far from it. Just mean that I didn't 'play their game'. So to speak. To what I can concern the same thing applies to the MA world. Sure it is good if you can jump through the hoops and pass the criteria for whatever belt syllabus it is that you are studying.
But I have been playing this game for too many years. Hence I will bow down to no man. Like I have explained elsewhere on philosophy, there is a knowledge beyond that of the ordinary press and generally accepted consensus of normality, sometimes. I find this with my secret service hippy girlfriend, and everything is cute.

You might be able to fight for ages until you are black and blue but I am sure that one ninja punch could not just kill you, but eliminate your entire family in the process. Don't believe me. I know what some of you guys have been saying about me, so don't even act all goggle-eyed to me.

I can also say that Jimi Hendrix was (voted) the greatest musician of all time, cos he played sweet music. So too Bruce Lee I think is generally recognised as the greatest MA. He would be on a popular worldwide poll I am sure. Look there is more stuff I want to say, but I have heard the final internet café whistle.

Peace now and mods, please don't delete this time. Also did any1 see that kid win his gold in the Olympics judo. I think he was a Korean. Anyway he lifted the opponent up and threw/dumped him on his back! Sweet.

OK so the family comment was below the belt. I still think that it's sick some of the pictures you've got on display and if you think that's funny then you deserve the worst I can throw at you.

<axbxixr, Admin>

Re:Philosophy - 2008/08/25 10:05 I wouldn't delete it. I never did. Hope all is well with you now. The most important thing is that a person can live with himself and thus have to do the things he thinks are just

<me again>

Re: Philosophy - 2008/08/25 10:53 Hi admin. I want to use language to cut through all the rubbish (in the world) like a knife. John

<OspreyTKD>
erm… what???

<me again>

189

Hi Osprey and Ax

Well a photo of a guy with his head up his own ass, and another of a guy's member are not things I want to see really. Er, oh yeah. I am reading a book on the Navy Seals, and it has reached a point over half way through when they are surrounded and taking fire from all sides Hopelessly outnumbered and taking heavy casualties. Marcus Luttrell in lone survivor.

I just wanted to know have any-of you else ever found yourselves in this hopeless situation, fighting near impossible odds. And unlike this fire-fight which was over within some 48 hours, my hospital battles both went on for a good seven months each. Sorry to hark back to this but well sue me..

And like the seals I don't forget who my friends are. So I go back for them. My good friend Lindhi from Zambia I talked to today and I'll be damned if we're not going to go back to at least visit her.

Likewise I have been trying my best with Tabith, another Christian who I have been visiting since I got out.

I don't know if <any of> you realise this, but the police are crooked as muck. I saw this new gal in a train station last week with a Stanley knife in her hands, standing in the middle of the tracks, clearly in quite some distress and wanting attention. She said that they had taken her kids from her, among other things. Anyway the policewoman actually turned her back when she began cutting the veins from out of one of her arms, and thus didn't see it and let her get on with it.

I suspect you lot are always on the right side of the law. They tend to stick to their own kind, beefed up fighters like the martial artists who visit these kind of sites I'd imagine. You know it's all like, 'who did you bone last night' or lets go down the stadium and support the Rams. But if you, or they, can't even help someone when they are in distress like that, then I don't think they should even be wearing their badge.

<pennmartkd>

I have absolutely no words to describe the confusion I am experiencing after reading this post.

And so it goes on. As you can see, not all of the guys entirely understand what I am going on about. Perhaps they are just not used to reading my way of speaking, like maybe they are reading it too fast, or skim reading it, and missing over the vital points. Or maybe they just don't have the empathic sensory skills to understand my emotional output. But either way that's really not my problem. Hopefully some of them have been able to follow me, and I think I have done a reasonable job at fighting to retain my dignity, despite being surrounded by mainly men who have mostly dedicated their lives to ripping other's heads off. In arguments AND fights. I am happy to have kept this (my dignity). You know last night I was on the verge of losing it. I sometimes get like that in the evenings, feeling low and unloved. Then it seemed like they were all mocking me and I just wanted to tell them all where to go in no uncertain terms. If you have read the above posts closely then you will see that I have twice had my messages

191

actually deleted from the site because they contained a swear word, the ef word in fact, and that warrants an automatic removal as I have now learnt. But I have been pushing it. I like to push it. My old philosophy teacher at college told us that he thought that it is a good philosopher's job to always ask questions, to test the boundaries of the conventions of normality, and this is exactly what I have been doing.

So some of them perhaps won't understand where I am coming from. Some of them won't know where I am going. Man even I don't know that. Instead I am focusing on the present, and the immediate future and past, things which I can both remember and feel closely. I have at the moment, got a good feeling of control over my life, and hopefully I can build on this strong ground. And despite being on the verge of throwing in the martial forum towel last night, I have had at least a few constructive remarks, or at lest comments on my speeches, and for this I am grateful. They have been part of the forces which have given me the strength to continue with my struggle, continue with my discussions and arguments. I cannot always expect to win. But after the mighty loss I had which was being sectioned, well I think that God owes me at least a reasonable period of comfort and security. This is what I am hoping anyway.

Hi my readers. Here we go again. I have had a wash and a good sleep, gone to the internet café and checked out the MA and new Koei warriors forum, not to mention the news and my emails. And here I am again chatting with you now. I'm gonna tell you exactly what I have been saying on these places as well so you can see exactly where I have been coming from.

15: Network Subversion

Interesting to hear you guys speak. I am a Buddhist AND a
Christian! I bet there aren't many of those around. Also I just
got banned from Koei dot com, but you guys seem to be quite
a bit more liberal and I hope that I will have better luck here.
So what is God? Well it says in the bible that he proves
himself with his rainbows. Have you ever looked at one and
just wondered, I mean really gone to town about it?
Er. Christianity can help you when no-one else will. Point I
say He, but I don't think that God is a single entity, much as
love, or rainbows don't have a gender. How then can Christ?
With regards to Buddhism, I first learned about that through
its philosophy. The way it teaches that rain falls from the sky
because of clouds, and so too its true with Karma. I'm not
trying to disprove anyone here just put my opinions forward.
Also the idea of atoms is just a theory. Much like the debate
between the light wave or particles? I have studied philosophy
and religion at college under a very good Christian scientist.
He didn't force us to believe anything, but gave us the
freedom to make our own choices. This is the only way.
Peace every1.

Well I had prepared a load of other stuff but it all seems kind
of irrelevant now. I want you guys to trust me and say that I
do know what I am talking about. For example the point I
made that the Spirit can beat both the mind and body, and I
gave concrete examples. Sometimes you have to take time to

reflect on the truth. The generally accepted consensus (for example that 9/11 and 7/7 were by these cave dwelling Jihadists is NOT the truth. In order to learn this you have to commit to meditating on the root of all things. This kind of understanding is attainable if you use your powers towards it. I have done it and I am only human like everyone else in here.

People all too readily rely on authority of the assumed order, the natural order if you want, but actually the establishment, to assume the correct state of things. One such assumption is that of the validity of money, territorial boundaries and possession of material goods. These things are assumed to be correct and valid by the majority, and that is the way it must be at the moment. 'Cos if you dared to challenge any of them it would land you in serious trouble with the police/government/and the whole of the rest of the ancient regime. But love (different from sex), like that which we share with our families and close friends. That is of a different higher value.

Don't take what I have been saying as gospel. I'm not trying to kill anyone. Just have a rational debate, raising serious questions and hopefully provoking some well considered answers. Nor do I want to insult anyone's families who have lost families to the terror attacks. On the BBC blogosphere conspiracy pages there are reams and reams of evidence supporting the theory that the terror attacks were staged. Just look at the way the buildings fell in a controlled manner for example. But I understand that you don't want to talk about politics here. Just remember that in a fight you go for the weak spots, or least need to measure your strike before making it. In the same way military attacks go for the supply lines, look at Russia's quick leap into Georgia to halt the aggression there for example.

I have read Musashi Miyamoto's The Five Rings as a classic of warfare fighting, and for any of you who are serious about learning battle strategy will read this also. Perhaps you will see it as somewhat incomprehensible. But I felt that I could understand that I knew what he was saying. It's not all about fighting, although I can see it may appear to be just that. If you take it out of the context it was written in it can quite readily be applied to everyday living. The idea of the elemental structure of the different realms of combat, shouldn't be rigidly stuck to as gospel. But rather looked at in the way that things in the world, from people to emotions, literature to films, can be broken down into different groups/sub-sets.

Take films for example, as my last point. There are clearly good films and bad ones. Some like Crouching Tiger Hidden Dragon, have expert choreography and are based on legend, with good actors and some convincing Chinese ninjas to make a good all round blockbuster. Others such as Step Up are just rubbish. Okay, I haven't even seen it but I don't have to. What I'm trying to say is that knowledge both underpins peoples convictions and actions. And so a knowledge of the circumstances of a fight for instance, will empower you with the decision of what is the best type of move. Sometimes you have to take action, in order to stand up for yourself. Other times you have to act the responsible adult and refrain from doing so. I want you all to be as empowered as to the max of your capacity. And hopefully a few of you will be able to engage me some way further in this discussion?

You know I have got no idea what they are going to say to this. Clearly my ramblings have just shot over the top of quite a lot of the people in there. It is nice to be able to have a forum within which to discuss my ideas and such forth. And maybe one or two of them will recognize what I am saying for the power it is. But even if not, no matter. There are other sites which I contribute to now, as you well know, and I am sure that my influences go further than to just one place.

Something else which I thought was good which I wanted to tell you is that you know the Koei warriors site? Well they have granted me the category of soldier. I just think that that is cool. Obviously I am not a soldier, but perhaps from my strength of conviction/loyalty to the cause they understood something and that is why they did it. Like I am a fighter, I got kicked out of the koei dot com site for fighting you might say. This even reminds me of an experience where I got told off for fighting when it wasn't even my fault. Like I didn't even throw the first punch, if indeed I hit him at all. And this very same thing also happened some years earlier on a primary school outing if I remember correctly. Then I just mopped it up with the teachers, and wrangled out of it that way. But now the guns are primed and I'm ready to go!

Hi guys. Well I have just had another afternoon with my mum and sister. First of all we picked mum up from the station, then we went to feed the birds just me and her, Cathy dropped us off. Then we eventually found a couple of birds and managed to feed them some bread before some dog

197

walker's dog scared them off. Then we went for a nice meal in a local Tai restaurant. It was nice, and gave me the chance to have a long chat with both of them, both about my internet encounters, and also about Cathy's room at uni and also about my mum's parents who are very old now and both in need of plenty of tender love and care, her dad especially. After the meal we went to the bookshop Waterstones to browse, and then that was it and I escorted mum most of the way back to the station. It is very important to me my family and they both provide me with a great deal of emotional and spiritual support, for which I am very grateful.

Now, as you might expect, I have charged back to the internet. Desperate to see what those MA guys have said to my latest contribution. And joy they have responded since this morning! But just imagine how gutted I was on discovering that it wasn't constructive criticism but as blunt as you could get. Quote by pennmartkd;

You've got definite issues pal. It's very hard to take you seriously as any kind of philosopher when you follow a statement proclaiming yourself as such with such a well thought out and eloquent statement as:
"You know what? It doesn't even matter who that guy in the park was. I don't care. You don't go around threatening to put a fist through my head or I will pop a cap in your ass punk."
…
Clearly he doesn't appreciate the finer points of my speech. But it makes no difference. Being on the forum has given me the opportunity to discuss my somewhat unorthodox views about fighting. And for this I am also grateful. Hopefully there

are others on this site who do see what I am saying. Maybe they will get back to me in the future. Sometimes I even paste my thoughts from this book right onto the site. But I'm not going to this time. I don't want to burn all of my bridges now do I? Meaning that this book I am writing is precious to me, and if they realised that much of what they have said online, is being taken apart by me piece by piece in a publishable form, well I don't think that they would be too happy. But screw them. This is what I think, and what I feel, and whatever they say online should be accountable for anyway. Else-wise they shouldn't even be saying it!

But I admit I do like to court controversy. Sometimes what I say is purposely outlandish, and intended to be that way just to provoke a response. It is not that I am wrong, but neither am I purely right. More like I think that what I am saying has the impression of truth to it, the hint, and by making it as a declaration I am able to judge from the response people get, certain things. It also shows that I am brave enough to say things that no-one else dares, and I think this takes something as well. It is like I have been telling them online; it is one thing to be able to fight someone, and quite another to be able to outshine them ethically altogether. I want to move on from there. OK here is the response I gave on the MA forum site;

Bruce Lee was an actor sure, but don't underestimate the dramatic arts. They are able to reach and entertain the greatest number of people. Saying that Mr X is better than Lee is like saying a machine gun is better than a Samurai sword. Sure it may be able to kill more people in one go, but does that make it actually better? Or is it better to fight with no weapons at all, given the chance? Or what about fighting with love (which definitely does not involve killing?) Or communication?

Anyway I was chatting to a gal a couple of years back in a Chinese medical store who told me that she too thought that he was the best. Did you know that the martial arts isn't just about causing pain to people? That's Ju-jitsu. There is also something called drunken master style, which Jackie Chan is an expert in, which also involves humour, although can be applied to a lethal extent as well.

I don't want to fight any of you guys. Your strengths are probably things like discipline, muscular endurance and control and strength. Me I have just got my philosophy! Ha-ha. But the spirit is a powerful thing which any Aikido black belt should be able to tell you.

In hospital I met quite a few fighters. One Guy, Al, I think he was from the Bahamas, well he was the toughest guy there. And he had the best sense of humour as well. I first met him in the intensive care unit four years ago, and he didn't like me much then. But we get on well now. I also met this other nurse who told me he could do a hundred push-ups. And another, Damien, he had a good sense of humour and practised some traditional form of Kung Fu in his spare time, to which there are no belts he told me. I think it was what Bruce Lee was first trained in as well before he did JKD. I also met a second degree black belt TKD, or at least she was going in for her 2nd. And another brown belt of some other form of TKD, although she told me she'd never get to black because in order to do that you had to do the splits! Like it was a part of the syllabus. She was cute as well! This is another long email.

Take it easy class.

Again I am being controversial in some of the things I say, I know. But I planned this essay even in the train station waiting for my mum, actually typing into a note memo on my phone, thoughts for what I was going to say. And now I have said them. Different things, about the very real people I knew back from hospital (although I can't remember all of their names) to something about Bruce Lee, and also a nice informal style to it as well. A lot of the guys can't understand it seems. Some probably write me off as a nutter, a w***er, whatever. Even still while I am getting responses I will continue to post. And even when I don't, I will still anyway if I think that it will do me any good. Like if I will get anything out of it.

It is very much like writing a diary, only this one is online. One of the other times I committed myself to writing was at secondary school for drama class; we had to keep track of the day's lessons in a log-book. That was pretty enlightening even if it just went in the bin in the end. And when I got my first book printed, well I spent quite a long time working on that as well. But as I think I have mentioned already, a key difference between here and there is that I am largely keying in text I want to be published straight out, without that great deal of editing and formatting which my other book went through.

I have already told you about what I did on the new Koei forum earlier today, and so I suppose that is pretty much my internet experience dried up for another day. My mum asked me 'What will I do when I go over to Africa and am deprived of this facility?' Well like I answered her, I'm sure that me and my girlfriend will have plenty of things to do, like most husbands and wives! I'll leave it on that note. Peace now.

I saw my granny yesterday. She lives over in Bures, and is doing well considering that she is dying of cancer. I think it meant a lot to the both of us meeting again; it's been some years now you know. Well I also had a nice time travelling down there on the train with my dad and sister. And on the way back on the train me and sis had an interesting chat about Christianity. Like we had something of an argument about reaching God, seeing as she is a Christian, and I am a Christian and a Buddhist, and it is clear that she doesn't really agree with this, not that she understands my 'other' religion at all. Well anyhow today I came across an interesting writing in the Bible which is from Psalm 119:57 (Heth).

You are my portion, O Lord; I have promised to obey your words. I have sought your face with all my heart; be gracious to me according to your promise. I have considered my ways and have turned my steps to your statues. I will hasten and not delay to obey your commands. Though the wicked bind me with ropes, I will not forget your law. At midnight I rise to give you thanks for your righteous laws. I am a friend to all who fear you, to all who follow your precepts. The earth is filled with your love, O Lord; teach me your decrees. This speech is perfect for my commitment to the elements of love, and charity, and hope, and giving and all of these other things which make us better people. And isn't it funny that I just opened the Bible and that was the first part I laid my eyes upon!

I also saw a good programme on TV yesterday, where Jerry Springer traced his family roots back to Germany. His parents you see, actually came from Germany, or an area of Germany which is now Poland. They emigrated to Britain to escape the fascist persecution, and that was where he was born! I never knew that. So he tracked down the resting places of both of his grandmothers, and one was gassed and one died peacefully in a concentration camp hospital. Watching that show conjured up some memories of what it must have felt like for the Jewish people at that time, and made me decide to commit to learning more about Judaism if I possibly can. This seems to be the most persecuted against and disliked of all religions, even to this day. And don't forget that my granddad is actually Jewish, and so it is a part of me you might say. So I feel an obligation to learn more about this one of God's faces. Wish me luck.

Ah man, I just put a long one up there and it didn't register, man! I'm gonna try again.

God calls out to each of our souls; we can either find him or we can't. Don't think that you are just going to wake up one morning a Christian; it doesn't work that way.

You have to actively engage with his teachings. Look for him in the Bible. No, don't believe every word! If you did that then He would be a mass murderer among other things (having wiped out cities with thunderbolts for trivial reasons, for example). That is not the way to read it. You have to read it from your heart. Be open to His message, but remember that it was written by men (you know, sinners). So it is bound to contain both inaccuracies and plain lies. I don't for one minute believe every word in there.

But how about the simple phrase, God is love. Contemplate it for a while. Don't just condemn it with your intellectual/logical brain. But try to feel the meaning. So God is the connection people make when they touch the mind and hearts of their loved ones. God is when he shows you hope. God is the seven colours in the rainbow, and all the other miracles out there.

And if you don't believe in miracles, what a sad life you must live! Faith is so much more than one man or woman. But that is where it started.

As to the Psalm I copied above, well I just stumbled across it the other day in the Christian café, when I opened the Bible, and there it was! What a stroke of good luck, hey!

It means that you should commit yourself to God, like the person who wrote it. Not God as in the big bearded bloke in the sky, but the little one in your heart. Ah I'm rambling on again. This stuff may not be relevant to Martial Arts, but bloody well is to Christians. So I stand by its inclusion in this thread.

Hi readers! Here we are again. Another good day is drawing to a close, the darkness is sweeping in, and I sit down to write. Above is a posting I have just made on that Martial Arts site, in response to some biting criticism of my earlier psalm, which I have also copied for you to read. My defence pretty much speaks for itself, as indeed do most of these posts, or so I would hope.

16: A Conspiracy?

At 3:01pm on 28 Aug 2008, busby2 wrote:

I find it amusing that the truthers believe that WTC 7 (and also WTC1 and 2) were brought down by Controlled Demolition when there is no evidence whatsoever to back up the contention that the buildings were prepared for CD. All buildings prepared for CD are stripped out and prepared for CD over weeks, if not months. The evidence of preparing the buildings for CD would have been seen by those working in the buildings, like maintenance engineers.
FACT: you cannot prepare occupied buildings of this size for CD without many people noticing and blowing the whistle! The NIST report recognises this.
If these buildings had indeed been brought down by CD in a novel way that nobody has explained, this would have been the first time in history that this had been carried out on occupied buildings without anyone noticing that the buildings were being prepared for CD. And yet this is believed by the truthers, the same truthers who reject out of hand that WTC7 was brought down by fire simply because this would be the first time in history that it has happened!! As for Ynda's comment "If you do believe NIST then evacuate New York now: skyscrapers are not safe!", there maybe some truth in this! According to the NIST report it took an hour for WTC7 to be evacuated when the building was half occupied and all exits were unblocked and working perfectly. How long would it have taken if WTC7 was fully occupied and if some

of the emergency exits were unsafe because of fire or smoke? Surely it would have taken well over 2 hours, and I question whether that would have been enough time to save everyone in the event of a major fire. Moral of the story: if the fire alarm goes off in a big skyscraper, evacuate immediately! I believe that saved the life of one worker high up in the second tower to be hit. I read that he left as soon as the first plane hit whilst his colleagues continued working whilst people were jumping from the adjoining tower. His colleagues never got out as they were still working when the second plane hit. It is interesting to note that the new WTC7 has far wider emergency stairwells and far greater protection from fire damage than its predecessor. It could now be the safest skyscraper in New York!

At 3:59pm on 28 Aug 2008, frasay wrote:

Hi Busby,
To agree with you is to ignore the first hand witness accounts of Barry Jennings, who says on video that explosions were going on in building 7 before the twin towers fell.
Do your own research into this on youtube. Busby, you're argument seems to me to be that because you personally can't imagine how someone could secretly rig a building with explosives, it can't be done. There wouldn't have been many people in the building at night. Why not rig it then over several weeks/months? Have you seen the film, Man on a Wire, in which a small team infiltrate the Twin Towers and rig a cable across both towers? This seemed impossible,

before they did it. I'm fairly sure also that huge bridges have been secretly rigged with explosives during war time.

How can you dismiss witness testimony of Barry Jennings? How can you dismiss all the other witnesses who say they heard explosions, or were blown off their feet by explosions. Also, how do you explain the refusal of mainstream media to show us the videos of building 7 collapsing for at least 5 years after the event? Why the cover up on building 7?

As can be seen above, there is still an interesting and well argued debate going on about the events which took place 9/11 even after all these years. Also just quickly, here is the reply that I have blasted in before I go.

Well Bubsy, if that is your real name, if you're not a government spy then you sure are a bigger sucker than Blair ever was.

9/11 was clearly a planned demolition. There is plenty of evidence from the third tower, to the investments, to the subsequent wars, to even the Bin-laden family having personal jets out of there right after it happened! I actually wouldn't be surprised if they were actually sheltering him somewhere untouchable, just so they could keep up this apparent charade of a search for him in Iraq/Afghanistan.

Most Brits now don't support either war, certainly not the ones I've talked to. That is too many innocent civilians are dying. Haven't you even considered that all of those 'official' stories are just too good to be true?

There is an old saying 'the first casualty in war is the truth'. And I think that is certainly true here. Take it easy. <Controversial I know, but sometimes it takes that to eke out the truth!>

<Another Martial Arts post I made.>

I wonder if having a fiercely high metabolism acts in direct conflict with spiritual peace? It's just that none of you have appeared to offer me anything more than a nod to all of these treaties which I have thus offered/procured. A certain amount of my writing is to make friends. To comfort myself. To express myself and assure myself. But it is also to explore ideas. Of spirits, and the more sedentary realm of martial combat. These are words and I am asking for feedback and suggestions. Don't be afraid of me, I won't bite!

PS, just to prove that I'm not a complete lazy bad man, last night I did about half an hour's ninja dancing to my sister's dance CD! and: Just as I hope to teach my baby daughter about God, as she grows up, and teach myself, I can try to teach you peops, and my friends, as well.

<This is a post I planned to make on the Inter-Gamers-Network site, which I never got round to.>

Did you know that the first time I properly realised how I could change the outcome of events in the world was about a month ago when I made a comment on a video game website (which also has public input), criticizing Square Enix's (a games producer who has created arguably some of the best role-playing games ever to grace the earth with final fantasy

7,9 and x-2 each of which I have completed!) decision to make final fantasy 12 a big let-down, despite arguably the most amount of hype and greatest expectations (and longest wait) a game has ever had? Practically the entire production team was scrapped, from the director to the battle director to the musical composer. And that guy Noremaya Uematsu, has created without a doubt the most impressive game musical scores for any game ever! The music was so beautiful and enchanting, the minute I heard he had gone I knew the game was doomed to be crud. Obviously the team tried to make the game a success. And on the veneer, it appeared to be just that.

But after half an hour's play or so, it became apparent to all of us die-hard fans, who like our games but don't expect to die over them, that the game was much too hard. Like what's the point of having plenty of options, if you have to unlock all of them to make even the slightest headway in?! And it took ages playing for like a real shortcut-scene. That just won't do. Plus the tunes were (as I had predicted) boring and rubbish compared to the earlier masterpieces. All of this I said on a direct post to IGN. And you know what? The next day Square Enix themselves, that big once world dominant Japanese power player, announced that it was changing the next game in the series (ff13) to dual format! Now I don't know if they realised that I had a 360, or had just guessed, but either way I am quite sure that they had read what I had put and taken it into consideration when making their decision. Which shows that even us little people can influence the big players.

Of course after that the internet was burning with rage! What were they (SE) doing! In abandoning their once beloved PS3 exclusives for the Microsoft machine compatibility. And seeing as I have no proof towards my conviction, no doubt the argument will continue for aeons to come about the true reason for this change. Which incidentally could make the demise of the PS3 format as successive games producers jump ship. But the real issue, still concerns will the change make any difference? I mean will ff13 live up to its expectations? They still don't have the key members of the team (already discussed) which made the earlier game.

So what is to stop this new offering from being any different from so many of these other new fangled games which place presentation over plot, and essentially amount to an enjoyable experience but nothing revolutionary or breathtaking as we all had once come to expect. I hope to be proven wrong, but I won't hold my breath!

17: The establishment is...

...a shady network of individuals who control where you work, where you shop, what you eat, what you watch (on TV), what you listen to, what you read, and what you think. They are not governments; they control the governments of the world. They dictate what is right, and what is wrong. They command who fights what war with whom and they dictate who wins. They decide whose economy succeeds and whose fails, by determining the international exchange rates they are able to put any continents or countries out of action (take Zimbabwe's recent fall from grace for instance).

They promote a macho versus feminism struggle which on appearances appears to be the natural way of things, but they can actually subtly promote to maintain their power. To them we, the little people, are at the bottom. They are the all powerful Doctors who decide what drugs you will take, what operations you will undergo and how long you will stay in hospital. They are the police who decide when you are arrested and how long you will stay in a cell for. They are the government who decide what wars your country will fight, and how much tax you will pay, among other things.

They are the media who will decide what most of us watch on TV, and what the more gullible of us will think. Have you ever wondered why voter turn-out in this country (Britain) is at its worst ever levels since universal suffrage began? It's not because we the Joe public are too 'lazy' to go to vote, as so many of the TV shows would have you believe, but because we are feeling rightfully pissed with the way the politicians never listen to what we say, always renegade on their promises and always stab us in the back.

They have led us into wholly disastrous wars, fighting innocent civilian populations in the name of 'Christ', and all the way expecting us to believe their lies on a daily basis, and continue to fund their guns with our taxes. They did it in Vietnam, Iraq and now Afghanistan. And they have tried ever so hard to do it in Russia and Zimbabwe too! They stock our farms with sick and dying livestock, then force mass culls of the animals when they fall unwell, instead of looking for a cure. You wouldn't kill a child if he or she fell ill!

If a newspaper dares to pick-up and question any of their antics, well God help them. Just look how the editor of the Mirror was sacked when he uncovered some gruesome pictures of British soldiers doing wholly unwholesome tortures in Iraq. The whole thing was quickly covered up and made to look like a scam. But a close attention to detail will actually prove some uncomfortable facts. Never mind that was what they were sent there to do. To maim and to kill. Which any of us 'truthful' historians of war have come to realise.

The government and media always present to the public a general 'sanitised' picture of war. Not because they believe that it would upset the public, but because they want to pretend that it isn't happening, that the dead millions don't exist. What's more unfortunate because of the years of believing their lies, of having no benchmark with which to question the 'validity' of their truth, many people are actually trapped into believing the lies. They discuss this 'artificial' reality amongst their friends. Blaming the world's troubles on some sneaky Al-Qaeda or the Taliban, who no matter the number of 'high profile' targets being taken out by carpet bombing of residential cities, there are always more to come! Why is this? Is this because the woodwork is just teaming with 'evil Muslims' chomping at the bit to kill another soldier, and are in some way genetically inferior and hence always bound to hate the occupiers and try to kill them? Are they incapable of learning not to fight? Do they not fear the bullets and the bombs, like everyone else?

Or like the Vietcong: are they recruited from the streets and the hearts of the dispossessed, a wild animal human soul, desperately clinging to its honour, its pride, its dignity its freedom. Surely not. Surely all of these carpet bombs are killing innocent human beings. No better no worse than someone born within these 'cruddy' British isles! No better no worse!! Forget the past for a minute I pray of you, look to the present, to the future.

Where is the honour in killing literally millions of civilians in a war that you'll never win? Wasting some trillions of pounds every year in just needless death and destruction. This is not honourable. This is not civilized. This is not war even. It's not even terrorism. Words fail to express and explain this evil, this 'establishment' this dictatorship over the human mind over all things good and equal.

And who will dare to stand up against them? To shout back to that barking army instructor as he assumes an air of invincible pride and authority as he bullies his troop into exercise? Who will dare oppose the Doctors who are trying to medicate us to death with their anti-psychotics, their mood-stabilizers, their anti-depressants? Who will dare to escape those walls and fences of that mental hospital which has kept us imprisoned for oh so many years? And who will dare to question the authority of the Doctor who put you under section in the first place, perhaps for putting through a car window, perhaps for doing nothing more than arguing with him. Tell your landlord that you don't stand bull-troublers and he evicts you. Tell your Doctor that you're not going to hospital again, show your consultant inside your rape scar on your bum, and he will keep you there. He did me!

So what can you do inside? Chat, go to chapel, fancy the nurses, the basics that's it. And what can you do when you're out? Well first of all; get better. Then get off the meds. Stand up for yourself. Argue with your Doctors. Believe in yourself; no-one else will. Listen to music. Pray. I am the Walrus, I am the sunscreen (Baz Leurman). Only joking. Er, make friends. Chat to people. There is no going back. And we all stick together, we who have faced the gates of death and live to tell the tale.

Write. It's your book, you can say what you want! Laugh. Dance! Feed the pigeons; even they need food you know. Remember how when you had no-one else, remember what that was like? Hope that you will find that one perfect woman whom you can marry and spend the rest of your life with, whom you can see God's face in, and be happy with, who can provide you with comfort when you are down and possibly have children with or adopt, who can be your left arm in everything you do and every decision you make.

And look after your friends. Visit them when they go to hospital, once a week every week they are in there for. Give them money if they don't have any. Give them a piece of your dream to hold to their breast from your own. There is enough for them surely. Try to be happy. Remember that there are days when you will feel low, when your enemies will scorn you and shun you. Ignore them and remember sleep is a great healer; hopefully tomorrow will be better. Don't place too much hope on your old friends; there is no telling when they will be gone.

But always try to give the benefit of the doubt to your new ones. The establishment is there. It is real and it is hard. It had centuries of time to solidify, to compact its roots, to engulf the world. Can it be beaten? Yes I would argue. But it's gonna take more than just one guy. A hell of a lot more!

I am not sure if it can be beaten by a majority. Currently it holds most if not all positions of power in government and such-forth. Look at how Georgia openly invaded South Ossetia (as I remember vividly watching being recorded on the BBC a couple of weeks ago), and then expects to get away with it! And then Russia swiftly and effectively reacts to stem and then stop the invasion; they are called the 'aggressors' and the 'war-criminals', when in fact it wasn't them who started it at all. Only they sure as hell   stopped it!

Then when it goes to the UN, they quickly wash their hands of the whole affair, and place 'frontier integrity' over acts of war (by Georgia), in siding with Georgia to deny Russia the right to declare the citizens of South Ossetia as part of its own. Even though the majority of them hold Russian passports, and have actually voted with an overwhelming majority FOR combining with Russia! This is not democracy. This is the West enforcing the borders it wants in Eastern Europe, against the will of South Ossetia's native population!

When Russia went to a separate coalition of Asian nations, did they have any better luck there? Not even Iran, with the fiercely Muslim Ahmadinejad dared to side with them. Instead only one inconsequential country (I forget its name) dared to break from the ranks, and support them. So what does this show? That Russia is weak? Nothing of the sort. They are the bravest of the lot at the moment, I would argue, for standing up for what they believe in.

Despite all of its high and mighty posturing, I don't think that they have anything to be afraid of by the UN. Here is an organisation set up in face of the defeat of the Nazi fascists to maintain world peace. And despite what good it may have done since then, it actually nailed its own coffin shut with the war it allowed in Iraq. It could have prevented that war. With but one veto against the invasion, the whole thing could have been averted.

At one of the London rallies I attended with hundreds of thousands of protesters, I clearly remember a French QC justice of the peace, telling us how flagrantly the whole invasion violated article 3 of the UN manifesto, that no country within the group shall attack another without due provocation. This is an international law which was quite clearly broken!

But that's the thing about laws. They are used by the powers that be to enforce their rules when they want to. What about the law to tell the truth? That one seems to have gone out the window a long time ago!

So what are we left with now? Ah, before I go there I just want to share with you two more memories from marching with Stop the War demonstrations in London. One is marching through the streets of the capital, singing war chants, and dancing to the music being played by the big band who was marching with us! Can you picture it? There were like at least two helicopters watching us from overhead, people gazing at us out of the office windows from buildings either side of us, police manning the cordons either side, and even the odd public barbarian hurling abuse at us, but still on we marched and it was great! The other memory I have was of the end of one of these rallies when, after setting camp base in a square and listening to some rather boring speeches by b-class VIPs, we got to the real meat which was a disco. Some DJs and bands took the stage, and played their music and we danced and it was great. Yeah, I love that stuff. Funny how it wasn't a Christian event but we shared a communion on that day!

Anyhow back to slagging off the establishment. Please don't just take my word for it; next time you see a news article on

TV, just stop for a minute and ask, could there be more to it than that? Could there be another version of events; what could the other side's story be? Don't automatically assume that the BBC are unbiased, cos I can assure you that even they have their pay-masters. And if the face doesn't fit, it's not going in!

Most of us have known for a long time that most of the Sunday tabloids are bent as a fork. And some of us will even remember the 'good old days' when The Times and The Guardian took the opposing ends of the respectable broadsheet joust. But now even they at times, most of the time, seem afraid to question the generally accepted 'truth' which the rest of the press propagate.

Actually I am sure that nowadays you are a hundred times more likely to get a reasonable and well reasoned view of international events from a man or woman on the street, as opposed to the clearly biased press. At least the person you sit next to on the train will be friendly and openly listen to what you have to say rather than just expect you to believe their story no question! And nowadays many members of the public are beginning to question the 'official' version of events.

From what happened on 9'11 to the recent Georgian conflict, intelligent and well reasoned voices can be heard emerging from the chorus, speaking with the intellect of a free and reasonable adult voice. This is something which for so long has been lacking from the public domain. Suddenly people are beginning to question, backed with incontrovertible facts, the 'truth' shown in the papers and TV. I think that more people are questioning and re-examining the popular consensus than ever before!

So where is all of this going to go? For one thing I think that there is going to be no turning back. And to the disgust of the media power-blocks, the public individual voices will grow and strengthen. Politicians eventually I suppose will have to start acting more responsibly towards the pre-election manifesto pledges, which currently don't mean anything. Hopefully things will change.

Obviously there are always going to be 'stock-heads'. People who cannot see the truth if it were staring them in the face. Who will continue to support the old power-bases, the old prejudices and hatred on which much of the world's societies seem to have been founded. And I suppose that wars will continue for a long time after my death. A world without countries, without money, without war which John Lennon imagined is yet a long way away. But I see the first changes happening today. And I pray that this is one dream that just might one day come true!

I don't personally know what to make of the 'moon landing' conspiracy theories. Clearly that could have been a conspiracy, but somehow I doubt it. And by questioning them, Buzz Aldrin and all of those astronauts and cosmonauts, who did it, we are actually taking away from their achievements.

I used to agree with the generally accepted public opinion that the rest of the conspiracies were fiction as well. Until I began to look that little bit deeper into it. And the further I went, the more I saw to make me doubt everything else which I had previously held to be true and correct!

I'll start with the war in Vietnam. From the outset this appears like a simple war between countries on the issue of Capitalism versus Communism. Only it was a continent, with external backing besides, against one country, with some Russian made tanks and Chinese missiles. And despite these eastern reinforcements this is by no means a 'fair fight'. Now I realise that this war was over long before I was born, in the seventies I think. And seeing as it took place all that was over there in the US, well not a lot of people over here know about it.

But for a long time I have questioned the supremacy and validity even, of our armed forces. And certainly the US army don't seem to be that different from ours over there. Now don't get me wrong, I now recognise how evil Hitler and the Nazis were, and am very proud in all of our ancestors' efforts in defeating him. But this doesn't mean that warfare is good or right. In-fact it is not. Lives are sacred, and should be respected as such.

Truthfully I suppose the first knowledge I had of Vietnam was that of 'agent orange', or Napalm as it is more commonly known. This is a chemical agent which when dropped from bombs at a great height, rapidly diverges in chemical clouds to burn and annihilate human flesh and other organic matter in an instant. The armies excuse for using it was to clear the

221

foliage of the heavy jungle areas they were attacking. They entered a beautiful country with ancient and historic temples, and left a wasteland.

I don't propose to go over every detail of this war, from the mass relocation (pacification) of the civilian population in South Vietnam to cruddy purpose build towns, to the 'interrogation' and torture methods used for getting info. out of 'suspects' in the later days of the war.

The funding was ridiculous. The US economy was crippled with this ongoing war, which eventually the public got fed up with and stopped. But it had to stop some time. And all admiration must go to the North and South Vietnamese who survived the conflict, and to the civilians who died, not to mention the freedom fighters who took up arms against the invaders.

What you have to ask yourself is what would you do if some foreign nation, attacked your country, started dropping bombs on your cities, and terrorising your life. I would hope that you would fight them any way you could. We did in Nazi Germany. What a pity we seem to have turned into that demon we once ourselves so very much despised.

But I am still a fighter. I don't accept general public opinion. I ask questions, form my own opinions. Sometimes these agree with most other's many times they don't. That's not a problem for me. From school I'm used to being different, I can hack it, can you? I wanted to earlier point out that there is now quite a good argument for suggesting that John F. Kennedy was indeed taken out by the state. I know this isn't the official story. That the official suspect was indeed shot dead.

But did you know that JFK was actually planning to stop in its tracks an impending war with Vietnam, which he had anticipated and wanted to stop before it had even begun. I have this good information from a reliable, fat, history of the war by Michael Moore called the ten thousand day war, and which once I had finished reading it, completely opened my eyes to modern warfare, and I'll never trust 'our' side again. Moore doesn't force you to believe his assumed version of events (as most of the weaker contemporary historians will expect you to believe). Rather he presents before our eyes historical documents and news reels of press releases at the time, and contrasts them with official politician's and army press releases. Then he adds to the evidence sources and findings which could only be unearthed some years after the actual events, such as subsequent findings, hidden army reports, and even happenings from the 'other' side, to build a complete picture. And if you, the reader, are in any doubt as to what happened in that conflict, I guarantee that by the time you have finished it, everything will be clear!

Sometimes the truth seems hard to perceive, hidden amongst a tonne of conflicting opinions. But with careful attention to detail it gradually becomes clear. And then once you have learnt who to trust and mistrust, eventually a sceptic becomes very good at cutting through the lies to perceive the real events taking place amongst a world of liars and b's.

The other major conspiracy 9'11, I think I have covered earlier in my writings and don't plan to revisit it. But suffice to say the evidence is gradually accumulating that this was indeed an 'inside' job as well!

I'm not trying to wreck all of our faith in the institutions which govern and inform us. Just to question some of their decisions and information. I do still actually believe that most of the people in this country, from the government to the press, are decent and are acting for what they believe in.

It is just the false information which prompts their misdirection and, consequently, if we can try to change some of these lies then it will be possible to change their output. Again this is going to take time, but if we can be strong amongst ourselves then I have faith that change is possible in the future. Peace.

P.S. It is nice being able to transfer all of the writing skills which I have developed by writing countless college essays, and re-submissions, not to mention the nightmare of that last book which I attempted, into a comment which I can flourish at. To be able to speak freely! To be listened to by real people in the public (via the internet). To actually feel that I am making a little difference to the world, instead of just another hamster trapped in the wheel of life. I finally have found a medium with which to voice my hopes and dreams and comments. It's all good.

I also want us now to remember the time we spent in hospital. Drugged up to our eyeballs, hardly able to move. Stuck inside all day, with no-where to go and nowhere to go even if we wanted to. With no-one but ourselves for company! These are hard times. I don't suppose that many of you will have been there, but I am sure that those of you who have will know exactly what I mean!

There's an old saying 'you don't know what you've got till it's gone. And how true that saying is. I learnt out the hard way. No matter whose fault it was, I've been there and got the t-shirt! It does change you. I suppose some people it beats. Some people turn out to be bad pieces of work. Always ready to stab a mate in the back to rob him of all he's got. But we're not all like that. I remember one kind woman who must have been in her late fifties, Margaret her name was. Always kind to me and she did read her Bible. Anyhow the police had separated her and her daughter, put the daughter in a young person's home and Margaret in the psych ward, just for grassing on some Paedophiles. I think they got successful convictions, and said they moved those two for their own safety.

But it must have been hell for her being apart from her daughter for all that time. Only being allowed one phone call a week to her on the phone. And despite what they may say, it actually appeared as if the two were being punished for going ahead and pressing with the conviction in court. But they both got out in the end, or so I heard, which is a good thing.

Or what about this other crazy woman who kept on making animal noises on the ward! She was a hoot, we would spend hours seriously, pretending to be cats and just messing around like that. The nurses didn't know what to do with us! We were supposed to be crazy right? So we damn well were! Ha, the things we got up to in there to keep ourselves amused. But quite a lot of the other patients didn't like her if I remember correctly. Anyway she didn't stay for long.

Then there was a young guy called Will, who I did fancy a bit if I'm honest. He was just young and like really funny. He kept on telling me about this new world order, which he had found out about on the internet, something like the Illuminati. And he had set up his own Facebook site, which had hits from really famous Americans on it. I told him that I thought they were probably just hackers impersonating those stars, which kind of put a rain on his parade. Then he told me that he thought it was probably me! Ha-ha. I also remember running down the ward corridors acting like hooligans doing piggy-back rides with him. Which was really quite funny given that I nearly dropped him at any time, seeing as I'm not that strong! You should have seen the look on his face!

Another memorable guy I knew from in there was Dave; I've forgotten his surname. He told me that he was British with British parents, and I guessed correctly that he had been in the army, in the parachute regiment possibly. He actually appeared to carry himself like an officer, with a little bit of self respect, and I wouldn't be surprised if he was that as well. Or maybe he was just a good man. Any-how me and him used to smoke like troopers in our dorms. Like bloody chimneys, all waking hours. Seriously , I even once set the fire-alarm off in the toilets where I was smoking these green tea to get the buzz out of it. It's funny now looking back on it; hell it was funny then. But I hated being in hospital, really hated it. And if someone told me that I had to go back there, I would kill them. No questions asked: a straight execution! Anyhow that's just a few of the faces, I remember from my stay in there. I find that I have made quite a few friends in the time we were in. But most of us seem to want to get on with our own separate lives, and move separate ways now we have got out. No hard feelings like, just it is time to move on.

So, those of us who've tried to hold onto our principles through this hurricane, inevitably I should hope, find out that once we do get through the net, that there is a blue sky above us and yes the free air feels oh so good.

18: Remembering the dead

You know not everyone does make it. I have lost four close, non family friends in recent history. René was a Portuguese man I think, with those intellectual good looks that I am sure plenty of women found attractive. He could speak at least four languages fluently I think, including Arabic and French. Well I met him at a homeless night shelter I stayed at for some seven months after leaving home, till I moved on to hopefully greener pastures.

Then I heard with some sadness, although an inevitability, that he had died some years later. And we think that it was probably a drug overdose which killed him. Maybe legit, probably not. Possibly even a combination of the two. I had seen him a couple of times on the street since leaving the hostel, and it is true that whenever I saw him he always seemed to be out of it, either on drugs or pissed. I also heard news that he was homeless again and actually had pneumonia when he passed away. We have lost a good man.

The next one who I lost, at least the next one I'm going to talk to you about, was another close friend of mine at the time. And don't even get me going into my past exes! We'd be here forever :-) Thankfully none of them are dead, at least not to my knowledge.

Anyhow this guy was called Nick. I actually dedicated one of my other literary endeavours to him, soon after his death. But that one never got past the drawing board so to speak. As in I am publishing this INSTEAD of that!

Yeah Nick was a good man, which it's a shame that I don't see many about in today's day and age. Most have their heads so far up their own arses it's unreal. And that includes in hospital, even the martial arts forum I've joined and everywhere else. There are plenty of good people about, but there seems to be just as many spineless back-stabbers at the same time!

Back to Nick: yeah I remember him well. He had a handsome beard, a brown wig to make Cinderella jealous, and a smile to charm the balls off a brass monkey! What's more this guy was clever. He told me that he was in the army, the territorial – some division I can't remember, back in the day. And you know what, unlike half of them who fabricate CVs faster than you and me can say 'pardon?' I believe him.

But he'd gone downhill. He was tall and skinny. A good 6'2" he did a lot of walking. And clever. We went to see films together at the local university cinema which was some fifty-five minutes walk up the road. I can remember seeing two good films with him. One called My England, or something like that. Set in the days of the Falklands Britain, it was about life on the streets for a young lad at the time. Pulled apart by involvement with the BNP, this was a powerful and moving experience. I didn't think that I'd like it but Nick persuaded me and he was right.

We also went to see Bridge over the Iowa Jima, which is one of Clint Eastwood's directions. I mean by that that he directed it; he wasn't in it. Well it was the second half to a world war two film about the Americans invading a little Japanese island somewhere far out in the Pacific, one of the last bastions of Japanese defence. But whereas the American film was more clearly done with a whole pro-us tone, this one revealed some deep sentiment for the enemy, here the Japanese. Showed how their once mighty war effort stumbled and then eventually fell by the end of the war. How even fighting to the last men the Japanese would do so with their heads held high. How precious the ideas of honour and family and loyalty were to them. How brutal and ruthless the American attack against them was. And how where their bodies may have fallen, their spirit ultimately survived.

Much as Nick's does him. I cried then and I am crying now. The same as I cried at Nick's funeral. Perhaps he died of a drug overdose, I don't know. I do know however that I miss him. And he was only 38. That's too young to die you know. He was going grey but, oh well. And plenty of people turned up at his funeral. Family who I had never seen before.

The truth be told the Nick I knew was something of a loner. He confided in me that he had a sister but didn't really see her any more. Also I knew that he had a girlfriend, a real stunner or so I have been told, who died of cancer some years before. And I guess he still missed her. I don't think that he ever had a real girlfriend again.

Towards the end I think he let himself go. He was still my close friend, and this is how I will always remember him. And I remember the one night they all kept me up cheering and chanting watching the footy, in the TV room which was right next to my bedroom at that hostel I was living in then, the bad men!

I think that that was also the night I heard someone offer him heroin. I told him not to take. I never have. Don't need to. My experimentations with Cannabis and fags have taught me to stay well clear of that trouble.

But I guess Nick didn't have the support or hope which I still have. Cos at 27 I am still planning to sort my life out, move in with my wife and be happy until my dying days. At 38 , Nick had already lost his love and I guess was living on a day to day basis.

You had never met a better bloke. He was honest, and intelligent and ready to laugh at a joke. After I slap-punched another lad at the house at the time, Nick was the one who escorted him back into my bedroom crying at the time for hitting me back (the other lad, not Nick that is).

And I discussed the idea of God with him. This entity whom for all my years previously I had spat out and denied vehemently, suddenly became a possibility. With my gal the other side of the world, here was a friend , a grown-up I could talk to face-to-face, heart to heart. Explore the possibilities of the Millennium. Explore the impossibilities of Love. We have also lost another good man the day Nick died.

The next death who I want to talk about was a friend who I didn't know well. His name was Steven I think, little Steve, little gay Steve. And let me make one thing clear, I'm not gay, and never have been. Although not losing my virginity until late in life, there have been times when I asked questions. And between you and me I may have been raped by a man. That happened the first time I went to hospital, you know when I broke my neck. Please don't argue with me about it, I have the scar to prove it.

Anyway I knew Steven when I was working at the Derby Cat's Protection Shop, a local charity shop where I have probably learnt my best work skills, seeing as I worked there as a shop assistant, part time for over two and a half years. Quite soon after being kicked out of my mum's house, I was at a loss as to what to do and so landed this job, which was a stroke of good luck, even if voluntary.

Anyhow little Steve was one of our regulars. I got to know and got on well with pretty much everyone there, both staff, and customers for most of the time I worked there.

So yeah I remember gay Steven would often come in looking at our Bric-a-brac, and pick up the odd treasure. Well I also remember the time when we didn't see him for a while, and then he started showing up again heavily drugged up. It turned out that he was in hospital. But he got out, and eventually moved in with this other lad.

I remember the time he kept asking me for a date. To go to the pub or have a meal with him or something. Well I didn't want to, but could hardly keep on turning him down. And so eventually I agreed to go to his for a meal, for him to meet me at the shop at closing time to go back to his place and for him to cook. Well I couldn't face it and left home early that day.

I think he was upset, but I did see him again. Actually the last couple of times I saw him was when I was busking in the Cathedral district of the town. Banging out the songs on my old acoustic, to pick up a bob or two. And he kindly donated, which was appreciated.

Steven also had a lovely smile, was honest and generous. And he had a loving aunt. So I was upset to hear a couple of months later that he had been killed, stabbed to death in his eyeballs in his own kitchen. That's not a nice way to go is it? And I know they eventually caught and imprisoned someone, who didn't get life, only about ten if I remember correctly. But then the whole criminal system is so crooked I just don't know what to believe. Another good guy down.

Next and most recently, was the demise of my old landlord, Roy Gregory. He was also the best landlord I have ever had. In his forties I think, I also know that he had a teenage daughter who was dying of cancer.

Well Roy was a good man. Honest and generous, which seems to be a dying breed today. Certainly none of those hooligans in the house of commons would make the grade, in-my-opinion.

I went on holiday to Kenya last year and when I got back I discovered that he had topped himself. Jumped off a building apparently. This definitely seemed very out of character for him to me. Here was a good, and strong man, the landlord of a few properties, who just kills himself out of the blue!

But I guess that the signs were there in the end. 'Cos it turned out that he had turned to his wife shortly before doing it and asked her to sell the houses, although she had refused, I think she had to in the end after he did it. I guess this shows that he had been considering it for some time.

I guess the pressures became too much for him in the end. Not just his daughter, although this clearly had a massive effect on him as it would any parent, but also there had been complaints put in about me behind my back asking me to move out. And I think they may have pressured him to agree to kicking me out without my knowledge, against his better judgement. Another question mark, another good man who'll be missed.

Lastly there is Kad, at least that's what I think his name was. A young Asian lad from either India or Pakistan, about my age, he moved into one of the hostels I was living in at the time.

He told me how he didn't get on at all well with his brothers, who owned takeaways in some other part of Derby. He was forced into an arranged marriage with some young woman over there, whom he didn't love he told me, and it was a marriage he wanted to get out of. He also told me that he had spent some time in psychiatric hospitals over there in Asia, and that he had actually been raped whilst in there. I shared my little secret with him and we made a connection there as well.

But I don't think that Kad was ever happy. He always seemed to act a little bit compulsively to me, like a manic depressive. I don't actually know what he was diagnosed with, or remember what meds he was taking but I suppose it could have been this. Anyway one of the last memories I have of Kad is fighting him in the garden. He started slagging me off and then it reached the point where I'd had enough and we took it outside. There was another lad there acting as ref, although I think he was goading him on as much as anything else.

Anyway it started with us circling each other on the grass, before I just touched him making contact. Then he let rip with the most ferocious assault of punches and kicks you had ever seen! Or so it would seem. In-fact he didn't touch me, his attacks were weak and thrown like a movie star might (not meaning to do real damage). I guess the poor kid had spent so long watching Kung Fu movies, he had lost touch with reality. But my counter wasn't so sober.

First I floored him, easy enough for someone who has ever done Judo. Then found my way on-top of him, and began pummelling his head with maybe two or three well placed

235

strikes. He had got me angry and now I was punishing him. Well he cried for me to stop, and looking up at the 'ref' he indicated that I should stop and so I did. And that was the end of it.

But the last I heard of him was a few months after that. I had left that place for another, and I never did get to the bottom of why he died. No-one seemed to know, apparently he was just found dead in his room one morning, reason unknown. But I have my suspicions. There was a real slimy man who was living in that house at the time, who considered himself something of a 'player'. Actually he was just a scum-bag but no-one dared say it to his face. And I strongly suspect that it was he that plied both Kad and Nick with some dodgy drugs, which finished the two of them off. They did you see die at round about the same time. However I don't have any proof, only my suspicions, and I guess it's over now.

19: Life is like a Dream

We roll out of the dream world of our sleep, to trudge through the days wearily and heavy hearted, before rolling back into them once more at the end of the day. Our moments are picked up by high spirited people, and then put down once again by the haters. We barely try to make head or tail out of the gibberish which emerges from the box day in on day. Yet another murder, yet another innocent victim, yet another war, yet another hurricane. Yet another load of self righteous political pomp being spouted off by the latest political candidate. Republican, Democrat, Labour, Conservative, Liberal, what difference does it make, they're all the same. Yet another sermon in church by yet another preacher telling about yet another Christian doing yet more Christian things.

But if I've never seen God, how can He possibly exist? Yet another meal, with yet more e-numbers. Yet another car model fresh out of the factory, with yet more shiny gloss paint sneaking by yet another speed camera. Yet another Olympics. Yet another gold medal. Another hypocrite, another death. Another story no doubt envisaged deep from down within the belly of the beast. Another conspiracy, another good for nothing and another do-gooder. Another cancer kills another patient, prolonged by another miracle cure which costs the tax players another million or so. Another lie, another white lie, takes a whiter shade of pale. Another song by another band hoping to sell another million records to another gullible million young people.

Another map of lyrics, planning another quest of music, over another damaged ear drum and into another restless head. Another can of 7up next to another mobile phone and another bunch of keys which opens, who knows where? Down another maze, out another rabbit hole, into another class room or another TV room, full of more sneering faces, and more hidden angst. Run away from yet more problems, unpaid bills, bills which have been paid but they say you didn't, escape the law, escape the Doctors, escape your parents, escape the angry stares and the insolent glances. Try to escape the ever-roving eye of the eyes in the sky (satellites), and the spies who seem to map your every move, and track your every call.

You see your name on the front page of every paper, your innermost secrets revealed for all to see in glossy girly magazines your sister has just brought. Yet another train, yet another destination. Yet another friend, yet another life living her way down the road to oblivion. What is it all for, when will it all end? On marriage? On Blackbelt, first Dan? On holding a job? On my youngster's first birthday? On her eighteenth? On the first publishing deal with a publisher, when will it all stop? Another day, another dollar. Another time to reflect, another time to forget. Another piece of the jigsaw and another colour of the rainbow. Fin.

Hiya peops. Thanks for responding and engaging with me. Let me tell you a little bit more about what I think:

I saw God's face when I last looked at my fiancée. I hear Him at night every time I talk to her; He made me really happy when I heard our baby say Dada over the phone.

God is a concept. Read Corinthians 1:13. It says that God is love. 'As a child I thought as a child I spake as a child. Now I am a man I leave behind these childish ways.' And you know I took this issue up: God being love. Not a shining entity, a force of divine power but a feeling. Something as simple and perfect as a feeling. Much as I get from when I am with my loved one, when I kiss her, when I love her. It has taken a long time. We have had plenty of obstacles in our way before we finally tie the knot in hopefully less than a month.

And through all of these hardships, who was there for me? Not my family; I have had a hard enough time bringing them back into the fold in recent months. Not music; it all sounds rubbish when you are down. Not friends, not principles, not God. You've got nothing when you are alone and then you are truly alone. But the thing is that I have done this before. I have played this game one too many times, lost one too many friends.

I know how the game works. So the fireball of misery can go as quickly as it came. Much as the tide drags the seaweed back out to sea. I am a Buddhist as well as a Christian. I remember as a kid going to church and 'playing the game' but it never worked for me. It still doesn't.

I have been to congregations when the crowd screams in holy ecstasy, but hold on a minute what are they playing at? Well I suppose if it works for them. But, you know what, I have met plenty of good people: Christians mainly, both in and out of church, who were always willing to listen to my problems, to spend time with me even when I thought that I didn't deserve it. And I have had plenty of times when I have had no one and been completely alone.

But now I have grown a little older and a little stronger. Now I find that people aren't as strong as they make out, the bad ones that is. They can mostly be knocked into place with a quick ninja strike, and then once it is over it is over. Failing that, or if that doesn't work, leave them be. You don't need their lies, deceit, false posturing, or false prophets.

You are right that there is only one God. But I don't know if you knew this; He loves all of His children. The Jewish peops, the Christians, the Hindus, the Muslims, the Buddhists and the rest of them. I think he even has time for the scientists and the Atheists.

His is Jehovah. He is Christ. He is Allah. He is Buddha, Brahma, and Atman. He is the word (Logos from the bible). He simply is. Whatever there was, whatever there is and whatever there will be. If you can't feel 'Him', if you think that 'He' has abandoned you. Don't worry, He hasn't. If people seem selfish, deceptive and generally just bad men, that's right, they are. I think they are too, most of them.

Some people said that the Bible needs to be interpreted as if it were cast in stone, figuratively speaking. Well did you hear about what Moses did with the old holy commandments written in stone? He smashed them on some holy mountain and started again. That is what we need to do now I think.

It's true that the majority of churches I've been to teach the Bible in some dogmatic literalistic fashion. There is no getting away from this. But not all of them. I have been to churches where the congregation sang out of tune, thinking somehow that that dreadful racket was going to please God. As if He is some external being. He's not. He's in each and every one of our hearts. That's what it means to have a heart. I'm not talking about the Aorta, but the old fashioned meaning of the word. Too much of modern life seems to have been deceived by modern scientific/technological values and the real meaning of things seems to have been lost. And I can give examples:

Just as the world was once thought to be flat, so too the atom has never been proven. Sure it fits in with the chemistry period table; sure it has been photographed using super-high powered electron microscope particle acceleration blasters, but does that really prove anything? One thing I have learnt from my philosophy classes is that any philosopher or scientist should be careful not to promote the answer to a question in the way the question is phrased. Unfortunately that's what most of the scientists are doing.

So you tell me that God can't be studied, that He is beyond human comprehension. That quite simply He is 'impossible'. This is all fair enough to assert, but like the above-mentioned scientists, you are making a statement of the truth. There is no questioning, no reasoning, no listening? No fair examination of what we know. An assumption that the individual is the epicentre of knowledge and that this is all there is.

Do you really think that I would be able to make all of this rubbish up if I didn't believe it? The thing is I'm a Buddhist (Zen Buddhist in fact) before I am a Christian. But now I have found God there is no turning back. He is there amongst my friends, there when I try to explore my faith with my sermons. There when I travel long distances to see those whom I love, and in the rainbows as well.

Ah I have just been bitten by the bug of spite another poster has thrown at me. I will show you what she has said, and then also display my reply beneath as well.

<panda>

2008/08/30 19:12

I am fairly sure that you have to credit us if you want to put our ideas in your book.

<me>

Hi Panda, don't worry your usernames will be there. I am actually going to try to upload a PGN file onto the site once it is done, so you can all see what you think for yourselves. But if you mean credit you as in Pay you, well you can forget it. In fact seeing as the last book I did I made a loss of about a thousand if you want to have a stake, I mean like be properly 'credited' then feel free. I'm not expecting to sell many if any at all of this new one, and the cost was £800, so yeah, let me know what you think? Thought so…

That has really riled me off. I hate people who mess with my peace. I was going to give you another blast of spiritual writing but why should I bother?

All you ever do is stab me in the back? Most of you wouldn't know Jesus if he shone down before you.

Ah man you've got me riled. I'm still gonna put the post in, in a separate message. If there are still any of you out there who place the content before the words, seek deeper spirituality beyond a barren external hatred, or seek the power of Zen which is and has always been more than a pure physical repetition of moves, please feel free to read onwards. As for the rest of you, just stop harassing me!

Hi. I am anticipating that you are going to put some negative post in comment to my answer, and so this is a pre-prepared reply. I don't think that this thread is about Christianity at all. As debatably the strongest Christian in this room all I have received is negative vibes. Well not entirely, but there definitely has been a strong element of it.

Not verbal insults you understand. You guys seem to have perfected the superiority complex, that idea that you are better than anyone else you choose to crush. I don't know what goes on in your dojos, I don't even want to. In the same way you don't know what goes on in my life, or my head for that matter.

243

I don't like arguing; it just seems that I have to defend myself here repeatedly. Physical strength is not the quintessential nature of things. Sure it helps in a fight, but even then there are usually rules, such as who are the witnesses and who starts it. Also, are the police going to be involved? You guys can rub my face in the ground, well it's been done before. But you know that being a father makes me a man, and as a man I am strong. I'm not talking about the sperm but the love I show my family, which you definitely aren't party to. Any of you out there who are also parents will know what I am talking about I should hope, and peace to you. And as for the rest of you? Keep on playing with those pick-up sticks. See how much good they will do you on judgement day.

PS. If you guys want to test your knowledge, why don't you ask your Senseis about me. See if any of them know me, what they have to say about my version of the truth. I would be interested to hear what they say. But I fear their hearts aren't open, their minds aren't open, to the universal truth of love, and so they will fritter their lives away like the rest of us!

Hi my readers I am now talking to you on a level that none of these internet poos are privy to, which I am telling you in the closest confidence.

I don't want you to take everything that I say as gospel. Sometimes I do say things which I think are right and true, but am not 100% on. Like for instance the issue of Tibet and China. For a long time I supported China's stance against the wide Western condemnation. However this began to quaver after the recent Chinese brutal assault and repression over there just before the Olympics began about a couple of months ago. It was almost as if they thought they could get away with it before putting on this big international 'circus'. And that is just what happened.

My mum kindly reminded me a couple of evenings ago, in a brief chat, that the Olympics never before used to be seen as the great event, rather more the poor second man's world championships. And it is only more recently, perhaps with the Chinese events being the biggest exposition of this trend, that it has been going for pole position so to speak. With the most events, from Judo to Tae-kwon-do, shooting to beach volley-ball, it certainly has something for everyone. And is now the apex of sport. Much as films have the Venice film festival, music the Brit awards, fashion various fashion shows and so on. This is it.

I've diverged. The China issue was not my mistake, I stand by my decision to say what I did. And now I don't support them. When I saw the photo of an eleven-year-old Chinese factory worker smiling in front of a video-phone photograph, I thought that this was just taking the piss. Whilst China is mopping up the markets, Africa is suffering and this is not on. Suddenly the deep and profound Chinese Zen philosophy seems weak and false. I am still a Buddhist, still support the much hard done by Burmese monks. So peace.

Also here's a hint: If you're ever in hospital and they come for you, don't fight them. OK you might be able to take one or two of them on, but I really doubt you could fight and defeat four to six burly guys armed with hypodermics. And even if you did manage to lay them all out, where would you go then? All of the doors are locked.

So they will grab you, one pushing your head down which really hurt me what with my neck and all, one to each arm and one for each leg. Forget struggling it will only make it worse, like the more you struggle the harder they press you into that submission position, and boy it hurts.

I've had it done to me a couple of times ago four years back. Then there is the seclusion rooms, one at the city (one each ward) and one at the ICU. I have seen plenty of people go into them when I was in. I think they usually do it to punish, or calm a patient down. Thankfully I didn't have to suffer these indignations the last time I was in there. Only the time before. But if they put you in there, a bare room with a plastic mattress, possibly a plastic glass of water, there is no telling when you will get out. I would say that it is better than the room at the police nick, but only marginally.

Although the time before last it did seem that I was taking the brunt of the punishment at both hospitals, this time I learnt to surrender right away. I didn't take any trouble from any of the patients, but the minute those security nurses came to take me to seclusion, just followed them there. Sit down on the bed. When they offer you a little green tablet take it. I guarantee it hurts a lot less than the injection in your arse! And that's it, maybe you will fall asleep. You will be off your head for a few hours maybe, but they're all nutters in those places, and the Doctors are the worst of all!

Hi guys, okay there are a couple more thoughts that I would like to discuss. One which you all will be privy to and the other which only my literary readers will get to see.

Okay, one of you asked me where do I get my information from, like who are my sources/teachers? Well I suppose it wouldn't be enough to just say God would it? Seeing if to you that is only a word, a figurative concept meaning nothing and approaching the abyss. But it is God, and everything I own it is because of Him.

I have tried ever-so-hard to explain that He is greater than any of you non-believers could possibly imagine. He fills the skies, the mountains and the squirrels. He fills the butterflies' wings with flight and the air with bird song. You probably recognised that a ranting lunatic such as myself is of no stable mind. That's certainly true. And I guess you think I'm crazy. Damn it I've served my time in these places, so I suppose that 'comment' would be justified also.

You probably also think that I must be a little bit crazy to enter these walls ranting away like I do. Ha ha, that's funny. You know what, I'm not scared of any of you! What's the worst possible you could do? Kill me? You can't even touch me; you don't even know what I look like. But say you did, say you did attack, say I was mortally wounded, well I've been there before. But the thing is this is called a civilization for a reason. There are laws in place, and enforcement officers at hand to stop any unfair assault like that from happening.

Whether you do or not, I recognise that there are times that they turn a blind eye to such outlandish behaviour. But my past dealings with these benders have given me a pretty good idea as to when they move, and when they turn a blind eye. So basically yeah, you can't do jack.

Secondly, I want to discuss another 'friend' I had in hospital. His name was Paul B, or Beef was his nick name. Classic. And this young man was the very definition of what 'being built like a brick sh!t house' means!

He told me he had a black-belt in Tae-Kwon-Do, no Jiu-Jitsu, sorry. Now I have never met one of them before and so was intrigued to learn more about this ancient martial art. I knew that Judo, the sport which I played at as a kid, was derived from it and assumed that it just added some strikes and kicks to the mix to provide the basic move set. How wrong could I be!

I actually gleaned a little bit more knowledge about Ju-jitsu from a book that I got off Amazon actually while I was in hospital. Some kind of Penguin encyclopaedia of the martial arts, it gave some moves and history to all of the basic ones, excluding Ninjitsu and a few other lesser well known ones. So I discovered that this is a combat set of moves designed to inflict suffering, maim, and even kill the unfortunate geezers upon whom it is used.

There is a good reason there are no such things as Jiu-jitsu competitions, because if there ever were all of the competitors would end up either in wheelchairs or dead! Ah.

So he also came across as not just physically strong, but mentally too. His one weakness was that he would fly into rages, usually in the middle of the night, where he would throw beds about the place and even put his elbow through a strong glass window.

But Beef was cool. He wasn't impressed by my Judo book. I guess his martial mechanic is now a part of him and that's the way it's gonna stay. And neither was he convinced when I dragged him to church. But he was a laugh and good company.

I was just this minute feeding the pigeons and do you know what? They all took off and flew away for no apparent reason. All except one that is, a cute 'gal' pigeon who hung about for a few minutes before flying off to join them I suppose.

So what possibly could make them go like that? Forfeit a perfectly good feast of white Sunblest bread bits, to over the trees and off somewhere else? I'll tell you what, there's only one thing that pigeons like better than food, and that's more food!

I know exactly what happened 'cos I saw it happen last time. Right when I was in the middle of feeding a flock of them the bread, an Asian lad and his brother appeared with a bag of seeds, and the minute they dumped it on the grass, that was it. Now pigeons like bread, I know that for a fact, they'd eat it until the cows come home, and then some, of this I have no doubt.

But they just LOVE seeds. It's probably in their genetic make-up being birds and all. So they flew to eat the seeds, and I just had to find a few remaining stragglers to feed the rest of my loaf to. You know I buy these loaves for one purpose only. And it doesn't make me happy when these bloody 'Pakistanis' do that. I think they may well have done it to spite me, and, you know what, it worked.

So next time I see them doing it, well I don't want to cause any trouble. I've got responsibilities now and a wife and baby to look forward to. But man, one of these days…

Hi. OK yeah I have just written a long twenty-five A4 page essay on things like God and what-for, which is cute and I would start typing it in now besides the fact that there is not time. It is nine o'clock now, and I am not too happy that I wasn't able to connect to my gal tonight! Can you imagine it! I don't know if it's because the network is down (maybe the satellite had a crash?) but all of the numbers I tried on both my cards didn't work, so I just sent her a text instead after trying for a while. Hopefully she will have got that.

I am planning on typing up that mammoth essay tomorrow. Right now there are a couple of other minor tasks which I have scheduled in. Like I wanted to copy a message from the chess board I am interacting on right now in a joint 'world versus grand-master' correspondence game, where each side has two days to decide on the best move to make. Then we take a vote towards which one we should take and the one with the most votes wins. I have previously contributed a few times to the ideas on what we should play; I mean I always know what I would play, and guess what, they always go for something else! And you know what? I always go with their move as well, ha-ha.

But it is interesting to hear (or see the text) of what the different players have to say. One guy today made a comment which had absolutely nothing to do with the game in hand, whatsoever. It was some really random Portuguese love poem which he found for us out of the blue. Maybe he just felt like writing it? Anyway that is the kind of random thing which I like and so I will copy it here for you now, to see what you think.

Waitaka: (English translation of a Portuguese love poem by an unknown author.)

"A tribute to the women I did not love: There were women I did not love, because I had to choose to love others. But these loves that I loved made me happy. These loves that I loved made me cry. These loves that I loved made me grow. These

251

loves that I loved made me live. These loves that I loved made me be the one I am. Even so, I cannot escape from feeling an empty spot on my chest every time I remember one of the women I did not choose to love."

I hope that you'll agree with me that that's a really sweet piece of work, and I like how it has absolutely nothing to do with the game discussion right now! Sweet (from a chess web-site). Good night.

20: Cooling down in Church

Hi. I was feeling hungry and so I ate. I was feeling thirsty and so I plan to drink after finishing this. That sounds almost biblical doesn't it? Well I would argue there definitely are parts of this script that resemble this, for the simple reason that the two are basking in the same power, the same dream.

Wow TV is distracting me; what was I going to say? Er, I really can't remember. Oh yeah writing, my style of writing is very organic, experimental. It really just comes out (as you might have imagined).

Okay, I don't know how some people generate these convincing and sophisticated plots, with deep characters and amazing fictional worlds. To tell you the truth I've not really read much 'ordinary' fiction. Obviously I've watched a lot of TV and films; who hasn't?

But when I was a kid I really focused on science fiction novels, mainly Isaac Asimov. As an adult I have changed to reading other more relevant bits and bobs. From the plays I have studied at college, to other imaginative writings, at college I also worked on my writing skills. I am going to do a separate heading connecting this art to the more physical one but later, much later…

Actually it has been prodigious the amount of rubbish I have had to churn out for those lecturers, a good deal of them having to be done again as they 'simply weren't good enough'! And as the years have gone by and I haven't shot to the top of the academic ladder, my priorities have changed. Suddenly it becomes clear that this is all just a game.

These teachers are only sinners like the rest of us. The system is not perfect, far from it. Actually I'd say that it's about as crooked as a stick. Sure it does do for some people, but not me. I want more.

I want to meet God, face to face. I want to hear his call and line up with his soldiers around me. I want to carry the herald as we march into war. And I want to watch us win!

I just want to spend a little bit more time justifying some earlier qualifications about God. You really should see this book as one man's attempt to prove that He DOES exist. I said that God is universal, and that we are essentially following the same Holy Spirit if we are Christian or Jewish, Muslim or Sikh, Rastafarian or Buddhist, even Marxist. This is clearly a bold assertion and I can see lots of people not just accepting it as fact because I say so. After all, it goes in the face of the teachings of many great religious teachers and doctrines over the years. Not to mention that perhaps the greatest religious leaders were multi-faith. Just look at what Martin Luther King said: 'brothers and sisters of the world unite!' And he was shaking his head as he said it! I wonder did he think up these words himself, or did some script writer prepare them for him? And Mahatmah Gandhi was another amazing religious unifying leader of people, this time in India, to whom people flocked like moths to a flame.

But just because thinkers aren't necessarily well received in their time doesn't make them necessarily redundant. Shakespeare didn't become mega-popular until after his death. So too for many famous painters. And even today half of the world seems to scorn Marx's writings, even though the other half follows them! I'll never forget those immortal words from the beginning of his manifesto; there is a plague sweeping over Europe. The plague of Communism!

But his writings were not mega-popular again 'til after his death. And then the revolution he predicted for Germany, actually took Russia and China into its power. Even though the Russian one eventually folded, there have been other political warriors who have taken up this dialectic and led the wars since his death. But these weren't conformists but revolutionaries, like Jesus before them. And to a lesser extent me.

We need to be careful in exploring this idea not to hurt anyone's feelings. As a matter of fact we should always be careful not to hurt people's feelings no matter the subject matter.

There was a time when people were hung for less. In the early years of the Vatican, the Restoration period and so on, women who acted out of order were burnt on a funeral pyre as witches. Arabia was actually invaded for a different set of religious beliefs throughout the crusades. That isn't to say that they were wrong, just that they didn't conform to the more powerful (militarily) force of the 'Christian' nation and so they were doomed to lots, and lots of bloodshed. Looking back, we should ask ourselves if it is hardly any wonder that this Muslim nation has grown into a righteous and angry people. Is it just possible that they have ancestral memories of what we have done before, and blood does not wash away easily (from the souls of the traitors, Kufr in Arabic).

Let us move away from this fundamentalist polemic and back to what I was saying. On the train last week I had an interesting chat with my sister, mainly about God. On the way back from Bures, Suffolk and it was in Bures that I started the argument with her about God. My point was that as a Christian AND a Buddhist I have a wider point of view then most other 'monotheists'. Her stance was that in saying that I can't be a proper Christian, 'cos it actually says in the Bible not to follow false prophets.

'But I know it says that in there', I told her. And the argument actually started to get quite heated. All of this in my granny's house, and quite a bit in front of my aunty! Well my aunt came in and tried to cool us down, with the three of us coming to some kind of a temporary stalemate to agree to recognise the difference in the other's opinions.

I wasn't happy with this outcome. Call me bloody minded, but I think my aunt was probably just trying to diffuse the situation. Anyway on the way back I continued the discussion, continuously pestering my sister to talk when she was clearly trying to listen to her iPod player. You know I can't remember exactly what I said now, probably just exploring the limits of the Bible as a concrete book comparing to the multiversity and diversity of people's different religious experiences. Or something like that, and I was happier by the time we got off the train. Then the next day I even remember I thought of another religious point, which I called her on her mobile to tell her. She was in the car with her friends (hopefully not driving!) and anyway we chatted for a bit more which was sweet. She is a pillar in my life.

So yeah, there are many different powerful texts out there. I was first especially driven to study the Upanishads which I think are Buddhist, and other early similar work, and this immediately captivated me and dragged me into its dirty depths. Full of stories of hunters and tigers, it is a sweet legend.

But not just a story. It's like – well – our lives are made up of stories, and when one connects to you, like this one did me, you start to believe in it. Forget that realism they advertise on TV and everywhere else.

Here is the perfect dream; the perfect fantasy which everybody can share in. That special feeling you get from listening to beautiful music. R Kelly's I Believe I Can Fly, Coolio's A Gangster's Paradise, The Fugees' The Score. I know these are all black songs, lay off me, they are good ones. I am also a fan of George Michaels, (not because he is gay, you dope) but because he can sing, or at least he could. And he did some great tracks.

This brings to my mind another memory from my life. Do you remember the time he was caught doing gay batty boy stuff in public toilets in America somewhere? Well I somehow got it into my mind that he did this in a Derby park. Ha. I don't know how I got this into my head, but you know at the time I was sure of it! I guess at that difficult time of my life, (just before and after leaving home at 19) there were a lot of things in life that I wasn't sure of.

But that isn't the end of the story. 'Cos many times there I was asked for, or offered a cigarette at night (outside, near to a park's toilets I somehow thought that George had been frequenting!) I don't know if what they really wanted was gay sex, but thankfully that never actually happened, I swear!

The closest I ever got was when some man pulled up next to me and offered for me to jump in the back and go for a ride with him near to the park. Well I considered it for a minute before telling him to sod off.

There was another time, when on the way back, this young man pulled up in his car and wanted to fight me 'cos I was singing. Prat!

Anyway the specific memory I had was of walking back in the rain. I had been reading a Shaolin Kung Fu book by Wong Kiew Kit, and had even been trying out the moves near the playground, by the lake. It was the middle of the night, pissing it down, and with only ducks, geese and swans as witnesses. Well any other more sensible people would have stayed well clear of that place late at night. But I like going out at night. I remember forcing myself through the creepy, sinister trees. Not to mention I really liked walking back then. I walked pretty much everywhere. Man, I've just thought of another story related to this, but we'll save that for another page.

Anyway, so yeah it was dark, cold, pissing it down, I was tired from the combat moves, a little bit lonely and depressed (this was how I generally felt at this stage in my life, not having a girlfriend or anything), and what's more the wind was very nearly blowing my very wig off! Seriously, on that night in particular it was a bloody gale force 5! I remember on the way home the rain eased off, and maybe the wind did too. But by the time I got home I was soaked as a trout, dying of hypothermia and shivering as well. I think I changed to watch a Bruce Lee film on the terrestrial channel on TV or maybe I watched the film before I   went out? I can't remember.

This doesn't exactly solve the conundrum we have faced ourselves with, does it? I'm not just arguing for a specific god to any particular text, but a universal One, who loves all of His believers. He even loves everyone else.

He is not male in my opinion. One of his ancient names is Sophia. The goddess of wisdom, of truth. Not a lot of people know that I guess, but I guess a lot of knowledge seems to have been lost down the years. And I'm not talking about medical/mathematical or scientific knowledge. We seem to have greater engineering knowledge than ever before.

I'm talking about spiritual knowledge, theoretical knowledge Dionysus style! I suppose a certain amount of this does still remain in the hearts of the true believers, the loving mothers, and has survived in pieces down the ages, but only in pieces. Ah these are the things which can only be conveyed parent to child, brother to sister, friend to friend orally. Physically. It takes guts to put yourself and that little box which contains your life in it to one side for a minute, and just be free. I'm not saying that I can do it all the time. But I try. I try to be a good person, a good Christian, a good Buddhist even.

I can't really teach you very much about the other religions because they aren't in the list of my top two. I mean I did learn about Islam and Hinduism in college. Not that I didn't already know about them, having read books on both before. But in college I learnt more. And what I probably learnt the most about was Philosophy. Now there's a tough cookie.

From the Greeks of antiquity, to the various Europeans over time (Plato anyone, he was French: I think and therefore I am; (Je me pense donc je suis) to more modern academics.

These lessons also gave me a forum to further explore my ideas of how everything relates to Philosophy. Our final exam was to try to equate Christianity with Philosophy. This was do-able, and actually required us to draw pieces from all of our earlier studies in class. Most of us had attended the majority of the classes and we had engaged with the teachings allowing us to do just this. But for the skivers, those pick-and-choosers who attended one day and not the next, well I don't think they passed. Let alone if they even made the exam at all, they wouldn't have known enough about the required subject matter to do it I'm sure. Philosophy isn't one of those subjects you can just bluff your way through. This isn't GCSE. At A-level standard we are set exams not just to test our knowledge, but also to consolidate it. To give us the opportunity to explore our own minds, and form some kind of personal philosophy bringing in everything we had learnt and pulling it into some kind of framework which we could relate to.

I'm not going to go into what Philosophy means, or what they say any more. If you want to study it, take a class. But this was my chance to explore a lesser known realm of metaphysics, which if philosophy is the higher science of things, this must be the higher science of that. To engage with the metaphysical application of things you are trying to deal with the truth directly. From people's minds, to concrete science, to universal truths, to universal relativity and conditionality, to patterns and language and so on. The list is great, and pretty stunning and humbling really.

The first thing a study of meta-physics takes is an open mind. Then the next thing which is required is a good overall knowledge of things I'd say. (And I'm not talking about 'who wants to be a millionaire' trivia neither!) You shouldn't necessarily believe everything you read. You should ask questions of the assumptions which you may have been taught, or may have fallen into believing as a child. You should place as a priority the learning you have made in life through personal experience, but when two conflicting points of view, fuelled by personal experience, come into conflict, who's to say which is right? Where is the benchmark we can rest on when we are tackling such broad topics as life the universe and everything. God, the human spirit and life itself. Who can be the adjudicator when no man is innocent of sin? A certain amount of scientific understanding is necessary in order to give a balanced hearing to all of the views. And I would say that a scientific mind can indeed tackle the questions effectively and events, if it is fairly applied, but it is not essential. Emotional personalities are just as valuable, if not even more so, for some realms of the truth I would argue. For what might be lost by paranoid winks can just as easily be gained by a human approach which none of the scientists, commanders, politicians and atheists have even considered.

They threw the baby out with the metaphorical bath water, you might say.

What I'm trying to say is that everybody's view is valuable. And everybody has a contribution to make. If I had it my way teachers would seek out the answers from what their pupils know, instead of sticking to a rigid mark scheme. Sure this would take longer, and a different approach and attitudes to learning. It would mean that less essays and exams were actually set, but more time was spent over them. And can you imagine what this would do to learning? It would revolutionize it.

God is not an exclusive premise of a secret 'seventh' society, only accessible to highly qualified or powered candidates. It doesn't take years of travelling or research or training and study. It doesn't even take excellent writing/reading skills or anything else like that. You don't even have to have a strong network of family or friends, 'cos you can make them. There are a lot of good people out there. Let us work together for a better world, instead of just continually arguing, or struggling for the betterment of ourselves or our own personal selfish possession base.

I have earlier said that we don't need money, wars or countries. I don't know if you picked up on this, but this was also a reference to sweet lines within the late John Lennon (and Yoko Ono's) epic ballad, Imagine. I'd seriously recommend that you try and get yourself a copy if you've never heard that moving song before. I once sung it at an old school concert which I was invited back to after my accident to do one last performance with our folk band. There was Chris on the violin, Stuart on the Wheezy-box, Brian on the guitar and me on the drum. Plus I sang a song. Well I couldn't understand why my drama teacher cried on that day. Never mind that I got some of the words wrong. It certainly is a powerful song.

I'm not going to dwell on the past. And music can certainly conjure some powerful emotions. But without taking away too much from the music, I think that there are often both powerful messages and words placed in many of the songs.

Here my namesake seems to have been stressing that we as a human people can live in peace and harmony, despite our differences. If we only learn to share what we've got, to piss off the law (the police), and just recognise each other for what we are, surely everything is going to be alright? Well this isn't so much a reality, a possibility, or a strategy even as it is a dream. But I for one am a dreamer, and I subscribe to his faith. An actual line in that song actually goes; 'Imagine no religion' and I remember having to argue the point for us to perform it at a church we were also performing at. By saying that he is also saying a lot more than just a Pagan message. And I think I won the argument, because I remember singing it there.

Sure John may have been an atheist, in the conventional sense of the word. He didn't seem to subscribe to the idea of an all powerful guiding spirit, which many Christians do. You know I have already told you that neither do I. I was brought up a Marxist you know? A pragmatic scientific school on the world. And I will never leave this. You don't, as you grow older, forget your past. But when you learn new ideas, they just supplement the old ones. Perhaps new friends emerge. I'm sure they will. But you're still you. You are still you. We still try our best.

What was I saying? Ah my memory's pants hey? I always forget what I was saying!

Oh yeah about John Lennon. His dream apparently was quashed with his death. A single assassin's bullet ripped through his head and put an end to the dream. Bad men. And you should know what I think of the 'official' theories by now, I wouldn't trust them as far as I can throw them, which isn't very far!

Did you know that my namesake was a staunch opponent of the Vietnam war, and so any of them could have done it. Do you really believe that they couldn't have carried out a hit and framed some-one else for it? These are professional killers you know. They spend their lives training to be the perfect killing machines. Do you really think they would do all that hard work on the bodies and neglect to develop the strategic element? Of course not. These guys know what they are doing and don't mess about. And if they want you dead, well you can pretty much count your days numbered.

Especially a poor innocent soul like old Johnny boy. His spirit succeeds him, but his body is long gone. Dust and bones.

So what does that leave us with? A failed dream which seems to be as ill founded as the USSR's Yeltzin's drink habit? But as his song keeps its place hidden away in your parent's attic or basement there is a chance that maybe, just maybe, one of these days someone will actually listen to the track, hear what he was saying, and actually do something that will change the world.

This still doesn't get to what I started saying. Something about religion? You know music is an important part of my life. When I'm not hacking away there at the internet confounding people's expectations of what sensibilities expect you to say, or feeding the pigeons, or writing these journals, there is nothing I like better than watching the music channel on cable TV! I think I have tried to tell you that I have learnt a thing or two from my lessons in class about philosophy, and also various other things in life. But you know I have learnt a huge amount from the songs on music videos. Not just the rhythms, not just the pretty picture, but listen to the actual words, trying to make out what they are saying and what they mean. Sometimes I think that they are talking to me.

Not the songs so much as some of these actors on these TV shows. For example today there was a drama programme whose audience started laughing when I laughed. As if they were watching me and laughing in response from a direct feed. Of course I don't have any real proof that this is happening; it is just a suspicion. And why would they do this? To mock me ? Well I'll tell you one thing: if they are using my life for their bloody voodoo doll then I damn well will use this platform to advocate my cause. Damn it! I'm probably just imagining it, but you know when that drama show I mentioned stopped taking attention off me and began actually acting insular and self contained style, they were taken off the air; no lie! They didn't even run the credits and, after the break , halfway through the show, some medical drama started without so much as an intro-screen. Now if that's not weird then I don't know what is!

I think that these guys are also experts at mind control. Not just media manipulation with carefully selected coverage of world events in the media, such as on the BBC over Georgia, to influence the mass public and other decisions who have key roles in the decision processes of the world, but also for the individual.

I think that they are totally clued up, not just on this, and not just on surveillance on anyone they want (including civilians in British cities), but they do so without the constraints of any law. These guys and their paymasters place themselves above the law.

They have tried to get me before, and I'm not going to try and dig up from the past all of the shreds of the picture to justify my claims. You would probably write them off as coincidences or worse my imagination. But please don't try and tell me that all of these years I have spent locked into struggles/meditations with another chess player haven't taught me a lot about using my mind in different ways. Chess teaches observation and analytical skills, which I have retained even in these twilight years of my life. So I think that they do like to keep ears and eyes on me, and throw me off track if they possibly can. Yet I have tried to explain that we are both on the same side. Despite our rapidly diverging ideas on many things we both are Christians and we all are trying to achieve a better place in human-kind. So despite the different means we use to get there let us hope that we get there in the end.

And even if they never do show their face, the fact that we share this same ultimate goal protects me from the worst of their wrath. And the closer I get to God (meaning the closer I get to my fiancée), the less power they have over me.

Suddenly I find myself in the open world. Discussing my ideas with other listening people. Some more open to my version of the truth, some sceptical. But that's okay. Surely if my philosophy can't withstand the duress of open criticism, then it doesn't deserve to stand at all.

What was I saying again? I want to escape these conspiracy/army/political ideas and move back to my argument that in order to recognise the connection between the various religions we have to study them. And not just with the old hard eye of the scientist or the scholar, but with the open arms and heart and mind of the believer. And this is the only way we can give these different creeds the chance to shine.

And that is why I am grateful to our philosophy and Religion teacher, Daniel, for taking us into a Mosque and a Gudwara, to listen to the preaching of the specific believers inside. There is no other way I would have got into those two places. But we went, we were actually accepted in, we listened to them and it was all good.

Religion, I would actually argue, like faith, is a human teaching. Meaning that it is a teaching passed on by communication. There are books, but it is the actual speech contact, like when you meet someone and share in their faith with them.

So in the books written by academics we can learn certain things. And in the children's picture books we can learn others. Isn't it funny how you remember gems from primary school? For me it was the story of Rama and Sita, a play we were in. Rama the prince fought many demons including the demon king to rescue his princess Sita. To do this he drew a magic circle around her to protect her from the beasts, and told her to make sure she didn't step out of it. In the story he was also joined by a certain number of allies, including the monkey king Ravavishnu or something like that. And I even remember being one of the monkeys. Cute hey? I may have even had a mask I think I may have also been a shepherd too in one of the nativity plays, but I can't be sure. I never did get the star roles, but that didn't stop me from trying. I do however remember the girl who did get them. She was a champion athlete, a scholar and very pretty to boot. She even went on TV once which we all watched after it was recorded on video. Anyhow, she didn't like me needless to say.

I was also a monkey in Joseph and the Amazing Dreamcoat play we did at another primary school I went to later. And I remembered to pick and eat the fleas from the monkey hair too, which we all assumed is what monkeys did.

So yeah that first play is based on Divali, the Asian festival of light. And is celebrated by the lighting of little candles, which look quite magic in the dark. I think it is also accompanied with lots of lovely Indian sweets. Any excuse for a good nosh up! I can't remember if she stepped out of the circle or not.

In fact I think that Sita was lured out of the magic circle by the Demon-king who also had about twelve faces, oh I can't remember his name. But as soon as she did, he reverted back to his demon form and stole her away to his demon kingdom somewhere far away. As I guess you have already gathered I can't even remember this story very well, but it is just one very nice memory I've got from my early years which I wanted to share with you, and these weren't that many!

So the actual Hindu story, another one, which I think I learnt at school, and many years later shared with my old teacher at university, was that of the Hindu's belief in God. The Hindu doctrine suggests that God has many faces, or spirits if you will. From Brahma the elephant god, the creator, to Shiva the warrior god. Sometimes portrayed as a woman, the destroyer, to Vishnu the preserver. And then there is Atman the everything to which we all are part. This is clearly a very deep and complex theology, but also a very accessible one I hope you will agree. And every Hindu I have ever talked to has always been a lovely person. Don't believe the lies. They don't believe in many gods, they are monotheists like the rest of us. And I was immediately drawn to them on the grounds that my first faith of Buddhism is actually derived from Hinduism. A subset if you will. The Hindu saints Krishna and Arjuna, are also Buddhist ones, and the beautiful story of the Bhagavada Gita, which can be interpreted as arguing both for and against war.

It is a test in which death with science, humanity, poetics, language, family, love, war, the truth, God and commitment, play a part in at the same time. I have been blown away on reading it, and instantly converted. It was probably after reading this that I began to suspect that I was multi-faith, as in all of them.

But to be properly multi-faith you do have to know enough about them to make that serious decision. Here's the Hindu story anyway. A group of people once came across an elephant; the first person who grabbed hold of its trunk clearly thought it was a snake you see, given the design. It was pitch black you see. The next one touched the leg and thought it was a giraffe. The next the belly and thought a hippo. And the last an ear and thought it felt like a sleeping bat. Then it was only in the morning that the villagers suddenly discerned that animal for what it truly is.

And so to this story actually is a Hindu metaphor for their belief in God. Part of him is a destroyer, part a preserver, and part a creator. I know that in the Hindu calendar there are many other festivals, but I don't think you have to know everything about a particular religion to make a commitment to it. All you have to do is discover for yourself the truth from wishing that set of beliefs, the sincerity, and if it satisfies you. If you learn something from it, if it helps you grow commit to it, hold it close to your heart and never let it go.

Then we went to a Mosque as well. I can't be bothered to go into the same detail with that religion, but anyway it did also have a strong effect on me. Not just in the temple, but before in studying the teachings of Mohammed (peace be upon him) before. So I am sorry I have slagged off individual Muslims in here. This was not an attack against their religion, but rather just a few key individuals who have grieved me in particular times in the past.

I think I ought to spend a moment here dissecting the war on Islam, seeing as half of the world seems to either be geared up to blame them for the sins of the world, or at least blame them for much of the world's terror, 9-11 especially.

Now I can't either prove or disprove what happened in 9-11. I think you know by now that I don't trust the official version of events. I think there is valuable evidence to prove that it was an inside job of a colossal scale, carried out by the most effective and secretive killing force the world has ever seen. But I don't have a smoking gun, or not enough proof anyway to satisfy the 'anti-truthers'. Some people will never agree with you no matter the amount of evidence you put before them. They seem to get their head stuck on one idea of belief and then remain there until the end of time.

But even if 9-11 was done by them, which it could have been, that doesn't mean that all Muslims are bad! And I realise that there may have been a certain amount of antagonism between different cultures, not just because we invaded Arabia in the middle ages, but because people are just generally afraid of what they don't know. It has been that way for a long time. But instead of being afraid of them, of blaming all of our theoretical problems on them, let's try and open up the channels of communication and discussion. Such as if they did do it they should be punished. But we've practically wiped Iraq off the map now, and are in the process of doing the same to the Afghans, so don't you think that they've suffered enough? And don't give me that crud about having a commitment to the mission, or whatever rubbish the commanders come up with. I am quite sure that the natives of both countries want the US and European soldiers out, and to take their tanks and barbed wire and guns and walls with them. Some people don't understand what they have done, the pain of suffering their politicians have created over these years of conflict. So can change come? You tell me. I have already said that I cannot do it on my own!

I'm not going to dwell on this one any more, only to say that Islam seems to stand for pillars of morality. It is interesting to recognise that they accept the Bible and Jesus as holy. And my studies of this have only brought me joy.

So what about the other religions? Well I want to next look at Judaism, and Jehovah, who I think is their god. My grandfather is a Jew. And despite them nearly being wiped off the map in World War two, there are still a couple of them kicking about. I knew this one guy (I've forgotten his name) from uni, who was Jewish. He also was a really good man, like he was honest and decent. I could just tell on meeting him. This is all good. I am happy to believe in Jehovah. Sometimes it is not the words you see or hearsay of a religion, but just the feeling you get from it.

For Buddhism, well I think that I've already begun telling you about it. This whole book is a part of my journey and in this way and others; it is also a Buddhist treaty. One of Buddha's first promises is that the truth can be found from the causes which are the root cause of all things.

It is whoever learns about it. It is about the happiness shared from listening to good music together, hearing a good speech, seeing a good play. Where Buddhism is also the source of power for Zen which is also a super-powerful martial art which teaches not just to be strong in mind, body and spirit, but also to recognise that all three are one and the same. And if you don't understand what this means, I guess you should spend some time thinking about it.

Not just with the rational mind, but with the emotional one. You need to meditate to find a space in you life to put aside, and draw a magic box around. To protect, and thus try putting the important things of your life in it. It is not just about God. But He does love all of His little Buddhas, of this I'm sure.

Seeing as we are being good comprehensive academics let's look at Sikhism. Well I know that they don't get on very well with the Muslims. That really isn't my concern. I did once have a Sikh landlord who was a hypocrite among other things. He's like the one who put me on the streets, which was a part of the chain which found me in the hospital last time. And he kept on bollocking me for putting my feet on the foot-table at his house, even though my feet were clean and I always took them off when asked.

This guy doesn't know God; he's a bloody megalomaniac, and I really wouldn't care if I never saw him again.

That also reminds me of the Doctor who did actually put me in hospital. Well he was there with my dad and my social worker, and they suggested that they thought I might to need to go in. Not to mention I had just been kicked out.

Well, man, he didn't have to say another word! I got quick out of there and with nowhere else to go spent the night on a park bench. Then cold and going blood crazy (seeing as I was also soon off my meds) I went to withdraw some money from the bank machine, which swallowed my card. Then on going in they said that they would order a new card whilst I had to wait to chat to someone. A short while later two police constables came and told me that they were taking me home, which turned out to be the hospital for the next seven months! Bloody pigs.

But this all being said, I do have a close Sikh friend, Sunjeev, who helped me when I was preparing to visit my girl for the first time in seven years.

We have seen films together too, been to church together, and share an affinity which comes from something of being a roughly similar age (he's a bit older than me) and of the same outlook in life. I've never been to his house; he visits me in his car.

Yeah and while I don't know any of the details about the Gurus, or Guru-Nanack the latest and last one, I do know that if Sunjeev is a Sikh, then it is a good religion. Simple.

The last major religion is Christianity. We have already discussed this, but I want to explore the Christian light because it is important to me none-the-less. I feel Him when I go to church, when I am with my friends, my family, when I feel a connection with my community, spiritual or otherwise.

I used to meditate. When I go to church I try to pray. I also try to bring this level of enlightenment and everyday conversation with God to my everyday life. I try not to swear, but if I have to I will. I hate do-gooders who tell others off when they swear in distress nearly as much as I hate prats who swear all the time because they think it's cool! That's it. We explored most of the major religions to both recognise that they are all different, but also the same. If you can't understand what this means even now, I think you haven't been paying attention this far and should start the book again!

There were two more things that I wanted to say to you just now. Suppose that I am. Suppose that I have generated all these crazy ideas and theories about God which are purely myth, that I have no proof to substantiate my claims. That all the conspiracy theories are just that, theories nothing more. That every religion is nothing more than a diverse group of people clutching at straws in their hands. Suppose the vacuum I find in my head when I sit down in church is just that – a biological void, devoid of all meaning and life. Suppose that those messages I think I hear are just my mind imagining things or me speaking to myself. Suppose that there is no such thing as Karma, or that the crimes and terrible things that I did in the past will remain as concrete objects in history forever. Suppose there is no such thing as the secret service, or spies watching every move. Suppose that if there were they don't care about me or couldn't care less about me. Or if they did exist they probably really don't like me, hate me even, what with after all I've done, all those years before. I'm not going to go over my sins again; trust me they are very bad and I did them. I have to admit it 'cos I want to get everything out in the open. So imagine that there is no network of somehow connected individuals, some knowledgeable in different things, and some with overview and some with different opinions. Suppose there was no conspiracy, that the Doctors really did believe in their work, and the people who go to jail really are responsible for the crimes which they committed. Suppose that God doesn't exist, and I am not spiritual, just a sad, mad loner. What then; where does that leave us? Nowhere I would argue.

The next idea which I want to explore is something of a tangent to that last depressing thread.

Now I want you to imagine that God is alive. That He is real. That He does watch you, follow your thoughts, smile when you do good things and frown on the bad. Suppose He watches everyone. Suppose He sometimes intervenes but more often than not lets them just get on with the job. Or imagine if He does not have power over man, and can only watch hopelessly as man murders each other, bombs and nukes each other and lies each other out of existence.

Suppose if He does exist. Let's hang with the Christian thread here for a minute. Suppose – ah no; I don't want to go there for fear of insulting my genuine Christian readers. I am a Christian and this is the last thing I want to do.

The Holy Trinity is a complex issue and I'm not even going to pretend that I understand it very well. And I certainly can't fit it into this surreal paradox which I have been playing with. Anyhow…

Suppose that there is a God. That He is Love. That when you fall into love you fall into His arms. Suppose God is in the glorious rainbows that shine through the sky. Suppose that He does exist for all those who want to believe in Him. Suppose that the simple act of belief, of hope, actually provides them with comfort. And in that comfort they can find solace. Suppose that He exists. Suppose He is just that; suppose He is more. Suppose these rhymes mean everything; suppose they mean nothing.

Suppose that He is a literary figure a concrete idol? I suppose that He is a living force, a breathing spectrum. Who breathes in all of his lovers and believers. That as well as the pre-mentioned names He is mother-nature. Just suppose.

An old Chinese graduate who I once fancied asked me, near to when she left this country for good, did I believe in fate. And despite what I may believe I wasn't able to come out with an 'enlightened' reply to that one. She was actually writing Mandarin Chinese I realise now. That is the beautiful language which doesn't rely on loads of words to have a striking impact where just one will do. And in that one can be a question AND a statement. A critique and a compliment. This takes me back to my days when I entered the dragon, entered

Buddhism. On its exterior it is nothing but a jumble of nonsensical riddles. Full of jingoistic clichés and signifying nothing! But what did I tell you about studying new religions? You have to do it with the heart of a believer! I know this may sound nonsensical to you if you have never even appreciated a particular faith, but really this is the only way! Probably the best way to do this is to talk to one or two of its adherents and see if they can point you in the right direction. Me, I went about it in rather a different way. For years I had subscribed to the lies that these post-modernists had presented to me. I thought that the good scientific and rational understanding of the world would stand me in good stead for the obstacles I had to overcome. How wrong could I be? For a start, A-levels have practically no reference to them at all, or at least that is what I found. I scabbed through school and the exams by sucking up to the teachers and swotting up for the exams. Really I did prodigious amounts of homework and revision.

I remember actually reading through a couple of entire textbooks page to page for my GCSE science! No wonder I got an A-star then, for that double GCSE at least.

But it all didn't mean trouble. I really think you can forget about these nobs right away who come out with the shining grades on their report cards. Who cares what results you get? Universities? Maybe but only because they're paid to. And what's more I think you'll also find that they are beginning to give more and more credence and credit to actual life experience, for all students old and young alike. So if you want to take a year out or two, go for it. The break will no doubt give you a well earned rest and hopefully you will meet one or two friends along the way. And even if you don't, at least it will give you an opportunity to sort your head out, and hopefully get your horizons into perspective. To figure out what, and probably who, is really important in life. And if you haven't met them yet, then what? Well I guess everybody gets at least one chance. And if it folds then what? Try again? Ah, I'm not really one for working. Never was very good at conforming and that seems to be one of the perquisites. But learning, is my second love. With the absence of a job I have become quite good at studying facts presented before us, from the media or what friends say, and dissecting them for the truth, before building them up again to fit into the whole bigger picture. This is the way I have been able to approach the war and the 'terrorist' attacks, by following the stories carefully, thinking about them, talking about them, exploring ideas, applying what I already know, to reach my own valid if somewhat unique conclusion!

So yeah, I should hardly say drop out of school or uni. Even if one of my good friends of the day did just this. I don't think Darren even took his GCSEs, but I am sure that he got a job straightaway and is doing well now on whatever his chosen career may be with some years under the belt.

Me, I smoke a different brand of cigarette. I listen to music to let the songs take me away. I enter fantasy worlds of harmony and beauty. And stories and relationships I could never be in.

Then I take this power of imagination and creation, and conjure it out of the hat whenever my need calls for it. Perhaps in meeting a new person and being friends with them. Perhaps it's reading a new news item and knowing what to make of it, what to expect, given the limited amount of information presented before us. Perhaps it is exploring good ideas with my wife, or a friend about something I know, maybe exploring a new idea with them or seeing what their output on any particular topic may be. This idea of being open is crucial to me. For the learning as already discussed, to playing chess (waiting to see what the next move your opponent makes may be and acting accordingly), to like everything else. There was quite a long time in my life when I tried to look at everything in numbers. As if music is just a mechanical, mathematical formula! What a load of rubbish!

And if there's one thing this grasp of the truth has taught me, it's that liars are just no good at all. Perhaps they have got something to hide; perhaps they are afraid of the new world order. That fabled idea that my friend Will from hospital (remember him?) kept on going on about. But I don't know if he even knew the significance of what he was saying at the time. I'll tell you that I don't believe these sites he was studying to get all of this stuff from for a minute. For me (a scholar of the truth) they were clearly traps set up for the vulnerable genius mind. Maybe they were made specifically for Will. I don't know about that, although I wouldn't put it past them. What they like to do is to cotton onto your one of more mental weakness and then manoeuvre things so you find yourself under their mental control. Sticking within the pre-defined limits and hence posing no real threat, they use the systems already in place (the police, doctors and social services) to deal with it. How do you fight this? With fire? Ah no, that is the mentality of a soldier and guarantees you're not going to win that game. They are the soldiers, the officers, the commanders. There is no way you are going to win that one. But I'm not stopping you from exploring the idea. By all means go ahead if you want to; you are your own person and this is the way it must be.

Some of you are bound to become soldiers. It is hard work and sometimes a thankless task, or so I hear. But I have heard that they pay quite well, and I also think they have got quite good job security and prospects. Whatever you do, be true to yourself. Try to hold your head up high at all times. If you want to write an emotional letter do it. If it upsets you, cry. I did that once when I was writing a letter to my baby inside my lover's belly who I wasn't sure if I would ever see again (being trapped in hospital for the unforeseeable future at the time.) Did I tell you about my good friend who was inside for some fifteen years? The only reason she got out in the end is because she ran away.

I don't think they are as bad now, in as much as they don't seem to keep us for as long. All of the old timers from both hospitals have moved on now, to my knowledge. And that is a good thing. These weren't prisons; most of the people in there haven't committed any sort of crime. But much of the small minded mentality, the superiority complex remains among the staff, especially the consultants in my opinion. It's not that they couldn't do their jobs properly just that maybe they didn't know how to take me. So Doctor Dave as my last psychiatrist diagnosed me eventually as a paranoid schizophrenic, which was a new one to me and Mum (who used to attend most of the ward-rounds I had).

But I'll tell you what – I fought them all the way. I fought the god-damned system from the minute I was escorted back into the building, until I walked out again seven months later. And I suppose you could say that I am still fighting them now. Only my fight has taken on a bigger scope, a bigger horizon. I am no longer in hospital. There are some good nurses and doctors and patients, for that matter, in there and after all a lot of them are trying their best at doing their job.

But I have quite easily been able to change my struggle into a global setting. In the game of chess there can only be one winner. I play it and enjoy the game, whatever the result. Whenever I get something out of it, but that is just the way I have come to look at it.

Back to this new World War; oh dear, inside I played with this ward: world war three. Actually I was fighting for my life. Seriously, when I take drugs my breathing gets bad like an asthmatic, only all of the time. Just in hospital I was heavily drugged up, and unable to do much walking being stuck in that damned building for most of the days, my blood unable to circulate properly (as walking promotes) so seriously I was struggling. Not to mention the harassment I got off different people in there, who simply didn't like me for whatever reason.

Since I've been out I have tried to stay strong, to stay close to my family, to build for my future instead of duelling as in the past.

Fire-fighters fight fire with water. Water is a cooling soothing force, which energizes all living things and the fish love it too. So in order to fight the meat-heads in the military and society I propose that love is the answer. Faith is the answer. The truth is the answer; these are three much ignored and despised little known jewels. But they are the jewels of the universal monarch, the true king of kings, the true Jesus Christ Buddha.

Well we have been taking on some pretty giant mammoths tonight, and how are we doing? You tell me? I think this line of argument has remained pretty strong and convincing and persuasive. Please understand that you might not even know me; you don't even have to like me, to read this book. I hope the arguments presented within are pretty solid and self-explanatory! I can quite understand if you reject some of the clauses I propose. But as each one builds on the other, from the very first page to the very last (even if there may seem to be some contradictions within), I very much doubt that you can reject the clause as a whole. Not if you take your time reading the words and trying to follow the ideas. I hope that you actually will be able to follow these ideas, as I have tried to give clear examples in most of the cases.

So fighting these secret services with water – what exactly does that mean? It means fighting deception and half/hidden/selective truth with the whole entire truth. It means fighting hate with love and industry with family. I wish I had a good job; who knows maybe one day I'll get one? Maybe I will, maybe I won't, does it really matter? As long as I keep arguing, keep on discussing I think that's the important thing. Keep on writing.

I actually feel very much like this is a chess game: John Robinson versus the world 2008, only God's soul is at stake! Ha, I bet He didn't think that I'd have this much power over Him. Ha-ha, God's my slave. Wow, I guess I could get crucified for that one! Please don't take it the wrong way. I was only making a joke; anything for a good laugh!

There are times when you have to try and make light of things. I know sometimes this may seem hard, but you must try. If we didn't laugh we'd only cry.

Again I'm sorry if it seems like I am preaching to you, but I am only sharing my experiences through life. Telling you a story, my story, academic, but as a human being, with a heart, a mind, a soul and a voice. I've already apologised for my sins, well that is what I meant to do in mentioning them earlier. Move on.

I'm gonna move back to that cute question Min asked me a few years back now. 'Do I believe in destiny?'

And what could I say? I love you? But that doesn't fit right. How about I want to stay with you forever, make it up to you, prove to you that I can be your man and I will stay with you forever? Oh gosh. But that one didn't work out. Of course it wasn't 'destined' to. I suppose she knew this as much as I did. Because you see I already had my gal over in Kenya, even if things hadn't quite progressed as far as they have now. I love you with all of my heart as I think you know. And I intend to stay with you, to support you until we are both old and grey, or one of us dies, whichever is the sooner. But M* was cute and she meant a lot to me at the time as well, okay? Boy we're getting quite heavy, aren't we? I said I wasn't going to go into my exes and now it seems like we're at it. I may as well mention C*, a stunner I met in hospital. An Indian princess. I'm not gonna to dwell on her for too long see; she is history now and I suppose that's for the best. But she was an element when I hit M* with that killer blow to the forehead. I did hate the sucker, but somehow just don't see the situation escalating to the state it did if she wasn't involved, that's all.

Yeah Chinese calligraphy is deep. I think the graceful and well written Chinese character ink blobs are pretty and powerful at the same time. And there are certain features among some of the words, even if no universal alphabet. I learned enough about the language to have Mandarin scrolls cut out all the way up both of my arms you know! Ha, pink unicorn, exactly.

So yeah, in Chinese they draw a box around a character to indicate that it is precious. This represents the Chinese recognising that precious things need to be treasured and valued. Not just possessions, not just them, but love, family and hope. I'd say they are my top three.

Where does that leave us now? I think I have just about shredded the parts I set myself. Oh yeah, here's another thing I wanted to say; oh, I've forgotten it again. Hang on… we've got some blank pages before us, some blank slates which I hope further positive meditations can create themselves on. I do very much feel that this time spent together, you and me, the page, the pen and the ideas, is quality time. We can explore things, sometimes controversial, which I believe. And I also believe that this not only creates a soothing and healing energy with which to surround my world, but yours too.

Don't just see this as a peace bible, although it is that. But it is also a fighting manual, much like the Bhagavada Gita (already mentioned Hindu text) before. In that, young prince Arjuna asked his uncle the general Krishna, why he should join in to fight in a war when he was a pacifist. Why he should lay weapons into enemies who had the same body features as him and his family. Why he should obey the orders of a commander in chief who he had never seen, and for all he knew had a completely different agenda as to that which they had been told. The world is full of liars, and half-truthers after all. They seem to have made a habit of taking it on themselves to 'alter' the truth, when they think it is for the best.

Example: I had to leave the hostel R* used to own when he passed away. I was told that his wife was shutting up shop. But I have seen two of the lads (who used to live there) about near to there. And recently was told that one of the staff had quit her job recently. But how could this be? I had understood that she had left her job when the house shut? I now actually think that they never shut it at all, but just took the opportunity of his dying to clear me out of there. Which was the first step to my problems you might say, 'cos one thing led to another and I found myself in hospital, which I guess you know by know!

Anyhow there is another idea that I would like to dwell on for a minute, and that's the one of Karma, which is basically a sub equation of the Buddhist nature of conditional truth. Karma is quite simple really: if you do bad things in this life you will be punished, and for good rewarded. The effects might not be immediate, but they will stay with you until released at last. I actually see this book as a good reward for all of those years of suffering I have done at the hands of the bullies in school, unable to control my life, or see a way out of that prison. But now all of a sudden I have a future. Things are going well. I am able to draw on my past and, in the form of learning, years of experience have been hammered into me, to clarify and expose them here perfectly for you, the reader. How many readers I'll be able to reach remains another question. I've been trying to put the word out on these internet forums I visit, and have been getting mostly good luck messages back, but one or two funny ones as well.

The most recent of which being a rather rude post from this kid who has been disagreeing with my definition of God. Like he doesn't believe. He told me that he comes from a family full of atheists (apart from his gran). Well I told him so did I, which I guess he took as a personal attack. So he spat something back. And what did I say then? Some nonsense about spirituality needing personal commitment. Which is very true, but doesn't relate to him in his difficult times (which he is clearly going through else he wouldn't have bitten my head off). Maybe next time I will tell him that spirituality can be shared amongst friends, but it is up to him to take the hand I am offering out. (Reply enclosed next.)

To D*;

You are honest; that is what I like about you. You are a lot younger than me, and clearly don't respect me like you should your elders, but that is alright too. You ask me for proof of God, and I have tried to provide it for you. But clearly this has not done the job. I did like it the post before last when you said something funny, something about haaaating me, or something like that. And I hoped, I prayed, that you were beginning to open up a little bit, loosen down a little. I don't know what you do with your life. I imagine you go to school; I suppose you like Koei games. Hell so do I – that's why we're both here, isn't it? Which is your favourite then: Orochi warriors, or Samurai Warriors 2? In all truth I think I would go for the exclusively Japanese franchise. It has better, more convincing stories, being based on true legends as opposed to some crazy demon-lord fantasy. But that all being said and done, with its three way tag-team system and impressive weapon points system, Orochi must surely come a close second.

See Danion, I am also normal. That is a part of me. I was once your age where the escapism those games provided gave me hope where else-wise there was none. We're talking about over ten years ago now, but I can still remember what it was like.

Now I do have other things to think of as well. Sure I like a bit of escapism, who doesn't? But as you grow older and wiser you do seem to acquire certain responsibilities that weren't there before. And if you don't believe me, just wait and see!

As for this whole God thing. I don't want to argue, nor do I want you to insult me. I seriously doubt that you can even begin to imagine some of the things I have been through in my time. Anyway peace.

21: Attack on Tae-Kwon-Do

I laughed when I saw that TKD youth kick that ref in the face! And do you know why I laughed? Because it showed for all the world to see what that MA is all about. Tae-kwon-do by and large tries to bypass the method of Judo, the movement of Karate, the peace of Yoga and the suspicion of Aikido to create a new fighting type which celebrates beating people up above everything. It also celebrates lying. Cos when I went to this dojo a few times, which declared on the billboard 'beginners welcome' they immediately jumped into a fast paced workout and move sets which were miles above my beginner's athletic ability and effectively told me to f*ck off. At least when I went to the Aikido class a couple of days later, they actively engaged with me when I demonstrated that I knew how to break-fall. And even got me to take part in a couple of throws, although I wasn't strong enough to do any more. The concept of accepting beginners is a critical one, and why advertise it on a billboard if you don't mean it?

No matter how long that discipline, there is a reason it has not got the films like Karate has Karate Kid, Kung Fu has Enter the Dragon and Drunken Boxing has Jackie Chan. It's because it is weak. Not muscularly, but spiritually. It does not tap into the eternal life of Gaia, but instead waves in the glory of Vader. And for this reason it is bound never to be anything but a second rate art. Sure its practitioners are good at strutting their stuff, or waving their arms and legs about in an excited and frantic fashion, all the while making deep and seemingly cryptic sounds from deep within the roots of their being, but you know what, they might as well be singing 'Puff the Magic Dragon' for all I care.

Perhaps my experience of them is biased. I have only ever partly known two. The first was my old social worker, Phil his name was. He saw me every now and again and told me that he had got some belts at TKD a few years back. I think that he said he got up to blue or green, one of the colours anyway. At this point I was pretty much in awe of him. Until he stabbed me in the back. Then one day, out of the blue, the whole world seemed to pounce on me. From being spat at in the street, to being kicked out of the hostel I was at, to having my dad and Doctor and social all agreeing that I needed to go into hospital again.

At this point I seriously didn't know what was going on. And don't insult this narrative any more. I don't want to hear your bla-di-blahs or your magic smoke patterns stories, got it? I am laying one on you.

Anyhow, I did see Phil that sucker three more times on the ward. The first he came to sit in on a meeting about me, and you know what I was fuming. How dare he? Well I made my mind up there and then that if he ever dared to come again, he wouldn't know what hit him. Well, needless to say he did and I did, hard. The little bad man. But I don't think it properly registered in his system. You see he tried to repeat the pattern and I punished him again. Again I used my left fist which is like a lot stronger of my two. You should have seen his face; he was virtually in tears!

I never saw him again after that!

I was actually very mad with my dad too, and hit him twice as well. If I wasn't ill when I went in I suppose it didn't take me long to get that way. And I vowed that if I ever did see that bad Doctor who was the ultimate assassin, that he would receive the biggest attack of all. I wanted to chin that man to within an inch of his life! Wow! Thankfully, I never did see him again; it was arranged that I didn't have to.

To kind of even up the score for TKD a little bit, I will say that I did meet a lovely couple of gals who did different versions of it, and the black one was something else, and they were both sweet.

But I'm still not convinced. I mean as a sport sure, but it really isn't as deep as some of the other martial arts specifically Shaolin Kung Fu and Hoshinryjutsu (the two I know best). Shaolin teaches you to generate power, true power from the soul and connect it with your opponent. Much as the Chinese use less words in their calligraphy to say more. Hoshin equally teaches that the spirit (that's God to you and me) is an inseparable part of the whole fighter. In shunning these deeper disciplines, instead on relying on the dogma of discipline, repetition and subservience, all TKD is doing is creating a mindless and headless army to stalk the streets and act way cool when in fact they are just getting on everyone's nerves.

Think about this the next time you students get out that mat; is this really how you want to waste your life away?

Now I have got your attention maybe you will begin to listen to me? I am not trying to talk about your houses, or creations, just levelling some criticisms to them. Look if you want to show me that you are worth more than all of this; prove it to me. Not by insults or personal attacks, but by demonstrating to me your value. Prove to me that you are worth more than this, can rise above this. If someone insults you in the street, what would you do, turn around and knock him out? Or ignore him. Chill guys. Sometimes I play the devil's advocate and there's a reason for that. Sure I'm trying to weed out the weak among you. And I am trying to demonstrate the validity of a principle which most of you reject. What better way to see if my theory of holy conquest is real by seeing if it can stand the test of time?

In a fight you throw punches, both fighters do. Sometimes you use combinations. I'm looking at Mohammed Ali versus George Foreman in the Rumble in the Jungle. Simple boxing, like it used to be, like it should be. None of this Prince Naseem crud. Two strong men slugging it out to the end. And even now looking back at that fight, I'm not sure that Ali did deserve to win it, despite his pride, despite his tongue.

So yeah, come on guys, take a shot or two back. Or agree with me. Man, I don't care as long as I'm not banned this is as good a place as any for me to have my say. Just try and stop me.

<Note I have just today (on the final edit) decided not to post that final MAs attack. Like my final blow ~I am instead choosing to hold back, to reserve my energy and fight for another day!>

Phew! I've just finished typing up a long piece of work. What to do now? Write some more.

I think in this book I have been trying to use logical arguments to prove that the Holy Spirit can be demonstrated, to be logically proven. Not God per se, which is after all just a word, but something which is both a word and everything. Not 'just' a word.

I have been using ideas to explore memories and thoughts, and chronicle things that happen to me and things I've said and possibly their response. This is very much an organic work; I didn't know where it was going to end when I first set out and I still don't, though I'm a good way through now. Even though you may disagree with some or several of my ideas, you can't argue with my honest approach to tackling them. And I have been honest, both in my attitude and in trying to give other people listening space before deciding on how to respond.

I am a thoughtful person. I do have philosophy, so one of MY threads has been to demonstrate that Buddhism and

Christianity can live together side by side in perfect harmony. What's more, powers derived from their knowledge can be used to unlock some of the fallacies of today's modern world. Not all of them: some. By deepening to the root causes of action, it then makes it a great deal easier to understand why people do things, even if they may be things that you don't agree with. It is very Buddhist to analyse the world in this way, in terms of cause and effect. And it is Christian to try and pull all of it together in a coherent, logical and honest way.

I'm not afraid of being the odd one out. I may have told you this before, but even in primary school I remember being forced to sit on the dunce's chair in assembly on several occasions. Bad men.

Then at secondary school I was an outcast through all of it, so yeah don't you think that I am kind of used to it by now? But since I have faced the stormy seas of adulthood, don't you think that I have met some good friends along the way? Some of the nicest, most honest and generous people. People with attitude, people with pride. God grant me to meet many more.

Unfortunately, I don't know if you have noticed this, but it always seems to me that when you are weak for whatever reason, that is when the predators pounce. And it is often the people in power who are the worst of all, or so I've noticed.

How does that old maxim go? Power corrupts while absolute power corrupts absolutely! Never a truer word said.

So yeah, there are obvious problems to being alone, such as being lonely, vulnerable to abuse and such like. But are there any advantages as well. For instance, it gives you the chance to move when no one else will. To figure out things before everyone else.

I remember once attending a football match and always clapping at least two seconds before everyone else did! I had to curb my enthusiasm so as not to stand out too much!

What were we talking about again? Ah, does it really matter? I just like spending the time with you. It's good to have good company and you are a good friend, or at least that's the way it seems to me right now. Long may it continue.

Full of metaphors and rhythm (with bits and bobs of nonsense and some typos as well along the way), some people can't hack my writing. I am too direct, too honest perhaps? No I doubt anyone can ever be too honest, maybe it's just that they don't like what I am saying? They don't like my political affiliations, or they feel I'm trying to muscle in on their positions of power? Damn right I am! I'm a revolutionary, that's my job!

So where are we going now? Oh yeah, I felt like I ought to say that I don't go in for any of the Oxford English crud at all. Maybe it's okay for newspapers, but in everyday language on the street people often use abbreviations or colloquialisms which would fail a hundred spell checks! You know what – I have decided not even to run this through one, when it is done. You can read it like I said it, warts and all!

So you've got words like 'init' which I often hear, even once by my registrar (senior Doctor)! Okay, well anyway, there are a lot.

I sometimes think that the powers that be also try to control our lives by putting a straightjacket on the words we can use. As if only the dictionary can permit what is and is not acceptable to say! What a load of rubbish! There is no right or wrong way of saying things. It's okay for school work to look new words, but that's all, in my opinion.

Bloody hell! I did have some other ideas I wanted to discuss, but first: babies are so special don't you think so?

When I was in hospital and very unwell, as I think you should know by now, well that definitely had a noticeable effect on my love and her baby when she was born. They both provided me with pillars of life and I would have been lost without them. But it wasn't always smooth sailing you know. Not even to mention the times I called her up in the middle of the night. And that's even if the hospital payphone was working! God, it was a major struggle getting access to a usable phone half the time. On one of the wards the payphone was dodgy (probably because people often banged the receiver down) or on the other I tried to use the staff phone with my calling card (it didn't actually cost them any money). Well some of the staff plain wouldn't let me. Then it was agreed I could before eight or after five.

Anyway back to the babies. Yeah, they're really clever as well you know! I only really found out this after doing a two month or so one day a week placement at a child-care place for one of my college courses. I got put with the babies to begin with. They wouldn't let me anywhere near the changing room, and half the time I seemed to spend washing the toys, but the other half I spent playing with the babies! Cool. Some of them don't say much, but most of them can talk if they want to. And they generally do know what you are talking about if you give them time. I even once had this one who tricked me and I got angry with him or her and was about to tell them off, before being stopped by a member of staff.

Yeah, we need babies; they are cool!

Some people seem to think that the martial arts are all about kicking the trouble out of each other, or some other outlandish macho principles such as pride, honour, integrity or some other rubbish. You know I shouldn't really be commenting on them because I have never really been able to do them, but that doesn't stop me from trying (to comment).

Part of my philosophy and its implementation is to find connections between seemingly disparate things. Or finding skills, knowledge and learning which we can take from one situation and apply to others.

There is definitely the quest for knowledge which, you may have picked up, underlies a lot of what I say. I also try to be reasonable at all times, and despite being a serious person, not afraid to take a laugh. I think that I have normally quite good interpersonal skills and also am quite good at judging character. The basic circumstances can go a long way in helping you to figure out someone. Even if they look like the butter wouldn't melt, but are actually contagious liars, don't trust them. They are not the kind of people you want to know, 'cos they will only stab you in the back when times get rough, and be off with your wallet! And lying is dangerous. It seems to be that if one person does it, they often think that makes it alright for others to do it also! What a bunch of softies.

Moving on, yeah I tend to be drawn to Martial Artists 'cos they tend to practice an ideal, somewhat physical but an ideal none-the-less. If only we had more ideals in the world I am sure that it would be a better place. And I do think that the nature of continuously trying to better yourself, in every possible way is a good one, with a lot going for it.

The more I write (and type), the wearier I get. It seems like the energy is slowly draining out of me and before long I am just going to end up a sticky mess of goo on the floor, like the wicked witch of the west!

But I've got to persevere; this book is my chance to show the world what I think, free of chains, about righteousness and truth. That there is hope shining through the darkness, a path under the sand!

I've talked a lot about MA with plenty of generalisations and some examples from my life as well. What I want to do now is compare it with English. That's right. But I have also attacked both of these 'things' too in here. Not because I don't like them, but because I think that they are both flawed as it stands.

It is these very 'holes' in the structures that give us some flexibility and ability to move them closer together, obviously not all the way, but some of it. Meaning that English, that diverse and sometimes seemingly long-winded language, can also provide the platform for change as well as self expression. Surely these are traits shared by the two?

Also, just as Shaolin Kung Fu teaches us to – power up – our punches before making them, so too we can – power up – our words before saying them. This is not a readily available skill, and not everybody can do it. It takes a certain amount of knowledge and confidence to do so. Obviously people are different, with different skills, yet we draw on our similarities and shared experiences on common ground to engage in conversations with each other.

Sometimes we use our intellect to assert ourselves above others; at other times our focus is on our family.

I think that I have covered all the topics I wanted to for now. I did want to put in a quote from Dr Glenn Morris from his form of Ninjitsu, Hoshinryjutsu, just to show that I am not the only one who considers spirituality to be important in the MA world, but I am waiting on a response from his widow to see if she will give me permission to use it. Just in case she says 'no' I can tell you that he did believe that the spirit was necessary to first achieve peace and then power, which is directly transferable to the martial world with the correct application and ideally instruction.

There are many people in our lives. If yours is anything like mine, some of them can sometimes be nasty to us, sometimes friendly, sometimes funny, sometimes helpful. We have to try our best to find our way through the world, make a meaning out of this mess, survive, make a living and possibly hold down a job. Whatever you are doing I pray that you do it well and have listened to what I have said. I'm gonna try and drag this onto the end of the page and the that's it, finished. I've said everything that I've wanted to say. Obviously some questions remain unanswered, but I hope that most of you reading have followed this exploration into the human mind and come out unscathed, and possibly even learnt a thing or two on the way! Perhaps about religion, or one or two of my experiences in my past.

You know I am going to Africa to move in with my fiancée in less than 2 weeks! This has been a long time in the making and we both have tried really hard to make sure that it's a success. I am looking forward to going over there, to eating Kenyan food again, learning Swahili (again) and being the only white guy in hundreds of natives!

As for you, what can I say? I may see you again if I write another book, or I may not. Either-way, take it easy.

Jojutsu
22 : White Belt

Augustine was a young French lad with a penchant for comic-books and peanut butter. He lived deep in the heart of the French province of the same name. He had heard it all before, all these rubbishers and their same old clap-trap. 'Sorry the homework was late miss, the dog ate it!' Or 'sorry I couldn't see you today, mon ami, but c'est la vie!' That's why the kid preferred his comics. At least in the pages of the fantasy worlds captured within, wars were no good, but people WERE.

One sunny Christmas day our kid was out for a stroll on a shiny if slippery countryside lane, when he stumbled across a dusty old parchment tome someone had carelessly left thrust deep in a compost bin. Extracting the somewhat soggy pages carefully, he peeled back the first couple to read what was there within. This was the beginning of his transformation. The book contained there within a collection of fantastic creatures and legendary fighters. Many of them fictional, a few of them based on real people. And every time August read a new story he felt a little bit inspired. Soon he was finding his attendance and school work was picking up. As if the characters from the written pages were overlooking his life, providing him with whispered words of confidence and inspiring him to always try and develop and excel in both physical and mental (metaphysical) skills.

So that soon enough, or before long anyway, people flocked to our trainee ninja. Once an outcast living on the fringes of society, August suddenly found lads to talk to, and girls to flirt with! It was bliss! Can you imagine it? A young lad, once self decidedly doomed to a life of loneliness and depression, suddenly with the partial reading of a single book, lifted up through the unspoken ranks of social hierarchy, and finding himself comfortably stationed with friends, a wife and baby, and perhaps most important of all, character. The thing that differentiates the have-beens to the wanna-bes, the liars to the lucky and the average from the above average.

All this and from reading one book? And what was the book's title? Jujutsu, C'etait facile. It was a book of stories and parables revolving around a single English lad, Jo, whom Augustine could identify with. Despite being somewhat older than August, Jo was brave, and not afraid to take on the bullies where so ever he faced them. This inspired the reader to take up the sword, or fist when none was available, and then challenge the mugs whenever they threatened him. Eventually he found himself actually getting into less fights, as word got out that despite his deceptively fragile appearance, this kid could actually fight. And so as his enemies learnt to keep a distance, so his friends were more than happy at spending time with the young champion.

Without actually knowing it, August had become the herald bearer of a cause so much bigger then his own meagre life had ever dreamt possible. He had started reading a book not for the closed minded. In that if you are expecting to read a conventional typically polarised portrayal of the world as a fight between the sexes, a drama of demons and knights in shining armour, with an apple-tart pudding at the end of every afternoon tea, you are bound-set to be sorely disappointed. This is the story of one man's (Augustine's) journey into manhood. A journey which began with the lifting of that old and dusty tome from its resting place amongst the firewood, and ending only with his death. Which was at present, still quite a long way off (or so he hoped!)

The young ninja walked a long and lonely path through the night darkness. From fields with sleeping stallions, to streets devoid of colour and life, and only left with the steady throng of midnight traffic, going on about their tedious business with no idea or inclination of the power this young ninja was fermenting under his coat. So far the ninja-in-training had been pushed about through life, far enough. He had stumbled from building to residence, childhood friends had grown up and metamorphosed into grown-ups, childish fancies into red blooded loves, and fighting video-games into real fighting. I won't pretend for a minute that Jo the ninja was any good at any of this. In fact (seeing as he had only been training for a month), he still very much only considered himself a ninja in training. But he very much did believe in them, much as he believed in the power of Chi (what else would have lifted him up from the pit of a life he had been living, and hurtled himself forwards towards the fast approaching destiny he now travelled towards). It was taking not just a little hard work. But as his bones became stronger, his breathing easier and his friends more reliable, so too did Jo's appetite for life pick up once again.

All of a sudden the challenge which he had set himself, of conquering Africa and coming back with a living and breathing Kenyan bride, seemed more achievable. He still had his work cut out surely, but what is it they say that the first step is the hardest? And Jo's step to Africa had been bloody gargantuan. He sure as hell hoped that it would be smooth (downhill) sailing from here!

23: Yellow Belt

Literature should flow. Suffice to say that despite this organic and biodiverse take on proceedings, the author sincerely hopes that the reader will be able to find enough to relate to within these pages, so as to find this an engaging read. Perhaps identifying with the familial (family based) structure of the characters, or otherwise find exciting and enjoyable the whole ninja theme set out here within. So while I write this for a chance to capture, or revitalise that own spark of magic and youth which my heart aches for within. And isn't it funny that the one time I felt like a man was when I was by my wife's side. That is, I would suggest, more than motive enough to promote a daily workout routine without exception. Which also, the author grudgingly accepts, means that this evening when I get back, I must go for a run around my local park. Determination means commitment. And commitment means exercise every day. Never-mind that it's Christmas. One of these days I may actually need these muscles which I am training. You never know!

'Interesting,' the boy pondered. 'I wonder what happens next?…'

It's not much fun not being able to communicate with my wife today (Christmas) of all days. I'm sure that she wouldn't like me washing my dirty laundry in public. And my big mouth could even precipitate my own demise, or at least that of our marriage. But I hope it doesn't. And this writing is one thing that I think, when I put my mind to, that I am good at.

It sure helps to have some soothing melodies playing in the background as I sit here perched on a friendly relative's couch. But one of my strings sounds flat when I'm separated from my loved one. Then this is another year without her. Another Christmas with no goodnight kiss from Santa's little helper. Another New Year's resolution left unfulfilled. Another lonely piece of mistletoe left there alone. Another candle unlit.

I hope they are having a nice time now, wherever they are, whatever they are getting up to. I suppose I should trust her more than I do. But the seed of doubt once planted is a terrible beast to pursue. It is the barricade of fear couples across time have had to face. Some have been able to overcome, others not so lucky.

So can one man and woman's love defeat the invading hostilities of an onslaught of third parties and terrible memories of things that might have happened, and other things that actually did. I dunno. All I know is that when I say wife, I love you, I mean it, I miss you, and I hope this time we can make it work x.

And so it begins… Jo coolly and calmly retreated to a place of repose and tranquillity. Somewhere where he could settle, bat his eyelids and put up his tired and bloody feet. A place of tranquillity from the chaos of the day and relaxation from the heat of the night.

As far as he could thus ascertain, the world in its present state consisted of a war between two forces. Light and dark, good versus bad or rich versus poor. Islam versus Christianity, religion versus atheism, TKD versus Hoshinryjutsu (kick-boxing versus ninjitsu). These were at present international battles taking place on a global stage. Very much in their midst, and very undetermined despite what the players and their odds may be.

But like Ricky Hatton and Amir Khan after him, learnt to their expense, even the odds sometimes lie, giants can be humbled, and one step at a time Jo used his clumsy and inefficient legs to run. His lungs wheezed, and his feet dragged. But today I plodded/ran three circuits of my local park. And tomorrow I have vowed to do four.

The road to ninja-hood is a long one. Many are the pitfalls and little the recognition. But for those of us who are committed the journey is important and the end a just one. Good luck, my brother.

Jo liked sitting in his quiet place and watching the words freely flow across the page. When he was with his wife he felt like a man. Despite the problems, doubts lies and fears. He still loves her and is still fighting for her. Just it's difficult to fight for a woman while she's two continents away. Not to mention perhaps not even   wanting to be saved.

But she took the baby to church today which is good news as far as I am concerned. And I've not been going to church, and have only said grace twice since being back. But I intend to start going again once I am in my wife's arms.

It was good seeing Alex and his parents (old friends) yesterday. And I can fight the powerful authority of these censors with the spirit of the pen, and the power of a mind which motivates it.

Relaxation promotes reflection. And music promotes harmonic thought. Even if it is cheesy pop sung by some geared-up mostly black singers.

Oh well, Jo considered, at least he had sat down and watched some nice TV since being back in my homeland.

He toyed with the idea of taking his TKD sensei; the Doctor's note he had asked for in his last visit to that dojo. He had rather felt bullied out the door. And grudgingly admitted that there are other training halls and facilities which he could join with less stress and heartache, surely? Just it stings a little bit when a man always used to getting what he wants, suddenly finds he no longer has that power. But then again, we all have to take a step back from time to time, don't we?

Where was I? Oh yeah, I had just told you that every great fight is decided by the preparation. At least, that's what I've found according to my experiences. That's the trick. And so for my next fight (or confrontation rather), the one I will have

312

with my consultant and dad, regarding cutting down my meds, I wanna do a bit of pre-game match fixing now. Two against one, not fair? Not at all, the odds are raked against them! Given the preparation I'll have put in by the time we meet.

So what am I up against? These two men: my dad, and or consultant or relevant man, trying their best to look after my best interests, seeing as I've had a history of mental illness apparently triggered by relapses into schizophrenia, largely because I stopped taking my meds.

Versus me, an intelligent and healthy young man, who has been complying with my meds albeit on a reduced dose. I have been well since getting back (except for a few world war three rows with my dad), and regaining my physical (and mental) strength by actively engaging in a low-level fitness programme, which sees me swimming or running a little bit every day. This is improving my breathing, which in turn soothes and enhances my mental performance. I still avoid booze and have a delicate constitution. But with the right care and maintenance I see no reason why I can't achieve all my planned goals! Here's hoping!

It is, in my opinion, a human culpability to always look for weaknesses in the enemies' defence systems with which to take-down and exploit. A sin which even I cannot claim to be exempt from. I guess the opposite of this is a willingness to befriend, or at least get on with, complete strangers, perhaps in a neutral situation, like people you have just met on the street. Moreover this side of the chalice seems to be an ability some of us are more adept at than others! What's more, some of us have been forced to learn this skill being thrown in at an early age (16) in the deep end, when a nasty road accident pulled the warm rug from beneath my feet and replaced it with a cold and lonely hospital one (even if only temporarily). God I don't think that I've ever been so goddamned lonely as I was on those wards. Unable to support the weight of my skull on its own, either because it was pinned to a board, or a metal skeleton frame (called a halo, what an ironic misuse of the English language!), else left free and kept on flopping down, to being unable to piss for myself (with a urine tube/catheter) collecting my urine in a bag! Seriously, for about two months! You've never seen anything so painful! No wonder I pulled it out thrice, only to have it reinserted! Bad men!

Presently Ninja-Jo had been able to find some quiet ninja time to himself in the dead of the night after everyone else had gone to bed. This is the time for goblins and ghouls outside, but here in the warmth and security of his dad's house he was able to train, primarily by swimming in the morning, dancing to cheesy music in the afternoon, and dreaming of being in my baby's arms again at night! A cunning and highly effective formula I hear you say? Perhaps. It does for the time being at least!

In fact Jo had been contemplating what the hell he was going to do with the rest of his life. His old plan (do a degree, get a job ad nauseam), now seemed sadly lacking, with the encroaching advent of the new one (train, get fit, train more, get fitter and stronger) ad infinitum.

He really could see no failure in this new adventure. Not seeing as his sickness benefit should support him and my family financially. Then, as I get stronger, I will be able to take out bigger and nastier enemies, both in the spiritual world and the real one. Until one day (soon hopefully) I will be able to reclaim my sweetheart's mind and body as my own. And hopefully in the near future as well.

Sitting down, Jo was able to find his quiet space again. It had been yet another hectic day. Another challenging morning run had led onto another enjoyable meeting with my old friend Sunny, to another bout of concealed and not-so-concealed abuse hurling on the internet. But because I'm not very good at concealing my verbal barrage, I always seem to take the brunt of the blame. So that means another strike on my warning count. That's three now, and five equals a six month ban! Woe! At least I'm not in prison; that's about all I can say there, but seeing as the internet forums do let me exercise one of my main joys (writing) to be banned from koeiwarriors.co.uk will at least mean I have to find my pleasures elsewhere! (Either that or start rotating my log-on IP address to access the system! Cheeky, I know, but seeing as I'm moving out from dad's next week, I think it will be inevitable. In fact, I think I'm gonna create a new account even if I'm not banned; a pre-emptive strike you might say! And I shall route all of my old mail through to the new

315

address. That old one only got bunged up with junk mail anyhow!)

So then, now is chill out time. Another night without my missus. But at least I am exercising every day in an attempt to crawl back some of that strength I never had. Oh well, here's to good intentions.

24: Ninja Beer

Last night Jo had his first encounter with ninja beer. A formidable adversary, this potion has the strength to knock the hind-legs off a donkey. And it's moreish too! You've drunk one and you've necked twenty, or that's my experience of it anyway! Well perhaps not twenty then, but five at least.

It's not cheap, not particularly enjoyable; man, I didn't even have anyone to go with. And spent most of the night getting steadily more pissed on my own halfway down the back of the pub! So why do I do it? You might ask. And the answer: because I can.

It's nice for me being back in my home country and home town, sitting in a local tavern populated by a decent age range of regulars. Catching/overhearing snippets of their conversation, and doing something my dad doesn't approve of.

Ninjas of the twenty-first century are proved as much in the oak-wrought fireside taverns as they are on the battlefield, Jo reflected. Anyway nowadays wars are all about long distance surveillance/counter terrorism as much as it is actually fought on the battlefield.

Isn't it time for a change?

Just as well too, Jo chuckled; they'd never accept him into the army. He bloody well has to invent his own army, a ninja army; yeah that'd do, a ninja army! And with this sobering thought he slipped away into the land of never-never.

Wavering in and out of the finer states of higher awareness and consciousness, Jo pondered on some of the subtler questions posed to the quintessential inner self.

Like which is the better form of exercise: swimming or running, which the better sex, the fairer one or men, which the best games console, which the best type of car: Ford or Toyota, the best entertainment wrestling or UFC, the best instrument guitar or a drum, the best book 'The Wizard of Earthsea' or The Bible, and the best colour, blue or pink? Sure, the questions were plentiful, and he thought he knew some of the answers, but he would be damned if he could nail all of them.

As the energy from a month's exercise coursed through his body and invigorated and inspired him, he felt lifted by the efforts. And even more lifted by the prospect of a new life, dancing, running, swimming and writing. So what if he will never work again! With these new found physical abilities it's not as if he cared.

Preparation is the key to success his old invisible Sensei had often taught him. And with this daily low level endurance work, he was preparing with the best of them.

Jo sat back in his armchair again. It had been another hard day nearly over, with the dusk drawing in its shady rays. He felt at peace.

Today's internet voyage had passed by: one warning and temporary (a week or so long) ban from one site, a flame from another; hastily replied, and a crude attempt to veil a direct attack at me in another (Martial Arts) site. Well I took the safety off when dealing with that one! They should have known better then to f£^$ with me!

Seeing as most of them hold blackbelts after all (IMO.) and me I'm mentally unstable shall we say, as already proved by my previous ban!

Oh well, hopefully we can sort this one out as well. I am happy that they are talking to me again. Just I don't like the thinly veiled references to mental illness targeted at me in their remarks. It's not easy having a mental illness you know. In order to fight it we have to hold onto what is good, from the dreams, exercise to the people and memories. This is a hard lesson which I have learnt, and it has taken a long time coming. I don't suppose I'll ever stop learning. About people, relationships, my daughter. A least I hope I don't. Until the day I die.

Jo found himself nicely settled into his dad's armchair again after another day well spent. He had successfully made up with his wife today (after yesterday when they were on the brink of divorce; he had been on a national demonstration in London the day before, whose heroic chants [mainly free-

free-Palestine] were still ringing in his ears) and he had been banned yet again from one of his favourite internet haunts, and had re-registered this new account under the username of Harorld (a misspelt Harold!).

So basically things were going swimmingly. Oh yeah, he was also couch lounging out to some neat CDs which he had bought very cheaply (3 for under a tenner), at Woolworths closing down sale the day before yesterday, and this morning I did another slow three lap run around Normanton park. I am definitely finding that it is getting easier each time I do it. Well the two days rest from running has helped a lot, giving my feet a chance to heal and recover from the daily impact they were suffering. I'm now even contemplating doubling up with a run in the morning and a swim in the afternoon, to try and build up my day's workout schedule a bit.

Oh yeah, also axbxixr has accepted my request for friendship on the M.A. Website, which makes me feel happy! (She was my friend when I first joined the site, but we had not seen eye to eye recently). Nice to know that she's still on my side.

Slowly Jo flexed his fingers backward and forwards, side to side. He gradually lifted his rotten carcass up from the floor from whence it had lain for all these years. Then beating it with a stick he watched as one by one the cobwebs dropped from its whole.

Another year, another life. But this one was going to be different. Now Jo had drunk from what might otherwise be known as the Holy Grail. This a fountain which others had immersed themselves in for years, but he had yet to savour. But now he had caught a taste of its sweetness, he was hardly going to let go? Not now, not now there was too much at stake.

And in that instant little boy Jo became a man. The instant he knew he would never more immerse himself into the fantasy delusional world of make-believe video games. Now he had found a new hobby; cardiovascular fitness as exemplified by running and swimming. He even contemplated drawing up a chart to record his progress? For if today he could swim thirty lengths and run three laps in one day, how many could he do in a month? Or a year of regular training?

Perhaps the chart was unnecessary; the main thing was that he stuck to the training regime. And maybe even one of these days he would be able to enter those Aikido/TKD dojos with his head held high and start proper training in earnest!

Jo sat down and contemplated. This morning is the morning before the day after (in other words I have yet to engage with my daily fitness plan).

Isn't it funny, he wondered, how these big celebrities and popular gurus pay hundreds of millions of dollars each year to hire trainers and join expensive gyms, whereas our trainee ninja has been able to get his work-outs for free. Or a pittance if you include the £1.90 the baths charge for a disabled swim in with the mix.

And slowly but surely his speed was picking up as he jogged round the park on these sullen mornings. And it had yet to rain on him whilst running! I guess I've got that to look forward to.

You might think that martial arts are purely about a bunch of well endowed blockheads beating out their workouts behind the closed doors of an exclusive members only dojo. Well I guess some of them certainly are like that, but not Jujutsu. Named in the wake of our Apogees genesis, here is an art form which exceeds expectations. Which is free to join and participate in, the only expectation being that you commit yourself to combat. Mentally, physically and spiritually. That means join God's army. In his absence we have to take up the banner and lead these sheep through the bad times and onwards to victory. The meek hearted only ever made slow progress. But the brave, sometimes failed, and at others prevailed!

25: The Advent of a New Martial Art

This is the start of a discussion thread centred around the philosophy behind the 'One inch Shaolin punch', the likes of which Bruce Lee so amply demonstrated.

I think that it's not just how far, fast or hard you punch, but when, who and how. In other words the context of the fight will have a great effect in determining the outcome. Maybe you started it, maybe you didn't, maybe you've got the odds on your side, maybe they're stacked high against you. But just as the Dragon is the only living beast able to enter the fires of hell and return unscathed, so too it is the courage of a hero that faces peril without flinching. And when he returns, if he returns, the once mad-man is heralded a hero with the dragon's head dragged close behind his heels. One punch can do all this; it really can. It's more about timing than accuracy and more the fact that you have the bravery to stand up and fight at all, than about timing. Peace.

Hi guys, if you or anyone else in here likes my style of thought and this particular take on Shaolin punching (as inspired by Wong Kiew Kit) please don't hesitate to make contact. I have in fact for some time now been working on my own school of Ninjitsu called Jujutsu. Don't even ask where that name came from, it's kind of a parody! Well I'll tell you then; I'm an author and the protagonist in my adventures of recent years has been a young ninja-in-training called Jo. Hence the name! If anyone here would be interested in joining my school, feel free to ask. The good news is that it's free. I don't charge, and at present the only dojo is the green gym (great outdoors). Please feel free to bring to this forum your own learning, from whichever styles you guys have trained in.

Me, I don't drive. So after a lifetime of walking places I feel quite grounded to the planet, both physically and spiritually. Oh yeah, and I should warn you, I do believe in God (or whatever you want to call it, Mother Nature, the Tao, the Force) and this is a part of my discipline. Although only a requisite of the higher level.

But that's Ninjitsu in its essence, isn't it? It is a higher level. Head-and-shoulders above the 'basic' move sets which make up the likes of the brutal TKD. It is designed to punch where others dare not, and with the velocity to settle the argument there and then. That's the idea anyhow. Yeah so feel free to discuss my new art form! Peace.

The solitary ninja carefully looked out over his surroundings. It was a dark night, and the wind was brisk and with a taste of animosity to it. He had spent his whole life marching towards this point. And on some days it seemed like he wasn't even halfway there! What had he achieved so far? A marriage, a baby which wasn't his, biologically speaking, but was as far as the love is concerned, had one book published and another on the way, and he knew what it was like to be homeless. Not to mention he had three strikes in hospital on his score-card, or four if you include his first. But that negative factor was less a part of his achievements and more a counter-factor.

As far as martial arts go, Jo was to this point very much a one punch bandit. Able to take down his enemies facing them and in a single blow. But if they didn't fall, or had anticipated his attack and braced themselves for it, well he didn't much fancy his chances then!

Sure he could think like the best of them, but if he was realistically going to achieve that first belt he had always dreamed of, he had a lot more work to do. This morning he had even set off on a run with the sincere conviction that he had to challenge a local blackbelt. But after the run was over, out of breath he realised that he might as well be signing his own death warrant. Some people we just don't like, but fighting isn't the only way out. (Plus I don't much fancy getting my head kicked in!)

Hi. My name's Jo. I'm a ninja in-training. On my good days (like last week) I am a young martial artist in a world of friends and family. Surrounded by dragons and giants with anywhere from one to a dozen eyes, we all share one thing, and that's a love for the martial discipline. Knowing that you've got the capability to culpably pound some of these other jackasses into the dust from whence they came. And even if not to beat them, then at least give them a good run for their money.

I train in the circuits of the park, or the warm waves of the pool. I eat vegetarian (and copious amounts of chocolate). I only drink alcohol on the new year, or at least that's the way it has been going.

I chill out with music, either listening to or playing it. And good company, such as that of my friends. I am multi-lingual, having forayed into French, Swahili and Mandarin. I can punch, and the upper-cut is my showy display piece. Although in a real combat situation I find the straight up, or even the slap, does the job just as well. Blackbelts I have known have taught me how to escape from a collar, arm grab, the importance of cardiovascular work, loving your friends and being pissed with my enemies.

I recognise that there is a lot more for me to learn, but I'm trying. One step a day and we're walking the path. Peace guys.

The ninja crawled back out of the hole where he had spent the last night sleeping. He was ready for another day of meeting ninjas on the streets, of training and spending the hard earned cash his benefits kindly provided for him.

Today's exercise would be another swim. Thirty or so lengths at a pinch. He had given up on the doubles for the time being. Much too much like hard-work! And I have already had a nice text from my ninja-wife and her baby this morning. They are both doing well and a joy to be-heard.

26: Macbeth rewrites

Is this a dagger which I see before me? Thy handle toward my hand? Come let me clutch thee: I have thee not and yet I see thee still. … And on thy blade and dudgeon gouts of blood, which was not so before. No! There's no such thing: It is the bloody business which informs thus to mine eyes. … Nature seems dead and now over the one half world wicked dreams abuse the pale curtained sleep, and witchcraft celebrates pale Hecate's offerings.

If it t'were done when t'was done then it t'were better that it t'were done quickly. If the act in its doing could capture success and be rid of all the follies of the murder which forth naturally brings about, then would it not be a good thing and a deed well worth doing for a price well worth having?

I go and 'tis done. The midnight bell calls summons me. Hear it not Duncan, for this is the call which draws thee either to heaven, or to hell!

I will fight the king on his day of his coronation.

I steal the crown from his head and place it onst mine own.

This act is one forbidden from ordinary men

and I am nothing more than a man.

But with God on my side I can fight

and now I can see freedom on the horizon

even if its grasp eludes me as of yet.

The freedom of power brings great responsibility with it also

The responsibility to not be afraid to open your eyes

to share and give to charity if you can find it

within your heart to do this.

Do not be afraid. I am not a bad man.

I have led a bad past but I have asked

God for forgiveness and the sun is shining

brightly today.

Sleep is a great healer, so is time and so

is strength.

But not the strength to whack someone,

rather the strength to refrain   from doing so.

So people would call this cowardice.

I would rather say courage.

Love is in the eyes of her beholder

and you are the strongest person alive.

Never forget that.

Wicked people persuade us to deviate from the

correct path, yet the holy spirit can and does

reside in not just all the babies, but the children and

men and women too.

Let us let it realign our souls and thereby help us

to communicate with one another, in order

that we might change the world to become a better place

if not for our children's lifetimes then at least for theirs'.

What? Is this a knife I see before me? Thy handle toward my
hand? Come let me clutch thee. I have thee not and yet I see
thee still! And on thy blade and dudgeon gouts of blood,
which was not so before! No, there's no such thing. It is the
bloody business which brings thus to mine eyes, wicked
treacheries which partake in the deadliest hours of the night,

when the true colours come to play. I will wash thy blood from my hands, and be done with these treacherous fiends.

But if it t'were done, when it t'was done, then it t'were done well that it were done quickly. Well it t'would be a feat no man could attempt. It would be the world of kings! To pick the crown from his scalp, whether he lives or dies, and place it onst mine own, would not the whole world bow in my glory?

They would be forced to look, and if not on my own greatness, then guilt at lack of their own! But there are demons at the door. I can hear their beatings, from my minds eye (memory) to mine ear, they are here and the war is oh so real.

Just as I am forced to call on the armies of love and karma to fuel thy rebukes, so too they have very real men, guns and strategies. Constantly changing with the smell of the tide of battle.

But I will not falter. We are staying put. Digging in our heels. First the challenge is at home, to bolster our love to beat these internal doubts. Then I take the blade abroad. A booma-ken, returning after each throw, each decapitation. And I will not fail! While this heart is still beating I will carry the banner and onto victory!

Jo contemplated his options. The odds were still stacked neatly high against him. In as much as it was still him against the world, well nearly but not quite. And some good the fragile friendships he had made at the last site when he got banned from there, once and for all! But I can guarantee you that anyone who's ever been homeless will know that there's much worse than this. And anyway those nimby pansies didn't deserve him. Yeah, that was it; it was their loss not his! (But I will still miss communion with a few of my close allies from there, specifically axbxixr and SamuraiKing, but I think it's time to move on).

And stepping straight into this new unknown foray, I immediately find myself making friends with a couple of new peops: one the site's director. Not bad for a start hey?! His name is Peter Mills, and also a gal called Madfrog. That's good because it enables me to start new ideas and fantasy stories of me (Jo) in ninja confrontations and the like. Half a way to express my feelings to real life events currently looming in my real life, and half a means to challenge and or coax some of these shellfish out of their shells and onto the dinner-table. And all this from a vegetarian! Oh well, what better way to break that resolution with a feast of human flesh! And they said I do things in halves!

27: Orange Belt

A point about Ninjas:

Some people don't believe in them. For instance we all know that Santa isn't real, don't we? But still a small part of our hearts still believes, still wants to believe in him. And so trying to capture that piece of childhood magic, we tell our children about him. Perhaps we invent a story how he and Rudolf made the personal journey to our house, to drink that sherry and eat the mince pie. The kids probably suspect that it is a lie, but we tell them about him never-the-less to capture their imagination and retain their innocence.

So it is also with ninjas. I've never seen one surely. But when I see an oriental man dressed in black from head to toe late one night (and shortly before one of my breakdowns) I think he could be one? Or when I see a good looking white gal with her face half concealed by a head scarf I think she might be one too! For when we were children we ate as children, we spake as children, we were children. But now as adults we can leave behind our childish ways. (Quote from the Bible New Testament letter to the Corinthians 1:13).

Don't be offended by me including a verse from the Bible in here. I have studied it and it holds a special place in my heart. (There'll be more of that later.)

I realise that most of you could whoop my ass in a one on one. But I'm not afraid. I know that I am a good person, and hopefully I will be able to earn your trust one day. Peace.

Now Jo paused for a minute. His enemies had fought him to a standstill. Trapped and with nowhere else to run he calmly lifted both arms into the air and let his Shinobi blade clatter to his feet. By this time hundreds of adversaries were facing him. Some of them watched on bemused at this murderer's gesture of peace; others didn't find it so funny.

Jo just let his eyelids droop. He was tired. It had been another long day. He anticipated night drawing the day into a close, her all embracing arms asking the world to sleep and rest for another day.

What happened next happened in kind of a blur. He felt a sharp pain at the side of his head and then another on his chin as the floor hastily rushed up to meet it. Then he was cuffed, bundled into the back of a meat-wagon and before you know it facing the monotonous walls of a police holding cell. He had seen the inside of one of these before. But as the night turned to day, a dim light cast its eerie eye over the place. Jo couldn't sleep with that racket; instead letting his eyes remain in a dulled kind of agony.

This half dream half nightmare didn't stop until seven months later when he was finally released from the psych ward. It had been a painful journey. And he realised now that he was too far in ever to return to normality. Instead he carried the herald and trudged onwards into the unknown!

My reference to Dragons was a poetic Eulogy and not merely twaddle as one of you rude boys put it.

Fighting in the dark, the ninja has to learn to pick up on extra-sensory perceptions not typically realised by the naked mind. Thinking on the straightforward path seems mundane at first, but then it's all a question of how far you're willing to take it. To lunch? To bed? To the ring finger.

These little words may seem like little steps to some of you, little flies to yet others. But without magic, how is the candle supposed to stay alight? And without fire, our rural fireplaces sure would seem cold and frosty on these bleak midwinter nights.

What I'm trying to say is partially a matter of perception, partly a matter of feeling, and partly common-sense. Who was it that once said learn to hear with the ear, look with the eye, listen with your heart and then you might find?

Take it easy Bailu and Madfrog. That's my alter-ego Jo you've just had a close encounter with. He's got me in plenty of trouble b4 including a ban from two sites. Let's hope I don't get banned from this one.

You say that Martial Arts is purely for display, with strikes never to be intentionally used in a combat situation. Well if that's your style of combat, how do you think you'd fare against me in a fight when I am punching to maim, injure and even kill?

Don't get this the wrong way but it sounds to me like you are a couple of big girl's blouses, wouldn't know a ninja if you met one, and are indeed pathetic excuses for men.

Please prove me wrong on this? Now I'll ask you a question: what makes the man, how many fights he's won, or how many he's been in? How about how strong his adversaries were?

How many gals he's nailed, or how many push-ups he can do (fifteen at the last count), or how many enemies he's annihilated. How many stages of mortal transition he's climbed (Buddhist reference there), or at how many enemies' tables he's dined. How many times he's walked into hospital, or how many times I've fought my way out?

You two seem to be under the impression that your schools/dojos know all there is to teach. But my lessons only began once I left school. Think about this, and take it easy!

Jo staggered in a rush to shake himself into some composure and regain control of his senses. In a flash the world around him had changed. Still populated by giants and Samurai in norm's clothing, the sun had changed from a pale yellow to a harsh red.

The trees looked somewhat taller, or perhaps the ninja had shrunk an inch or two given his recent encounters. The fire still burned, something dimmer perhaps, but he knew that the fuel to keep the hearth going was still there, that the chalice of truth had only been partially sipped at to this point.

Then shaking himself out of the daydream, he dragged himself to focus on the enemies surrounding him. Too many to count (or was that because of his blurry double vision?) He lifted his left up into a ready attack position, and his right he let settle into decoy mode.

Things were about to get interesting!

OK guys, let's get one thing straight here, if you ban me for doing nothing wrong, then you don't even deserve to have me.

One of you complained that I don't have any martial arts experience. Well that's not strictly true now is it? I did Judo as a kid, and have had a few other (critical) lessons with blackbelts here and there, which maybe you might have picked up on if you had read my posts more clearly.

I don't want to fight you guys, but if there are a couple of Judases in amongst you lot who feel desperate to get me banned 'cos maybe they feel I threaten them, well there's nothing I can do about it.

And so what if I haven't spent my life to this point in the gym? I intend to do so now, isn't that the important thing?

Jo is my alter-ego. Whereas I can't even run very fast, he runs in leaps and bounds. He is a hero and successful, whereas me, the author, can pretty much only sit here and write.

What I'm basically saying is this: I think you lot are generally a decent bunch of peops (community), so please don't any of you start teasing me or picking for a fight on the grounds of your status. That just won't do at all!

Cheers guys for not screwing me just yet! Now it wouldn't be the first time that should have happened (check the rip/stretch marks!) You think I'm joking? Today I went to Sheffield to meet my solicitor, and spent the first half of the meeting shouting at my dad (who subsequently left). Well at least this cardio training has given me that! As for Ninjitsu training, check out my latest dance video! All of the action and half the pain! Happy!!

Jo climbed out of the pool, soaking wet and more than a little tired. His hands had been used a thousand times in the 'karate kid' circle of breast-stroke. A pending critical combat/defensive manoeuvre if ever he got to use it. And as he swam, and ploughed through mindless throngs of young teeny-bopper style juveniles, he threw himself a passing glance at more than just a few of the gals! But seriously, if he ever got in a fight he knew, or at least he hoped he knew, that some of these spectators at least would be on HIS side. Not to pick up the pieces if it ever came to that, but to throw a cheer when one of his punches connects. When he tackles his foe to the floor, when he pounds them into submission and carries the trophy away triumphant.

Some things take time. Others repetition. Others money. And still others faith. Ninjitsu takes something of all of these. The faith to know that your strike will connect once you've thrown it. The money to buy the books, and time to read them. The hope to challenge the controversies of the past and the good luck to meet the odds and come out victorious.

Check out these references! And Peace!

KOEI Warriors (Forum)

Error:

You are banned.

Hi Paris and Mule,

First thanks sweetheart it's good to know that I've still got some of us on my side! (PS I'm gonna miss axbxixr; she was my help over on the other side*)

Second, cheers Mule, I can't remember what exactly it is you said, *scrolling down the messages*, oh yeah music… I LOVE music. I play in a one man band you know? Called… Well it's not exactly got a name, just me and my guitar. And yesterday I went out and busked (first

338

time since I got back from Africa, and I made... £5! Whoopee. That's a record you know!) Seriously I played all my greats from Dylan to Amazing Grace, to Lennon, to the Gallagher brothers. I appreciate that this music stuff doesn't have a direct bearing on beating the s#%t out of anybody, but there definitely are parallels between the two arts, n'est ce pas?

So music, or playing the guitar, takes time, study, attention to detail and commitment. Same it is with MA I guess. And I'm not in any dojo right now, but have got my eyes set on a local Aikido club which I'm hoping to join at the end of March. In Africa they hand wash all their own clothes you know! It's certainly an eye-opener (and hard-work).

As to the scoundrels out there who want to scalp me before even shaking my hand? I call them Judas. Unfortunately our world is full of them, and MAs is no exception. I think that it's probably best that we just ignore them and hope they go away. Buzz off like. As for the rest of you, TAKE IT EASY XXXXX

This morning Jo woke up with a yawn and a stretch. Then staggering over to his wardrobe he pondered which costume to adorn? Should it be the exotic red sari of the Indian dancers, flowers in his hair and bells on his toes? Or the proud and honourable suit of the Samurai, ceremonial sword at his side and trusty steed at his beck and call? Perhaps he could wear the shades and Afro of the Capawerist, ready to beat them jives and hit the deck on his head-spin? Or the red bandanna and white t-shirt of a free-runner, paying little heed to his own safety and maximum respect to the thrill of danger-seeking. Hmmm. Who shall I mimic today?

Sometimes ninja Jo does ninja dancing. At other times swimming or singing. At still other times he likes to spend time and chat with his friends. Did they know that they were speaking to a 21st century ninja in his genesis? Possibly. Did he suspect that some if not all of them held powers greater than met the eye? Of that he had no doubt! They were his friends after all.

He's not saying that he considered them to be ninjas themselves. Rather together they had helped develop the holy spirit. Which is a just and honourable cause, true in its intentions and decent in its approach. He didn't care that he didn't know how to fight. If anything he had spent the past twenty-seven years of his life fighting internal demons. And now if he hadn't slain them, had at least subdued them into submission, was he at last able to turn his attention to his physique and physical abilities.

But that my friend is another story. He still liked singing and dancing. Cooking and eating. Writing and typing. The free world is surely the 8th wonder of the world. Isn't it funny that you can only properly appreciate this once you know what it's like to have it taken away from you. Peace. In the beginning was the Word. And the Word was with God. And the Word was God…

28: A new version of Saint John's second letter

To my chosen lady and her baby, whom I love with all my heart, and not just I but all who know the truth will too – because the truth which lives in us all shall last forever and ever.

Grace, mercy and peace of the Lord be with you. It has given me great joy to find some of my family walking in the truth, just as our Great Father once commanded. Now dear lady, I am writing to you not just as a friend but as your lover. Not just as a lifelong companion, but as a soul-mate, someone whom I want to share the rest of my decisions with, if only you will let me. I want you to love me, and I hope that you can, in just the way that I love you. And you must forgive me for all of the bad and terrible things I have committed in my years gone by. They were in the past. I am sorry I did them, but that is all.

I am not writing you a new command but one that we have had from the beginning. I ask that you love me, in the same way that I love you. And this is love, and obedience to his commands. As you have heard before, he told us to walk in the truth.

Many deceivers, who do not acknowledge Jesus as coming, will reject and spite him. They go out into the world and throw scorn on his name. But our love holds us together, binds us and keeps us in his presence. Be careful to whom you show this love, but don't be restrained in giving it. And please when you do, love with all your hearts. Ignore the atheists. They cannot do you any harm. What is their power? What is the source of their powers? Nothing more then a rickety old bridge, rotten in its foundations and bound to crumble and sink back into the sea. The Devil has all the appearance and grandeur of a great man, but is actually crooked and rotten to the core. So do not be afraid of these people; you can beat them every time!

Never lose all that you have worked towards; your spiritual faith is your greatest treasure; never forget this. And even when times look hard and there is no hope in sight, don't worry, I am still here waiting for you (with my rainbow at the end of the storm). Anyone who acts from the heart is blessed. And he who does so without is a coward and acts WITHOUT Christ's blessing. The outcome of the journey is not half so important as the steps taken to get there. And if on the way, anyone else approaches you and asks you for direction or comfort, do not hesitate to show it to them. This is the way of the Lord and his believers. It is only in times of great difficulty and hardship that we find out who are friends truly are. Even if we never see them again. But bear true to your promises, to build character rather then weaken it. Stay happy my child and may all your days bring sunshine and joy!

I have much more that I want to say to you, but on paper there is only so much that I can write. As you are expecting, I am hoping to see you face to face soon enough. Then we will have ample opportunity to catch up on the times we have missed, and the lips we want to kiss! It has been a long year apart; I can't wait to see you again.

With all my love, yours John Robinson 09-09-08

29: More Ninja Stuff

Jo the ninja emptied the loose change from his pockets. He had about five pounds in silver, copper and gold. Five pounds of our monarch's head, keeping his mind occupied and his heart hungry. Oh how he longed for an age that John Lennon promised, of no possessions, where men and women shared their property and so too their love. As it currently stands, hard earned cash is miserly hoarded over. Oh sure they'll be happy to take it off you, in their Happy Maccy Ds or one armed bandits robbery machines. And there are even now places set up in this country to help the lost and destitute. From homeless shelters to midnight food stores. But not enough. Not half enough.

And how terrible it must be to be homeless for whatever reason, in a country like Kenya, where charity is frowned upon, and despite the external appearance of a God-fearing population, the only respite for the homeless is the bed of a stranger. This reminds me of my own personal experience. Ran away from home, I was left with the clothes upon my back, and a little cash in my bank.

Out of the fireplace and into the fire. Never a truer word said. God the subsequent seven weeks I spent in a Nairobi private hospital was as grievous a time I've ever yet had to face. Don't believe it if you hear anyone say that those hospitals are easy. And it's not even the food (staple basics, potato and spinach mainly for me the vegetarian, with the luxury of a Chapati or two every now and then, and Uji gruel for porridge! Ha! I even found maggots in that damn stuff! Boy you know what I did? Flicked out the maggots and kept on eating! I had to; the hunger had to be fed at all times!)

At least I made some good friends in there. From Chris to Pablo and Tony, to Catherine and Esther and others. But don't think that this in any way mitigated the sufferings of being imprisoned in there against our wills; it didn't. I'm just praying that I never have to go in again!

Loose change for a loose life. A loose heart. Free as the wind, but bitterly cold at times. He had learnt the hard way the strength of our currency. The security of the British Isles is without a doubt, both an honour and a privilege. Never more will I flee from my homeland. Sure I'm prepared to go on holidays, perhaps even extended ones. But I now consider my birth country my proper home, and I won't forsake her grace again.

Jo entered the multi-purpose gym by the same door he always used. It said on the notice outside Tae-Kwon-Do – Japanese kick-boxing – martial arts class – beginners welcome – 7:30. It was already quarter to eight, and still not a soul in sight. And so he waited, patiently counting the minutes.

Then after about another twenty, some weasly and thuggish looking Eastern European white guy sticks his head around the door, before he disappears once again into the darkness. So Jo had to wait a bit more.

346

Eventually the class began to filter in, and it was a rag-tag bunch of convicts with all ranges of ages and gender. From little old grannies swinging their handbags around with lethal precision, to Japanese 'blackbelts'! Whoa, a blackbelt! Something Jo had only ever dreamt about. He remembered meeting this lad Karl outside the hospital, who swung a stick about like it was a double nun-chuckers. He was hard. But this was different; this was special.

And so he sat down to watch. When the class bent down, rather than spending too long examining the cute and pert bum of the only Japanese gal in there, he turned away disgusted. Beginners certainly weren't welcome there, despite whatever the poster may have said.

So before long they got under way with a series of what is better known in the industry as fairy kicks and strikes. Lethal in their intention, but weak in their conception. This was flower arranging of the highest degree!

The thing about Aikido is that you use the enemy's energies against him. Tae-Kwon-Di just beat the crud out of one another. So the class was nearing completion. It had been a brutal some two hours work-out, and that was just watching it! And he sincerely hoped that he wouldn't meet any of these suckers late at night in an alleyway alone. But he was getting bored. His whole demonstration of watching the games had not resulted in him learning any new skills, or even done one push-up.

In a desperate attempt to get their attention, he ran into the wall and punched it so hard the skin on one of his knuckles broke. He did a four inch punch on the sucker, and was damned that it would have felt pain had it not been an inanimate object. Little bad man. Then he walked away. And I even have the circular centimetre diameter scar on my middle right hand from where I hit the sucker.

But this isn't even the end of our little treaty. For when attending some other class in that self same hall, he spied a number of contact grease points there on the paintwork, where apparently some of the other class members had felt it necessary to imitate his strike. And those other ones sure looked bigger. But whatever their size, he was there first.

30: Red Belt

Jo tried to settle down after that latest outburst. It had been a rough day's adventure over the previous day/s week/s and months and years. He considered that he was entitled to take a rest. He and his wife had struggled to hold their marriage together over the past period of about eight years, and against all odds it seemed like they were finally coming to realise the completion of a successful union. And at least that is what he hoped.

And when I say see the fruits of a marriage, I'm not talking about babies. It's much too late for that as far as I'm concerned, I'm afraid. Years of abuse of my sex parts, starting with a Catheterisation in hospital, and carrying on throughout my life in different ways had led to my being impotent. But you know I'm not even particularly bothered about that. Not if I've still got my wife by my side, and in her arms the new baby, Michelle. Hell she might even be expecting another, but I've accommodated room in my life for our first angelic blessing, and I see no reason why not to make room for another.

People have called me a spammer, and a troll at various other sites. I think that this is slightly unkind, seeing as I speak my mind. I go with the flow, expressing my feelings and not afraid to express myself fully on the written page. Just because they don't like hearing me say what I have been, doesn't entitle them to call me these hurtful words. What was that number one forum rule? No personal attacks? But if they deem themselves able to break it, then I have seen no qualms about returning the favour! Which might have some of the reason for why I've been banned at about three sites, at the latest count! Still I'm active at a good MA, one right now as we speak, and despite treading a fine line between emancipation and oblivion, let's hope that I have learnt enough from my mistakes enabling me to weather this storm and prevail through to the other-side with my dignity intact, and also preferably my site's membership.

Now Jo found himself walking down a long and empty road in the middle of night. The light had faded about an hour ago, and his only company was the busy A-road which his path straddled.

To the right was the park. He had just watched a film at the cinema, alone as usual, to return to his flat and his usual routine of doing nothing much with nobody important. In the park he found swans and ducks, the rain and the moon. And the cold. He tried out a couple of new Eastern moves he had studied in a book.

He imagined that he was Bruce Lee, and had just watched one of his films. A freedom fighter who was up against the world, with only his two fists to survive.

Nobody was listening to him. Sometimes this bothered him. He felt lonely and isolated. But what should he expect so far from home, in a distant land, with these strange and unusual people. They weren't used   to him and he not them.

There are advantages to being under-appreciated, like an attack is not prepared for. But the time for thinking is over, and the time for action is now.

But before he could move he felt paralysed to the spot. His hands were not chained, nor feet shackled, but the wind of circumstance had blown the opportunity out of reach. And what seemed like a definite chance to assert his authority had spilt from within his reach. So once against he was left alone.

He could still do pull-ups without too much trouble. There had once been a time when he could even manage five 'naked' ones, that is without a bar to grip and just a high ledge to jump onto and mess about with.

But that was when he had nothing else. Now he had the night, that beast, and the clouds to play with. He envisioned a future where he ruled the world as universal monarch, with a kind and caring circle of friends and family. A kind and caring, but firm and unseen authority, which pulls the strings of the world with but a careless whisper.

Perhaps he would never realise this dream. For a long time he had lived on a pure subsistence level, barely above the brink of death. And for a few brief moments, relatively speaking, he had even dipped below it. And actually died. And although it may have been quick, that certainly seemed to last for a very long time, and will remain with him always.

It was at these moments, that he had been examined closely by some of his enemies, and they had drawn the conclusions that he was both a weakling, crooked as a stick, and just a bad person. And so they vowed to destroy him with the power of a speeding bullet.

That was then; this was now. He had grown stronger, and power had brought him responsibility. He still had daily battles with his family and loved ones. He still had to keep on reasserting himself to obtain authority over the community around him. And it was a hard fight. But he was confident that his truth and love had a power over all the liars and haters which flood the world, and have dominated history up to this point.

Then without warning he felt a hard blow to the back of the head. This stunned him, and did not fully register. He looked around but saw nothing. So carefully he looked forward, and started walking fast. Then again he was struck, and this time the force of the blow sent him flying head first into the ground. And it was not so much the attack itself, as the impact of hitting zero, which winded him. I don't know if any of you have ever suffered this kind of attack. Being hit when you are unprepared. It takes you off balance. And he considered what he had done to deserve it.

Jo was as guilty as the next man, perhaps more so. But he had started various chains of positive karma to hopefully redeem himself of his crimes at least to a certain extent in God's eyes.

When the kicks began he was on the floor and bleeding heavily. Suddenly he was in the high street, and surrounded by a crowd. Some were innocent bystanders who walked on by, and yet others were uniformed and armed officers. Police and army-heads. Some of them wearing plain clothes, others beefed up. And they didn't hold back, not this time.

He desperately looked up to the CCTV cameras which had been installed in place to prevent exactly this kind of attack. But it was all to no avail.

And then, as quickly as it had begun, the attack was over. Now no-one was there, his attackers fled off into the distance. This nondescript and irresponsible bunch of rapists and hooligans who think that they can rule the world with their sex, just taking out whom-so-ever they choose, whenever they want.

Well he would change all of them, Jo vowed. With the strength of his fibre quill he was going to rewrite the history books. Put Napoleon back as the courageous leader of men he surely was, and the Vietcong as the brave and courageous group of self-defending freedom fighters which they truly were, and not the scum of Vietnam which the invading nations had labelled them as.

But first he had to get better. His neck was killing, being the weak point of his skeletal structure, and the strike that had connected with it had left serious damage. He had a splitting headache, that would take days if not a couple of weeks to dissipate. His breathing was buggered, and he squealed for breath like a stuck pig. And his wounds were bleeding heavily.

They had not damaged his spirit, only briefly knocked the steam out of it. He hoped that he would learn from this, to come back stronger and better prepared. And he damn well knew better than to challenge those particular fighters again, knowing that they fought without mercy or compassion, and would one of these days finish the job off he feared.

But he was not afraid. And just as these thugs grouped together in some kind of gay and wholly homosexual male bonding ring, so too he had met good and decent people from all walks of life, who had listened to him and respected the decisions he had made in life, and his right to make them, even if they themselves may have acted differently. And out of these good and decent people he had faith that in time he would be able to build their trust. To learn from them, and maybe even teach them a thing or two. And perhaps even make an unbreakable bond with them, the kind which cements brothers into a unity of kind, which builds nations, and provides support through prosperity and disaster alike.

He knew that lying on the floor he was a long way off from this potential. And so slowly, and with creaking bones, he picked his soggy carcass up off the floor and painfully made his way back home, to clean clothes, a hot bubble bath (surely the liqueur to sooth any injury) and bed!

At night he dreamt a terrible dream of beasts and creeps. And I regret to inform you that he never awoke. His injuries were too much for his pale frame. And he still rests in that dream today. Still walks the streets at night, alone with only the swans and the cygnets for company. Still suffers from unknown and merciless strikes to the back of his head, still is

354

kicked to the floor by martial artists eager to teach him a lesson in front of his friends, and proven again and again how weak and drunk he really was on that day.

This is a memory he will never awake from. And on the day Jo died, his body was totally and completely destroyed. In hospital they rushed him to an operating theatre, pumped him full of drugs to try and stop the internal haemorrhaging and keep the temperature down, and filled his neck full of scaffold and engineering works that would make the leaning tower of Pisa proud.

On that day Jo died, of this he was sure. He then began spitting out fire, reminding people of the same injures which he himself had suffered. People despised him. He was an outcast.

It took him many years to even contemplating healing these wounds, let alone to actually do it. And always the ogres were there to watch his shadows, and threaten to beat him if he ever stepped out of line again!

So he kept his head down. Kept himself to himself. Eventually he left home, eventually found himself a new life and a new wife far away from the brutal streets where he had learned to trust no one but himself.

And after a particularly bad dream, he fell into a deeper sleep. The rapid-eye-movement commonly associated with dreaming ceased, which the Doctors would have noticed if they had even been listening, and he still wasn't lying on the park bench, his mind in turmoil stumbling through the past and future desperate to find a foot-hand hold to stem the bleeding. And he cried to the pigeons but there was nothing they could do. Already in a dream, he could sleep no more. Instead he entered some kind of second coma, where he found little rest, but closed his eyes and let the steam train of his brain at least find a more comfortable pace. For a while at least. Then afraid that he was going to die of hypothermia, he awoke hungry and lonely, and cold and wet. So he stumbled off to see if he could mug someone for some change, or at least get one of his parents to answer their phones and lend him some much needed dollar.

The streets of his city seemed to know him quite well by now. Damn it – he honestly felt that lots of the TV presenters were even watching him when he turned on the box. Mocked him, and his misfortune. And this only set him off into another rage, another bout of roaming the streets in a half delirious state, vulnerable to the thieves who would take all he had got if he even had access to it. And would leave him totally and thoroughly alone.

Then one day all this actually happened. It had happened before, and it seemed to be his destiny. He was sure that people the world over actually believed that this was his 'fate'. Many had actually told him as much! And then, just as when all options and bridges have finally been burnt once and for all, a stairway appeared from heaven. An innocent spiralling staircase, which he had only read about in books and occasionally dreamt about, actually appeared before him. He had prepared for this day, and eager not to let this opportunity escape him, he stopped what he was doing at the time, dropped what he was holding, and climbed up the stairs. Never looking back.

He had had slip-ups, stumbles and falls along the way. He was alone and had nowhere else to turn. Even his family no-longer trusted him. But as he walked up that spiral staircase, sweet music filled his ears. Suddenly, above the fence, he could see couples and groups engaged in depraved and difficult sex. He watched this for some time, before shaking his head, and starting the climb again. It seemed like whilst he had been otherwise engaged, the stairs had grown steeper, and he had slid down a couple of steps in the meantime.

He wondered if he would ever meet a gal who would let him put his stinky maggot inside her, whether he would ever feel the sweet embrace of female flesh against his member, and thus prove all of those haters wrong. He knew that in order for this to happen he would have to challenge everything that he had been taught, to tackle some of the biggest criminals the world had ever known, and do something alone even as he was totally alone.

One day he would learn how to fight, to move, carry himself, kick, roll and endure. He would practise ninja dancing to gypsy music, seeing as there was no dojo in the world that would take him on. And he would face in combat enemies twice or even ten times his power with the odds stacked again him.

About the only premise remaining to him was that of courage, and on his bad days when even his family seemed defeated, even this seemed to seep away. On the days his painful injuries of old returned to him, when he could not eat because he could not swallow, and he could not swallow because it hurt to breathe. And he could not sleep, because the pain kept him awake. And he could not breathe because a demon had gotten to the inside of his lungs and was pulling him down and apart.

His snores woke the whole apartment block. And from cold glances to ignorance, he started to receive even more bitter insults on the streets. Even the little children, not to mention the young men, called him 'queer' 'poof' 'yellow' and such forth. So as you can see, even over here (Kenya) things have not been easy.

But ever the little fighter, on a day when the worst thing happened, which you can imagine for yourself 'cos I ain't going to tell you, you went outside with the intention of running a mile both ways. He got as far as walking down the street, reached a dead end, got out of breath and sat down (on a conveniently placed nearby bench). Then when he got bored of doing that, he did some push-ups, then wandered home. Halfway there he found the search party which had been sent out to look for him, headed by his then fiancée, and now wife. And joined them back to base camp. It had been a difficult time and he hoped that it was only going to get better thereafter.

This was not strictly true, not straightaway at least. But things did make a remarkable improvement in the long run. He hoped that together they would be able to help each other much more than they would ever have been able to apart. There would always possibly be bad days. He knew this. They both did. But hopefully the faith of both of them, not to mention the grace of the little baby, would weather the storms of life and carry them onto the rainbow at the end of the tempest. He would see first hand the little promise God made to Noah and his family when they stepped from the ark, and the dove which had been sent to find a safe place to land never returned. The rainbow, seven glorious and perfect colours, untouched by human hand or explanation, glorious in its simplicity and also a reminder of things to come.

Now he once again slung his satchel of rations over his shoulder, once again picked up his warriors seven dragon sword, and returned into the fray. He was not afraid; call it stupidity, call it what you will. And he knew that if he was seen he didn't stand a chance. So instead he relied on his ninja skill of invisibility to move unseen among the shadows.

They didn't know what he was capable of, for he was enacting the morals of legends few of them had even read, and for even those that had they didn't understand. I'm talking about King Arthur and the knights of the round table here, complete with Merlin and his trusty rook. I'm talking about the hidden kingdom realm high up amongst the mountains, that many brave adventurers have set to capture but none succeeded. That only the chosen few had caught a glimpse of in their travels, even if it be only possibly in the eyes of their companions. And they have shared with me through chronicling their exploits into writing (this is a direct reference to Julius Evolva's Meditations on the Peaks if you must know).

When every day becomes a struggle for life, for breath, it is not easy by any means. Some people look down on you, and the rest ignore you completely. But what a surprise it will be for them, when suddenly you metamorphose into all of those game heroes you have played on your video-console. In a flash the traits of heroism and honour imbue your armour, and your banner promises a new world which has only to this date existed in the dreams of the few and the tired.

How many heed your call to the banner, I've got no idea. At present they were alone in a strange land. But they now were planning to make the return home at some point. And when we do things will be both the same and very different. I hope to have danced enough to provide myself with the physical prowess to challenge the evil but dim mental institutions (minds) of my enemies, in a very real and physical way. And if they bloody well want a fight, then I'll bloody well give them one!

But now is a time for healing and rest. For spending quality time with my family, and messing about with dance moves for two hours in the morning to good CDs when I've got the energy. I cannot forget what they've done to me. But I also believe that I've got the capacity to change my meagre frame into one somewhat stronger, and then whip ass as a result! They will still ignore me, but oh how much sweeter will it be when I crack them between the eyes for all these years of injustice they've caused me.

And yet others may find it in themselves to approach and shake my hand. Little knowing that in so doing they are signing a contract, wrought in blood, and never to be forgotten. Making a promise among men to help one another in the journey towards complete emancipation of the Martial Arts into the world of men, from the barren wilderness from where-within it has remained for oh so many years.

Things are definitely changing, but they are still a long way off, of this much I am sure. I am actually at the tail end of recovering from a brutal illness which had both stripped me of my strength and confidence, and made it nigh-impossible to breathe let alone sleep, followed by having really itchy mosquito bites, feeling totally drained and sapped of energy and tired, unable to eat, feeling really sick, going to the toilet all through the night and the following day with the sh!ts, and having bad headaches and an irritable personality all within the space of about a week. It was an illness I wouldn't wish on my worst enemy, and he didn't know what it was called. All I do know is that I've never suffered from anything even remotely like it before, not such a succession of symptoms which despite their different causes of pain, I feel sure are all part of the same virus. Perhaps it was a mild strain of malaria, carried by one of those pesky mosquitoes. It certainly wasn't a cold that much is sure. But I think I'm getting over it now, after a week. And all I've suffered today is a cough and a runny bum.

I suppose that it could be a curse that Africa throws at her visitors to keep them away. To teach them that Kenya is not for the faint hearted, and just as all of the natives have built up a staunch resistance over the years of living here, so too the 'invaders' find themselves stricken and hapless under its power! But at least now I seem to have defeated it, I can sleep peacefully again at night. At least that is what I hope.

As for the rest, who knows? I still live in that dream land I told you about earlier where children are respectful to their elders, and the rich actually give to the needy instead of scorning them on the streets. Who knows, perhaps one day this promise we have made among ourselves will actually come true. Those few and gentle words whispered late in the evening, just as the smoke-yard is closing, that look of unadulterated compassion, that knows full well is never going to materialise but always remain as a dream, that call of duty, or respect shown amongst equal men, will one day step beyond the hospital walls. Beyond the playing fields of the video-games, and the programmers and reviewers who rate them, to create a very real new world in the one we have.

This is going to take some work. And it is also going to take more than just one man and my family's efforts. At present it appears like a pipe-dream, a fairytale of imagined ideas and impossible occurrences. And for a long time this is the way it has been. But things are changing. And no matter how many times they plaster over the walls, cracks are beginning to show in the prison foundations.

The number of people rejecting this 'comfortable' way of living is greater than ever before, and instead opting for a life of crime, has shot up here in the west (UK/US) in recent years. Murders are on the up, so are violent robberies and corporate crime, despite whatever the official police/governmental statistics may say. It seems to be that only every other day some new poor kid is stabbed to death in the dirty streets of one of the big city estates. And nobody seems to want to take responsibility for this. Not the parents, nor teachers, nor government let alone the kids themselves. They all seem to be innocent bystanders in a guilty world. And they are all guilty I would say, in their own little way.

So what am I proposing, a martial law where the streets are ruled by the sword, and respect driven into youngsters from an early age? Hardly, like that's going to work! I think they did actually once try that way in Japan, and look at what's now happened to them.

The truth be known, I do not have the answers for this one. How pride and respect for all morals and people can be brought back into the school playgrounds and cities, where it is now a very much carnivorous and dog eat dog world. Where any human intervention in the eyes of the police is deemed as criminal action, punishable by arrest, and where those who actually use their positions of power to stop wars from erupting (such as South African President Thabo Mbeki did with his interventionist peace talks in Zimbabwe) are thrown from office, and stripped of their power by the secret but formidable powers that be.

Damn it – they did it to me. But whereas I don't think Mbeki can constitutionally ever return as his country's president again, I never was anything. My name is not generally known. And so we are on a level playing field. I am still desperately trying to break it through into the big time, and with the loving support of my family I may even do it one of these days.

Peace now everyone. John Robinson 28-9-08

31: Blue Belt

Jo coolly surveyed the hills around him as they cantered into battle on his white Arabian mare. He gently but surely gripped the saddle with one hand, and his other rested on the hilt of his sword.

They had journeyed several continents, from the proud cobbled stones of Hong Kong, to the rolling hills of the sovereign British isles. And now they were God knows where, towards God knows who. But they were marching towards him, that much is for sure.

And each and every one of his ragged motley crew had proved themselves to him, in their own way at their own time. They were all warriors. He also thought that they were all men, although for some of the younger lads who had yet to grow a beard he had his doubts.

They had tackled and slain many wolves and hob-goblins to reach this point. Today he merrily thought back to when he was a boy having playful fights in the fields, to dodging the city traffic, as if every car was a beast, every driver insane.

But now he had returned to the empire. Every one the different but things were still the same. It was still a fight for hope and glory, against an unseen and unheard enemy. All he could hear right now was his horse's heavy rasp as she moved along.

And he wasn't afraid. Not today. Not with the knowledge that his wife and babe were back at home, waiting for them to return in the base camp. A warrior's life is difficult at the best of times. And now they faced an enemy with vastly superior fire power and numbers. But he was not afraid, and glancing to his left and right neither were his men. Or if they were they didn't show it.

Some had been slain, others deserted and still others joined. But they were a formidable fighting force, even if they were travelling into new virgin territory. The ground was fresh and the scrolls of history and fate just waiting to be written.

And Jo led his army. Not from the front, but on the front line.

Jo flexed his head above the surface of the water. He'd been swimming again in the pool of uncertainty and doubt. Fragile relationships and temporary internet surface providers. He'd been challenged and old friends had paddled to his aid, using warlike and epic boats the kind of which he'd never sail. Instead he had to be content with swimming, like an otter, using his two feet to kick and his arms to paddle. And paddle they did, over and over again. He felt himself getting tired; he had to stop and take a breather every couple of laps. But then he pressed on. Past the slow swimmers and the fast ones! And boy there were a lot of them!

He swam as in a dream. Through castles in the sky and songs in the clouds. Over and above busy highways full of people rushing to he had no idea where. Past busy gyms full of even more peops grunting and sweating for again unknown reasons and motivations. Past schools full of diligent, and not so diligent kids studying for unknown curriculums, to be marked at unknown places. Past country lanes with walkers with their dogs and spouses (but not necessarily in that order!) Past half-full cinemas, race tracks and battlefields. Past cyber cafés, and coffee shops. Past supermarkets and barbers. And still he swam. All of a sudden his arms had become wings, his toes feathers.

No longer of the human variety, Jo had become a bird. In this dream he could soar up to the sun, but not so close as to get burned Icarus style! And then he would dip and dive, and hurtle faster than the speed of a fast thing, like a bullet, to the horrified onlookers below. Before pulling out at the last minute, and in a wild swerving spin dart away, another mission objective well done! This was Ninpo, swallow style!

Speaking of swallows, he remembered that Happy Prince (by Oscar Wilde) his cousin had once told him about. A golden prince on a high column overlooking some random French town, who piece by piece donated the rubies from his eyes, emerald from his nose and jewel from the butt of his sword, to another distant relative (swallow), who then dutifully gave the jewels, and finally the gold from the prince's skin, to give to the poor and needy of the city. So that when winter came, there was nothing left of him but a barren statue, and a bird who had missed its migration to Egypt in helping out the people of the city. They died that winter, both overcome by the cold. And the city's mayor, on discovering the lifeless statue and bird corpse, was only too quick to have their bodies thrown onto the garbage, not knowing the good work they had done.

But the prince was given his kingdom, with his swallow, in Heaven. Or so the story goes.

I don't know if you feel moved by reading my recount of this precious tale, but it sure makes me cry when I read the original translation (from French). Oh to be a bird, soaring and diving, spinning and flying alone or in formation. With no more worries than to avoid the hawks, and find worms to eat! Ha! (Perhaps I don't want to be a bird after all!)

At least in my songs and stories I can fly. I can run, show off my chest hairs (all three of them). And press the buttons that in a real life situation I'd be more cautious about shall we say!

Ed. I don't know what they've posted after that and quite frankly I don't care. They are a semi-literate macho bunch of hooligans who can keep their interpretations of the Martial Arts and stick it where the sun doesn't shine for all I care. And so comprehensively and conclusively I am going to sign off there, unsubscribing from the site and effectively ending all contact with them.

I appreciate that they may have spent many years earning their belts, jumping through the various physical and theoretical hoops set by whatever form of combat they have been learning. And one or two of them may even know a thing or two about fighting!

But that really isn't my problem right now. I have decided to cease this, and indeed all other literary projects which I am engaged with at the moment, to focus purely on the genesis (creation) of my own Martial art baby, whom I have from today Christened <the way of> the weak monkey, or Si fa Dao in Mandarin Chinese!

It borrows from monkey Shaolin kungfuu, Chinese drunken boxing, little pieces of Aikido and Judo and quite a bit of the deeper spirituality of Hoshinryjutsu, to create a wholly new and genuine take on combat. I intend to sign out tomorrow from those bad men with one last post: 'Ow you've killed me. <Rolls over on the floor>.' That'll be my exit. Or maybe I'll be honest and sign out letting them know that I am going to work on my own new and unique style!

Now I can spend my time working into this new creation of mine. I'm going to have to put in place some kind of syllabus for it, which can be whatever I like seeing as I am the one and only Grand-Master! I want to have thirteen kyu before black belt first dan. And I was even considering setting up a dual belt system, where two separate and possibly different coloured belts could be worn by the pupil at one time, although perhaps they would only go into combat with the one.

This is to reflect the idea of spirituality and mind existing side by side, or love and hate, or yin and yang, or weakness and strength. Indeed a key idea of this form is going to be using the hidden capacity endowed by a position of weakness, or smallness alternatively to employ secret and unexpected moves which your enemy sure wasn't expecting and thus beat him, or at least punish him severely as a result. The immediate example of this move type springs to the ninja art of stealthy movement without perception. Or getting lost in a crowd you might say. If you are Mr Beef, rippling with muscles and striding about with an air of royalty, obviously they're going to spot you from a mile off! And the minute they do they're going to know exactly who you are, or have a very good impression at least. Your enemies I mean.

And so while other Martial Arts, boxing and Tae-Kwon-Do seem to revel in well built athletes, these are not going to be prime requisites of my style, rather associative factors you might say. Obviously it helps to be fit healthy and strong in whatever you do, and martial arts especially.

But I also want to place at the fore of Weak Monkey style, the idea of the human spirit prevailing over all other things. Improvisation has to be a part of it (although how I would test for this looks troublesome, and would have to largely depend on the ability of the marker, and his vision).

I also want to include the basics, such as running, maybe press-ups and swimming, pull-ups and even walking. I have even toyed with the idea of including a cooking demand to the syllabus, although perhaps this is my own insatiable appetite getting the better of me. And indeed seems more suited for the likes of a duke of Edinburgh or Prince's trust thing than any combat syllabus.

I do certainly want some kata to be in there. Although it seems clear that I am going to have to invent these from scratch, perhaps borrowing some of the basic strikes from all

MA and also animal movements from Shaolin Kungfu. I suppose a certain amount of deviation and original input should be accepted in these, as long as the overall themes and principles are judged to be appreciated. And these can be developed further in some detail, as I build up the foundations of this thing. Perhaps we will be looking at one kata per kyu, or certainly for the early stages. As well as the kata there can be a written test, and I would prefer to keep it written as opposed to oral to emphasise the importance of that much forgotten skill of reading.

We could even set essays at various levels, although perhaps not, (this is supposed to be about combat after all). I need to develop a set of tests which can reliably both gauge a student's grasp of the style and promote his future development, by not making it too hard or easy, but just right. And the tests need to be demanding and rigorous enough so that any old black-belt can't just step off the street and pass the lot in one go! And I am specifically talking about the pre-1st dan colours up to this point. I think that it is going to be slightly unrealistic of me to even begin contemplating 1st dan and above, when I have only yesterday awarded myself that first in this my own style!

So to recap: Weakling Monkey style is going to be about a fusion between spirituality and martial combat. I want to include a certain degree of written work, perhaps some coursework and group presentation even, to pay homage to the great traditions of our academic heritage, not to mention that they are good ways of testing. Easy to perform, mark and learn for. It has to be rigorous to an extent, but I am also going to be looking at doing new things with this one which have never been done before. More on this later.

For a start let us go through the kyu, and I think that there should be two for each colour, going up to thirteen before we hit the fabled black. And for each grade we can also instil a name for the victory achieved.

Let us start at white, this is the universal 0 kyu and denominates a beginning who is new to the sport. 1st kyu yellow is the first step on the ladder of Weak Monkey. It will include a written multiple choice test of some ten questions from a total base of about 40. These will test the student's knowledge of the foundations of the style, and other such basic facts. I also think that we should throw in not one but two elementary kata, to get the kid going in the right direction. If we add a two push up bar, maybe some dancing or jogging on the spot in a style favoured by the student, some sit-ups and star-jumps then I think we are well on the way to getting there. Let's not cram too much into this first level at this early stage.

We can save the basic strikes and blocks and directions for 2nd kyu yellow. This is still easy, but advanced easy. We can look at new kata, although a knowledge of the preceding one will still be required and perhaps even randomly tested for in the exam. The written exam is still multiple choice, but needs to be a new set of parallel questions, and that little bit more demanding. From two good push-ups we can ask for four. And the same number of pull-ups. Maybe double that in sit-ups. Other simple movement work can take place, including perhaps a longer dance session. And I also want to add something new to the syllabus, say a fight, or Karmic achievement. But I suppose we can leave that for the later stages. Assuming the questions and kata are new and challenging enough, and the strikes, basic kicks, holds, movements (break-fall) perhaps a throw, and blocks should round this grade off nicely.

It had been a cold hard night. And waking up in a gasp Jo looked out the keep window to realise that the worst of his fears had come true! At midnight last night the enemy, whose men had presumed pummelled and finally on the back foot, launched a parallel simultaneous attack across each of his seven castles and five other keeps. God knows where they came from or let alone how they had planned it. But to the castle guardians it appeared as if they just materialised from nowhere, and hostages were shot, houses burned and governors decapitated. From that day forth it would be known as the 'night of the burning embers' a chilling reminder to his people, never to let their guard down for the enemy were everywhere they now so realised.

Pulling on his Long Johns, Jo jumped on his horse to assess the damage first hand. It was true that he had lost about 40% of his live-stock and cavalry in the attack. His team had finally been able to beat back the oppressors, but not without copious blood of their own being spilt, and the battle had lasted well into the night. And where was our squire when all of this was kicking off? What was he doing you might ask?

Well it seemed that someone had slipped a sleeping potion into his nightly mug of Bovril, that he had spent the night suffering from the most terrible constipation pains and must have visited the John approximately 14 times. And that is no lie. So that by the morning his arse was tender and raw like a new born babe's.

Speaking of which he now had the dilemma of whether to tell his missus or not of the havoc caused them, and their very near defeat last night at the hands of an indomitable and shadowy organisation. Of how wrong their previous battle summary had been to let such an event take place, and what it would mean to the moral of his men.

He did actually like to share with her everything; he considered himself a just man, and held honesty as one of his utmost virtues. But he feared that given her frail constitution, and the energies the labour of birth had sapped from her heart, he was not sure that her body would be able to take the news. And so reluctantly he decided to withhold the info, at least until a week or two when she was a little stronger.

On visiting the keep's prisons, he discovered that of the few attackers who had been caught and survived awaiting his judgement, they were generally an uneducated and uncouth lot. They were strong alright, he'd admit that, but behind their eyes he sensed something that he could neither explain nor trust. It seemed that all of them without exception was possessed by some sort of demon spirit, and acting under the guise of a being far, far out of this world. God knows what they would ever do if they managed to break free, and so

374

without further hesitation he ordered their straight execution right away, and it was done. He now thought that if all his enemies were so possessed in this way, who, or what indeed, was the spirit controlling their outlandish and most terrible actions. Could it be a man, a single man? Perhaps an army officer, who had thus risen up the martial ranks and inspired this formidable army to walk in his footsteps, follow his banner?

Surely not. No single man had that kind of power and control over the hearts and minds of men, and women alike. So if not human then what? Some kind of demon, an ogre perhaps, or a Cyclops even, who had travelled a long way across many oceans to stake their territory here at his base camp? That sounded more likely. But why had they chosen to pick on him? Across the kingdom of Arcania there must have been at least seven different municipalities and trading empires which all operated quite independently of each other, albeit along similar lines. Why had they attacked his?

And then at that moment a shrieking thought pierced the back of his mind. Something so terrible it would keep him awake into the early hours of the morning for many moons to come. He remembered the name and face of his long lost half brother Jeff, or Jester as they used to call him. Could it be that he had returned to the land after all these years and was seeking some kind of retribution for pains suffered him just before he fell from grace. This was an option so repulsive to him, that he had to put down the Nescafé he was drinking. He could not bear the taste, once sweet now tasted oh so sour. And so he called on the servant girl to get him another cup.

If it really was Jester come back from the grave, he knew for a fact that he couldn't face him alone. The man knew all his weak spots, his vulnerabilities, and God knows the kind of havoc he could wreak when the bad moods which he was renowned for, overtook him. He prayed that he had got it wrong, that there must be some other kind of explanation. But the more he thought about it, the more he feared that it was true.

Now he was left with the by no means easy task of devising a strategy to battle and beat the bad man. He considered hiring mercenaries from further afield, but he never trusted these type of men, who placed money above honour and were liable to scram as soon as they tasted their first drop of human blood.

He sat down at the table with his new cup of milky coffee, and began to write. He would start three new divisions of the peasant army, recruiting the local yokels and training them how to carry and use a sword and shield. These types of warriors were usually inefficient on the battlefield, and served as cannon fodder. But every last man counted. And what's more, occasionally from among the ranks there rose a uniquely gifted individual of stalwart courage, who was worth at least ten thousand men. And despite being few and far between, these champions were worth at least ten times their weight in gold.

Secondly he would send out to the workshops and blacksmiths to begin the creation of new siege defences. One of his problems seemed to be that the enemy worked solely under the cover of night, moving without trace from trail to objective. Some new weapons would at least bolster his men's confidence. And finally he would send a personal carrier pigeon to Arthur, Percival and Sir Lancelot of the Knights of the Round Table in Camelot. He imagined that they were probably too busy fighting wars of their own, the crusades and what-not, but it was worth a try.

And now he fell back into the arms of his chair. It was still the early hours of the morning, and the sun's first rays were just beginning to break through the battlement shutters. It had been a long hard night. And no doubt there would be many more. But now at least he had devised a plan, a direction to take the fight to the enemy. And for the time being there was really nothing more he could do. So he set about finishing his coffee, before going for a shave and to face yet another day ahead.

32: Purple Belt

Confused and in disarray Jo watched as his army fell apart
before his very eyes. The vanguard had taken the brunt of the
initial attack, and most of the men there lay either dead, or on
the floor grovelling up to the heavens in prayer to some god
he didn't even believe existed.

As for the rest of his troop, from the sides, to the centre, to
the rear all were in disarray. Some were crying, others
sucking their thumbs. This is the moment he realised that the
true measure of a man is not how much an aggressive and
ruthless killing machine he is, but how well they can cope
under adversity. How well their moral constitution serves
them when everything else falls apart. How good are they at
making friends and building the trust of strangers whom they
had never met before in their lives.

And now with his army in tatters, Jo himself shed a tear. The
unseen and unheard ninja had moved efficiently and
effectively cut up his force before they could even see him, let
alone react to defensive positions. How one man could cause
such destruction was not within the realm of human
comprehension, but nevertheless he had done it.

Now from the side of the arena, even the bystanders who had
nothing to do with this fight, watched in terror as they saw so
many of their proud men fall from grace. Men who were
admired the world over for their honour and pride being
reduced to a quivering wrecks. And further afield he knew his

enemy were waiting and watching with glee as they witnessed his force being ripped to shreds. He doubted they had anything to do with this. He supposed that there were forces at play, and things at stake that were beyond the comprehension of even normal men.

But he was not defeated. So blowing into his brass trumpet, he signalled the retreat of whatever men left were able to hear. They would have to return to camp, regroup, draw new battle plans and a new plan of action. It was very possible that with this latest onslaught, the war was over. And it was only a matter of time before the enemy claimed their unrighteous property over the rest of the world. But as long as there was still blood in his wheezy lungs, he would lead his men in the fight against them. With the energy left to his arms he would carry the banner over the battlements and into the fray. He will never surrender. Even if down to ten men, even if he is standing alone against the beast, I will raise my sword high in the air and march onwards, to freedom. Staring the vagabond straight in the eyes I will not falter. And this time there will be no quarter!

Jo picked himself off the floor, dusted his suit down and walked away. It had been a hard week. There had been many traps out there for the unsuspecting ninja he now realised through personal experience, and to his peril. He wasn't about to give up now, and realised that he was too far gone now to ever turn back.

Friends had become enemies. Enemies had dummied and then remained enemies. And he did have some friends, even if he wasn't sure who right now.

And as he walked away into the sunset a soothing R+B melody played in his forehead. Jo would never be a fighter. He was a man that was all. Nothing more, nothing less. Then he clenched his fist, the one with the ring on it.

Note for all my pretentious posturing, I don't really think that I can claim to be good enough to make up my own MA, not properly, without at least one good win under my belt. So today I have decided on who to select as my next target. Simon, a man if only by the loosest sense of the word, he is hard quick and nasty. A perfect chance for me to prove my worth or die trying. It's gonna take a lot of ninja dancing, and kata practice, not to mention some push-ups to even get near to contending fighting this punk. And I am still getting over a nasty African virus which has left me semi-impotent among other things. But I have great confidence in my body's ability to recover. And then when it does I will get angry, and used to the rage to attack and quickly put him in a position he never knew I was capable of. I will let you know how it goes; you will gradually see my body transform over the weeks and

380

months, and then it will become clear when I am ready. My breathing will never be cured; it is always going to be my weak point. So what? I think that I have now demonstrated that I can hit over the internet. Let's see how with a little bit of iron, this can translate into real pain. JR 30-9-08

The next day Jo awoke feeling fresh and renewed. He felt like he could take on the entire empire single handed. And in this happy and joyous mood he meandered outside whereupon he found an exotic looking purple/orange Persian rug, minding his own business under the old apple tree in the yard.

Getting onto it and sitting there, Jo actually imagined that he was Aladdin, flying high in the clouds with his princess Jasmine on his arm. He closed his eyes to fully enjoy the warm experience of the sun's rejuvenating rays, and pretend he was somewhere else being someone else. He must have fallen asleep in this position, for when he awoke he was flying through the clouds, still on the carpet!

The gold tassels at the corners of the rug were sprinkling fairy dust onto the ground below, and everything took on a translucent and ethereal quality. Even germs seemed harmless and friendly in this generous kind and brave new world.

They dodged the clouds like a fighter plane, an old allied spitfire from world-war 2, repainted and given a new engine so it could take to the skies again for one last time. And as they played dodge ball with the clouds, they saw the vast and icy desert plains and mountain ranges far below them, where that other great leader of men Genghis Khan once staked his territory. This was the Mongolian outback, one of the most isolated and untouched regions known to man. And now he could call it his home. On his way back he flew by a thunderstorm, and just turned his head in time to capture in his lenses that magnificent tribute to nature which is the rainbow. God's gift to Noah, and man, after he stepped from the ark onto dry land as if for the first time.

On getting home he was astonished to find that the humble flat where he had once lived had turned into a magnificent palace. Where burly and big soldiers lined the yard, and saluted as he walked by them. And little kids ran through the streets to say hello. Yesterday he had been confused and alone. Today he was together and happy.

Once he stepped through those pearly gates and into the marble interior and plush gold carpets within, he smelt a fresh fragrance which at once reminded him of home, and yet he had never smelt before. There in the shared communal lounge sat his friends, some watching TV others playing chess. There was L*, that head instructor in the techniques of control and restraint, a pretty and charming bird who he got on very well with and also had a most charming smile. He actually thought it couldn't have been too bad to have been controlled by her!

Then there was little T*, a cute and short old time raver. With a vicious piercing of an 'e' on her tongue, a stud shaped as one, for any of you who know what this means. There had been a time when he would have done anything to get her under those sheets, but now they were just good friends, and he respected that. There was also K* that rugged native African, who told me that he had done more days in borstal then I had eaten hot breakfasts. This other fat guy I used to go to the pub with, (D*), and he kept on getting into fights and getting barred from them! My first proper boyfriend, this skinny lad; man, I can't even remember his name. But they danced the waltz together, and shared special moments which only two people who truly share together can ever hope to experience. It was, and always will be, true love. What matter was it that they shared the same chromosomes? This was the real deal (ed. joke!). Then there had been T*, or little T* as he was known, on account of his being about 5 foot tall. He had a beard like a monkey, and was seemingly keyed in to some mystery rave dealer, who used to charge and send him rave tapes, which could hardly be called music. Both T* and K* each had a ration of beatings for that gay friend of mine. And when I complained to P* the manager-in-chief, it was him who put me into seclusion!

Then there was L*, a big gal with a photo of her precious kids who had been stolen from her by social services after her life had fallen apart. I saw her by the now redundant bus-station some time after she had escaped. Then there was C*, this Asian guy who was funny as he was clever. (He was in there because he had burnt down someone's house, and then called up the poor geezer, D*, who was in bed at the time, to tell him to get out 'cos the house was on fire!) Dr B* a staunch but firm Doctor, who was kind but fair with his injections.

Also Will, another crazy kid, who he fancied like hell. Not in the same way a boy fancies a gal, nothing will ever replace that. But anyone else who has ever spent a long time living close to a member of the same sex, who is funny as they are innocent, clever as they are handsome, may well find themselves being drawn irresistibly and inseparably towards them. It was funny, for a laugh you understand. We went as far as kissing, but that's as far as it went. I found that gay sex hadn't been for me, and I wasn't about to repeat the experience! And reading about this now you probably think that I must have been some little sicko to have taken advantage of this twenty-year-old kid in this way. But, oh, if you had but seen those lips! And it wasn't just the sex, but the physical attraction, the attraction of minds, of two kindred souls, secret fighters and holy tribesmen.

Boy, when C* (another princess) found out, she wasn't too pleased. And then there was M*, her boyfriend. Demo Dave, Dave the para/Christian, Harry the army guy with his motto cut into the arm, John another army guy, Big-John the caveman, C* the simpleton, A* the landlord, Jess the black Labrador with a heart of gold, and Paul Bentley, also known as Beef on account of the fact that he was the very meaning of the words (built like a brick sh*t house!). I didn't not get on with him, and tried to explore things. But the best we could manage was some kind of mutual truce. Anyway he got my 360 fixed for me which is really good enough.

There was S*, a cute Asian nurse, who was luscious and pretty as hell. She kept on threatening to kick my ass, but never did! Another cute nurse, a temp who I forget the name of. She was up to her 2nd dan going in for it shortly I think, TKD. There was Al, this Indian, or something like that, who could probably kick the ass of anyone in there. Plenty of Russians and Japanese, including one, another John, who used to be a bare-knuckle boxer back in the day, or so he told me. And I believed him. He carried himself with the authority of someone who doesn't have to worry about the consequences of what they say, on the grounds that they were safe in the knowledge that they could handle the worst that these pied-pipers could throw at him.

There was K*, a pretty say 38-year-old nurse who would have loved me if it wasn't for the fact that she was out of my league, and anyway a nurse whilst I was a patient. But she was another one with an innocent and playful smile, which oozed confidence and personality, and showed that she didn't need to bow down to no man! He remembered after one particularly hard session of shouting at the Doctor and his team, to ask her (in charge) if she could unlock the bathroom for him to while away his sins. It was good of her to ask me if I wanted her to get in it with me as well! Ha, that'd be the day!

Who else was in this palace of his? R*, another spicy and cheeky nurse, who he could have throttled for about the first five months, but after that saw a turnaround and then fell in love with her as well. And New this Chinese guy. I don't think that New was his proper name, but after a debate in the corridor, I think I got him to adopt it as his English one. And people to this day call him by this alias which seemed to fit him well. And lastly there was Kim, a South-African bird a few years older than him, who also had been snatched up and swallowed by the system, and was another kindred burned soul. But she was still fighting in her own way, as indeed they all were. They had spent a nice early morning together reading from one of the slush books in the lounge's book-case. In this way they bonded considerably. And when she left and came back to find me still there, she said that she thought that I was the Godfather on account of the length of my stay, and strength of my connections. There was also L*, an Italian break-dancer who went to the pub with me sometimes. L*, a cute Zambian who teased me with her singing, near the end of my stay. And Tabith, a Zulu African warrior queen, proud and strong, moral qualities modern men and women seem to be sorely lacking in today's fast food age.

I practised my kicks against the lamppost, his pull-ups on the bus-shelter when it dried out. And those were 'free' pulls, with nothing to grip onto, you rely on the friction of your fingertips and the momentum of the initial jump to carry you into the movements. I think he did about five one day. I wonder, how many of you could do that? And the odd press-up, shadow fighting with one fingered Zen (against boxing), all the while pissing off the authorities and trying not to w!^* too much. Joy. This was heaven and that is hell.

Then he went upstairs, past the cousins' bed-chamber and into the warm entourage of his fiancée. Politely knocking twice on the door (he didn't like to enter unwelcome), he soon found himself in the warm and splendid environ of an African Queen. Fragrant and happy, he sat down to engage with her in long and engaging discussions. They never argued, but if they did, they made up afterwards. And they loved each other perfectly. He hoped that she would let him spend the rest of his life with her. Whether at home or abroad, he wasn't really bothered as long as they were together.

Ever since he'd had his Samurai sword snatched from his wielding grasp by an unknown and sneaky opponent, leaving him with the mute and impotent sheath in his grasp, he realised that the best weapon was the fist. But in hospital, even that is not enough. So you have to learn how to fight by other means. How to suss out and then call your allies to your side when you need them. How you can meet a friend you will never see again, but never forget them. In this way they will always be with you. And it becomes easy to learn how to see behind a whole person's conceptions, mental apparatus and what makes them tick, not just by looking at them, but even by being told their name and nothing more. And I wonder, have any of you there got this power? Can any of you so called 'fighters', not just form an opinion or judgement, but actually know the everything about these people I have mentioned in this essay by hearing their name alone? Before you've even met them? And am I lying about these past friends and acquaintances? I've not even changed a single detail! Perhaps you think that this is all rubbish, that this carpet is purely a product of my imagination, and this palace and its residents about as real as the fabled unicorn that was 'left behind'.

There is no way I can prove to you these truths. You have to determine for yourselves their validity. And if any of you really are blackbelts, I would hope that you can determine the truth behind these stories, make a split judgement in my claim of honesty, not just from the way I write, but what I've been saying as well! Please try to establish from what I've been saying that my writing is not the proverbial cream cake with a crunchy centre. This is not possible by meandering vagabonds, nor rapists or self-obsessed uber-quote-bots. You have to be emphatic. You have to know people, to pick up on universal traits, and also what distinguishes the men from the boys. I don't suppose many of you will be able to do it.

And yeah, I am talking to you, the Tae-Kwon-Do 'expert' who likes to strut his stuff and throw his kicks as if there had never been a plank hard enough to withstand one of his kicks. Or you, Akidoka who thinks that there has never been a puncher who can escape one of your throws, let alone draw a bullet through you before you even had the chance to smile. Boxers tend to be of a different breed, less pretentious and self-inflating. I will leave them out of this attack, but I am getting tired, and I want to retire.

So, wearily, after another hard if yet constructive and informing day, Jo left the company of his friends to retire into the comfort of his own chamber. And just before blowing out the candle he glanced up to his bookcase, dusty in as much as it hadn't been read for some time, but epic and gothic none-the-less. He hoped that one day he would be able to finish the books he had started reading, the one on Drunken boxing, by Leung Ting, A Doll's House by Henrik Ibsen (he had read before, but determined to again), and even a strange and mysterious tome called 'Weak Monkey' or 'Si Fa Dao' in Chinese, one of those funny books which actually seemed to write itself as you turned each page. Jo was again going to fall into the soft and soothing world of cuddly playthings and happier times. This was where he deserved to be. This, was his destiny. And now if he could sleep a night without squashing the baby, everything would be fine!

The group of uniformed and highly decorated officers nervously waited and tried to occupy their time, as they waited for the soon to be arrival of their boss, who they hoped would be returning to the meeting hall at any minute. With that second the great brass doors of the war-chamber burst open and in strode a commander-in-chief with authority far beyond his years. Brushing past the lower echelons of the cabinet, he walked straight up to address the acting general in command. Commander Jameson bowed his head as he fumbled with the words,

'S-sir, I'm ever s-so sorry for disturbing at this hour on a Sunday morning, but we have just had important news.'

'SORRY!' Jo barked. 'I'LL SHOW YOU SORRY!'

Jameson hung his head in shame.

'SEVEN O'CLOCK ON A SUNDAY MORNING AND THE BEST YOU CAN GIVE ME IS SORRY!!'

At this point commander Steward stepped forward to offer his condolences.

'Please forgive us, sir. If we'd have known you were taking a nap we'd have surely waited for a more convenient time!'

'Bah!' the commander-in-chief barked. 'The damage has been done. Now whatever is it   that you wanted me for?'

Again Jameson lifted his head and spoke, 'Sir. We have had reports through that the enemy is pulling back its forces from each and every front! From the Eastern slopes of Abyssinia, to the Persian deserts, to the Normandy sunrise, the dictator is on the back foot! It would appear that we've won!'

But Jo wasn't pleased. 'And why wasn't I told about this earlier? You thought that you'd just wait till this major battle operation was well underway before telling me of the news? Leave it a bit longer would you? The bloody war would be over before half of you had even gotten out of bed I'd bet? And what are we supposed to do now, just walk on air?'

His men all hung their heads in shame. They were ashamed for not having told him earlier, for leaving it so late and proving such a disappointment to their boss. They really were lost for words.

'Well, get after him!' he raged. 'Planes can't fly themselves you know! Get up off your sorry asses and lead our men in the counter attack! Jesus – I don't even want to know what to think this army would be like if it weren't for me!'

'Yes Sir, yes Sir,' they finished before filing out of the room to fulfil their allocated responsibilities.

BANG! Jo smacked his enemy in the chops and after standing there for a beat, dazed, he crumpled to the floor like the sack of beans he most surely was! Victory! Surely nothing could stand in his way now.

'Erm, I-I'm sorry, this has never happened to me before!' He smiled to the pretty gal as she showed him from her bedroom, to the front door of her flat and kissed him goodbye before he set off on the cold and lonely trek back down the street to his parents again. Damn it! How many times have I used that line, and they always seemed to believe the lies! I cursed all the way home, for being such a disappointment to the female race. Boy, it was another angel, waiting to be harvested and then sadly left alone on the vine.

Now I was back in the ring. He cracked his knuckle dusters, zipped a bent fork round in a circle and out the window, and telepathically empathized with a rainbow overhead. Who was this imposter who had squared up to him in the street. What kind of a punk, racist, ignorant, indignant, imposter would dare challenge my authority in the ring, and dare me to fight outside?

As I walked down the stairs, following the lanky lad Simon, and his mate, I considered, how hard could this be? So big deal if he liked watching Mixed Martial Arts combat programs on the late night cable channels back in the hostel. Jo could rip at least twelve push-ups on the trot, perhaps even thirteen! He was the undisputed peanuts champion, and could boil an egg as good as the Hilton! What could this cheeky monkey possibly hold to that?

As we got further down the steps, I thought back to my first fighting days at school, the wrestling lessons he had given his then best friend Ross, in how to take a headlock. He never had understood why Ross moved to Preston with his parents shortly after that! Or the fights I had gotten into at primary school, with the mostly Pakistani and Indian lads. Well they had sure taught him a thing or two. In fact the fights he had gotten into had sure taught him a thing or two about getting a good beating, even if it had mainly been on the receiving end! Even the bad man!!! fights I have been in with my gals, where the determining factors had relied on the strength of the slap, or length of nails, had certainly taught me how to fight. But even now I still couldn't understand why she (my ex) left me for some mystery factor, who lurked in the shadows. And how whenever we talked about 'him' in the future, she always turned a pinker shade of pale, and fell into a little faint at the mere mention of his name!

I will show all of these 'rude boys' who's boss. So walking down those steps, I now imagine myself to be entering the WWF arena, thousands of fans cheering my name as I clamber over the ropes, and into my destiny. The ref gestured for us to shake hands, and we were go. Pacing round the ring the Under-taker faced the Giant Haystack. An impossible match, everybody said would never happen. Two giants of wrestling, colossals of their age, stood shoulder to shoulder pulling off suplexes, clothes-lines and full nelsons like there was no tomorrow. And he was so sure of his formidable invincibility that by the time they had reached the bottom of the stairs the fight was already over!

GO! God shouted. And bang to the head, bang to the head, he tried to block and as if he read my mind he dummied. Then bang, bang, bang, a series of punches in quick succession. He wasn't even in range. The guy fell to the floor, as if I wasn't even there, my body wasn't my own. Then now on the floor it was kick, kick, kick, kick. The match was over before it had even begun. One of them had won, but Jo would be damned if he knew who it was. Until he woke up the next day with a headache that even your granny couldn't imagine and total body bruises to match. It felt like he hurt all over. Not in the slightly pissed and pissed off way a boozer gets when he is denied his daily fix, but the kind unique to what an amateur feels after he gets a thrashing from a boxer/prisoner type whom he underestimated.

The next time I met Simon was in the street selling the Big Issue. I challenged him to a rematch in the park in an hour. I'd teach that retard who's boss, or die trying. Simon smiled and said he'd be there. Then my sense got the better of me and I changed my mind. Did I really want to get pounded to the ground again? So what if he hadn't let me get into my zone before our last fight? He hadn't even let me throw a single punch? What was that all about? You're not seriously telling me that he was setting me up for this next *fight*. Ah, the guy's a bloody black belt. Or if he isn't he should be. As a post pubescent being I've never had such a beating before or since. And if he thought he could finish the job, as you might say, in the park, he'd have another think coming.

I wasn't about to face that sucker on his own terms, without have pushed and pulled my muscle mass into at least some sort of martial extreme. I've always been good with the imagination, that's my forte you might say. And it does have its pros. But when you're one on one, there are other things that matter as well you know. From how quick, to how hard you punch. And yesterday I even threw a kick in a real fight situation as well. It worked I suppose you could say, even if the guy who I attacked was my cousin-in-law and wasn't expecting it in the least. What I'm trying to say is that I want to build up my gunnery before facing that devil again. So what if he's quick, with a bite and good insight? He ain't got Karmic justice has he? And he sure as hell doesn't have 'weakened monkey style' cos I just made it up myself yesterday? So what the f!!! does he have? Karate? Tae-Kwon-Do? Bah! Those are flower dances, and yeah I have seen how gay and self-righteous what goes on in those practice-halls really are.

So, returning to at least some semblance of reality, I measured my options like a string on a stick. Weak Monkey Way (Si Fa Dao), looked like my best bet. I was going to have to get over this virus which has been buggering me for the last week, get mean, and get even. I will have to learn how to push like he had never pushed before, to run, to swim, and to hit and possibly even kick. Sure I'll go to those old dojos, visit the masters and refuse to bow to them. I'll hit those walls and break other knuckles. I might get arrested again, although I bloody well hope not. I don't plan on returning to Britain in order to lose another seven (months)!

And I'll get strong. People will look at me funnily down the street as I plod along. They will ignore me on the roads, and serve the person behind him in the queue in the post-offices. But this didn't matter. I have now set my sights on the next target, truly the next level up. Defeat would mean a crushing blow. But the stakes are higher now. I'm not just fighting for myself, but for the dignity and honour of my friends and family too.

This is all well and good, but without the training I am going nowhere but to an early grave. My Doctors would recommend against fighting I imagine, given that half of my neck is fused together in an immovable blob. And my mental vulnerability leaves me open to abuse from the nerds who seem to rule our world, without justice or remorse. But a victory, and what a victory.

Even to face Simon on a level playing field, to square up to him, then dance round him. I want to throw the first punch at him. And I won't even tell you which hand I am going to use, in case he is reading this and so goes into the battle ready. Let's just say that I will fight him, on my terms as opposed to his. Maybe I will hijack a ref to manage the bout, instead of relying on one of his to blow the parting whistle. And whereas the other (fight) was in a narrow and restricted space where I barely had room to move, the next is gonna be on a f!!!!!! field. A park. I will kata, and animal form (from my monkey style remember) him out of the ring, and then once he is on the ground, I will follow him there with target connections. And if he doesn't go down. If he stands his ground and gives as good as he can get? Well I guess then I will get a beating. But I have about a year to train for this. A year of dedicated ninja dancing, of parries, target practice and foolish wands, to engage with the devil. I can learn to be invisible when the expert has all of the exits covered. To lift with a blob, and breathe without blood.

It isn't going to be easy. But I'll be damned if my sights aren't now set. Cheers guys.

Such was it that I feel right now, that it wouldn't be too soon if I single-handedly scalped every one of my foes in their sleep. After what they have done to me, all of these years of being imprisoned in a box, not like a man but an animal. Now I will show them animal rage. And with his last remaining men he drew back into the darkness. Tired by the day's fighting and eyes desperately seeking some sort of solace that the cover of night provided. He knew that today, the worst had come true. But even now he could not bring himself to realise this. To him he was still an all-powerful monarch, leader of men, undefeatable as indefatigable. But the dreams of the night would batter at his soul with the week's events, the loss of many good men under his command, ripped to pieces by a seemingly invincible force.

This was a campaign like none he had ever fought before. And now that it was nearly over he feared for the worst. But counting sheep as they jumped over a fence he finally got into the dream world which took away the eyes of the vampires, and replaced them with the gaze of willowy clouds. It would be a good sleep. He'd sure as hell earned it.

?: An adventure into Literature

Okay, I am now going to prepare a dummy post for the internet. I think that I am good enough to do this now. And once I have prepared what I want to say I can package it in a 'Jo' format. This is a literal 'dummy'! First though I'm goin to look at the things we need to address:

1   Apology or anger at Osprey. How to treat him given my 'win' there.

2   Approach to my friends/enemies/abstainers/ignorers/administration/Derby peops/general public on the site. Should I reveal to them my true intentions, or keep it under disguise?

3   Don't be afraid, but stand strong an proud? Is this the best way? Or should I act like a coward, until I pounce?

4   Keep up the momentum, I have still got some followers: hold on to them?

5   Challenge the presumptions/science of the readers? It's how I started and by continuing in this way only consolidates my confidence, does it not? Not just general science, but martial as well. Not too specific, such as against TaeKwonDo in general (which is going to hurt people's opinions), but more tangential perhaps. Let's say attacking the notion of pre-training stretches?

6   Show no weakness, or admit that I am mortal as are the rest of them?

7   Tell them my plans to knee-cap Si, invent 'Weak Monkey' style, and eventually rise to the top of the Martial Arts world, in total, or keep it secret?

8   Oh yeah strength of the baby, do not forget that? She is not worth a thousand Bruce Lee 'one inch' punches, but many more besides that!

I think that is a good point to draw a line.

So here would be a sample letter, with how I could address them directly (or get Jo to say it), point by point...

'Hi guys, how are you doing? *Being courteous, never hurt a fly.*

First of all I want to say 'What's up with Osprey?' *Actually I am just going to ignore this nerd/once enemy. I don't think that he, nor DavidLoPan are worth my breath, for that matter!*

So then, thanks to some of you for supporting me. *They have largely stayed hidden, and out of sight. Perhaps thinking that there is a possibility that I might win, but not quite believing it. So not this.*

So you are a bunch of spineless tits. *Too hard, would piss off the admins, so a no go.*

I don't even care if you are ignoring me. There is something that I have to do which you can have no part of. *Or maybe you watch me with the bemused experience of a balding uncle, who thinks that he has been there, and done that. Well I guarantee that where I have got my sights set, none of you have been, let alone dreampt!*

I'm now going to plan a first draft for this story:

1   New parent goes on a holiday with pregnant wife to Tycross zoo.

2   It is an overcast day, and on the way there it begins to rain.

3   Then out of the mist a hazy image of Marlon Brando appears, and tells them to avoid the apes.

4   They go to get refreshments.

5   On the way to the shop they find a soggy leaflet on the floor, and on the cover of the leaflet the face of a laughing jackal. Then inside, an advertisement for a new mobile phone brand, say xt2k. They bin this in the nearest bin.

6   Next he cracks his knuckles when his fianceé's back is turned. He wanted to help her, but also knew that before he could do anything he needed to help himself.

7   He feels incapable of helping himself, and so punches a sign post with the gorilla pen on it, in frustration. His missus (Sarah) asks him 'what's wrong?', and he explains that he just

has a feeling that he has been shat upon, although he can't put a finger on by whom.

8   Then he flexes his knuckles again, and this time he punches the ground. Sarah ignores him and suggests that they go to visit the monkeys, and take care of whatever it was he had bothering him.

9   Then he looked at the normal people in the crowd, the everyday people going about their everyday lives. He shuddered at the realization that they would never know the reasons for what he must do.

10   He watched them carefully one by one, until they all disappeared out of view. Or something like that. Maybe it began to rain, and they had all brought coats or brollies, only he was left without. His gal offered him hers, but he declined, and got wet.

11   He got wet, but didn't care. Then he saw a little baby being pushed along by a mother eating an icecream, and he pulled a funny face which made the baby cry!

12   Let's have him taken down in the end by the zoo guard, or even the monkey can be put down? This shows that martial arts are not the ultimate way, and that the LAW is, or at least gives that impression!

13   Immortality let's us change that last point. As the guard closes in with the tazer, Jo can spin a backfist in to his face, cracking open his jaw, and leaving the sorry mess on the floor.

I'm not going to turn it around again, we have already had more turnarounds then a tacky pop-tart!

14   We could however have the guard whimpering on the floor, and begging for his life, as Jo stood with the Tazer, holding it perilously close to the critical position (of the guard's neck).

15   I also want us to have him blow smoke up in to the air, and watch for the patterns it makes. This is both a references to some of the martial arts website idiots, and other things.

16   Finally he puts the Tazer down, and walks away. He wanted to hurt him, to put him in a world of great pain. Then he remembered all of the times when he has been hurt himself in the past, kicked in to the mud by the schoolyard bullies, and laughed at without remorse. And he wouldn't stoop so low.

17   He walked away knowing that he has made the right decision. That by having let the zoo warden live, he had spared an innocent man of his life. He didn't want his baby's father to be a murderer, in or out of jail. And he had a hope, a certainty now even, that God had great things in store for their family. That he would get that post in the office, that he had been working so hard towards. And that his fiancée would give birth to a beautiful baby girl, probably the most beautiful baby in the world! As they walked in to the carpark, to get in to their Ford Siesta, the rain stopped, clouds cleared and a glorious rainbow crowned the sky!

18   On the way out he saw a little kid pick a purse out of the handbag of an old granny, and yelling he gave chase. Then on catching the boy, the kid started to cry, so he relented and let go. But he got the purse back, and returned it to the grateful granny, who hadn't even noticed that it had gone! She took it back though, and was then very grateful.

Let's put this in to the storyboard now!:

33: A Day at the Zoo

Jo and his wife to be, had travelled for two hours down to London, to spend a hopefully entertaining day at Twycross Zoo. His partner, Sarah, was expecting for five months now, although they hadn't found out the sex of the baby yet. They wanted to leave that for a surprise.

After they had paid the admission fee and stepped through those pearly gates they saw lots of different people looking at different animals. Big men looking through the aquarium at strange fish, kids looking at crocodiles and women admirably eyeing up the elephants. But what he and Sarah had most hoped to see were the monkeys. Not the orang-utans, they were anyone's cup of tea. But the silver backed mountain gorillas, that rare and now endangered breed of species, once popular from the plains of Siberia to the Chinese jungles, now headed for the way of the Dodo. And it is only places like Twycross that protects them from total extinction on the part of the brutal and merciless hunters, who take them for their meat and hides. They can fetch quite a bob on the black markets you know?

Half way there to the indoor monkey pen and it began to rain. Not a mild pleasant drizzle which frees the air of the day's sin, and gently brushes the skin. But that harsh oppressive rain, which like a headache, just makes the day feel bad. Jo had actually begun to enjoy the day at this point, but with this parting blow could take no more.

'I'm going to the toilet,' he lied to his missus, as he snuck behind a pen to light up. And as he fell for one last time into that inexplicable and irresponsible trap, as he held that dagger to his throat and gently pushed it in, he considered destiny. He watched the smoke rings fill the sky, saw clouds in their faces, and they spoke to him. He told himself it was nothing but he thought he could hear Marlon Brando tell him that on his daughter's wedding, a father was the proudest he had ever been. And that he would honour this pride to the death, if it need be.

With these happy thoughts playing through his head, and a still slightly dizzy and euphoric nicotine hit buzzing past his eyes, he returned to his missus happy and thoroughly satisfied. The minute he returned to her she new something was wrong. She could smell it on his breath and he had done so well.

'You've not been smoking again have you?'

'No,' he lied, pleadingly. But she didn't believe a word of it. Then she looked him up and down and held out her hand. He knew exactly want she wanted, and reluctantly handed them over. Then she took out a pair of scissors from her handbag, and neatly snipped each cigarette in two. Seeming to take indifference at the discomfort this caused him! Nothing more was said of it.

Inside the monkey pen, there were a few gorillas sitting about. But they were a far-cry from what Jo had imagined they'd look like from TV. They seemed somewhat smaller, and more boring. He tried pulling a face at them to stir a reaction. It wasn't that they couldn't see him, more like they just couldn't be bothered to react. And so he walked away pretty disappointed really. And looking back for one last time he considered what a bunch of weak monkeys they really were!

On the way back to the car-park, Jo told Sarah, 'Well I didn't think much of the gorillas! They weren't a patch on them on TV!' Sarah grunted something about thinking the same.

Then he said, 'Well if I ever get my own zoo, which I very may well do, at least you never know, then one of the first things that I will do is give the monkeys a larger pen, and possibly an outdoor playground area as well to hang about it. How depressing to be stuck in there all day, sitting on that same dirty straw eating bloody yellow bananas!'

It was truly a sad sight. But it was an oversight to suggest giving the sad gorillas an outside bit, seeing as they did actually already have one, the doting couple just hadn't noticed it yet.

But despite whatever disappointments the day had held, both Sarah and Jo unanimously agreed that the day had been a success. And they looked forward to their next trip to the zoo together. And as they drove away, the rain subsided, the clouds parted and a fragile rainbow filled the sky.

OK that's it guys, I hope you like it? (This last comment is not for publication). This final version wraps up the objectives nicely and comprehensively. It appears to an outsider to just be some story, perhaps with a moral. Whereas in fact it is a martial assertion of complete control and dominance over these puny people! I wonder if anyone of them will cotton onto this?!

Boy that was surely a bloody minded work of art! And most definitely the greatest piece of writing I have ever done before! It attacks, links, parries, throws and finishes in less time then it takes for a normal person to say 'Jackie Chan'. And with such grace!

But you know what, I'm not even gonna give them that! What, this rag-tag bunch of losers don't deserve a literary masterpiece of such acclaim. You've gotta be joking?! Do you really think that I'd put out a display of such greatness, so far above the heads of most of their miserable existences, only to have it mocked, and worse ignored. Nah, man. That one is mine.

Sure I'll give them a story with monkeys in it alright. I'll make one up right now:

Jo was a monkey: a silver-backed Siberian Gorilla in fact. He spent his days hunting little goats and chameleons in the jungle, and the nights cozying up with his loved one in his pride. Jo was a strong gorilla, his muscles were rippling and he could easily tear the ears off a hyena if one ever even dared cross his way.

Then one day Jo met another gorilla: Bob. Bob was bigger than Jo. He had bigger muscles, could climb higher, run through the trees for longer and just generally outdo Jo in every possible way. This made Jo upset. Very upset. So upset in fact that he used to spend the nights crying himself to sleep. He was no longer the 'king of the monkeys' but now just another o-rang-u-tang. Geeze. And as he got older his eyesight began to fail him. He could no longer catch the hyenas who teased him with some wicked and merciless sense of cruelty. If only he was ten years younger, if his joints weren't failing him, if the damn kids would have a bit more respect.

His family still loved him; they always would he hoped. But as the silver back turned grey a once very strong monkey became a weak one. In one of these twilight days of his life, he came across a little chimp playing alone in the field. She was practising some bizarre set of moves, so strange; he approached her and inquired,

'What are you doing little monkey?'

'Hi, my name's Sue.' She smiled, 'it's called monkey kung-fu, here care to try?' She laughed as she then lunged forward to push him over. Instinctively he grabbed her wrists to counter, and she fell to the ground laughing. 'See it's easy,' she said 'just follow me.' And they spent the rest of the day rolling about in the mud getting thoroughly wet and dirty. The next day one of the old village elders approached Jo with stern words and revoked him, 'I hear that you have been playing about with one of the youngsters' he hissed. 'Clearly this will not do.'

Jo instinctively agreed, and let her go. He wondered if he had begun learning the kung-fu style before now he might have had a chance to fight his enemies, the jackals and the rest of them, before it was too late. But that now it was too late.

He could not fight like David and Goliath, much less Casanova. The books bored him, and TV – well, that was like even worse. He still had his family, he still had his friends, and his lifetime collection of banana skins. What could any-other self respecting monkey possibly want?! That night Jo fell into a deep and peaceful sleep. He dreamt of jumping sheep and flying carpets. Gushing through the clouds and over mountain valleys. It was probably the best night's sleep he'd ever had. And God rest his soul, for it was the last one he had as well.

34: Brown Belt

Wow, I think that one's even too good for them! It is, if anything, a fitting testimony to mine and dad's old counsellor, who helped me a lot through a rough patch, even if not protecting me from my last fall. But I remember a couple of good MA stories he told me, about chi transmission through human contact, that will stay with me forever. And I think that he probably is a black-belt, even though he denied it. See there is a lot more to fighting than just boxing. In fact, the fact that his company only charged what their clients could afford to pay, demonstrates how just and honourable he is. These are, as I think I have already mentioned, dying traits in today's brutal and godless world. So let's try another one. Oh yeah, and one more thing, I think that God may have actually demonstrated to me His existence in very real terms when I was dying in the city back then. He showed me his rainbow, delicate and fragile in the sky, but beautiful and indomitable none the less. And anyone who knows the significance of these words can hopefully join us as His believers, and Him, in regaining His world from the treacherous and wicked men. I am not there fully yet. But I think that I have started down a path from which now, by this point, there can be no return. It is not about the money. I get what I can steal. It is about the love. And that is priceless!

Peace guys. But seeing as they're gonna want something tomorrow, let's see if I can't cut up some silly little diddy to satisfy their appetites!

Man, this is getting too easy! I come in here looking for a fight and what do I get? The worst any of your can throw at me is Osprey's 'Shut the f£^$ up', and now even he's fluttered off, perhaps to where he belongs? So what does that say of the rest of you?

Listen, I guess most of you know how to fight, and I'm sure that you all can last a lot longer under the sheets than I ever did. But you know it's still possible to have nice sex, with a small d!! Yeah, and more to dancing than black man's moves. In this same way there is more to unarmed combat than black men's fighting. And I realise that I am going to have to prove myself before making this assertion. But as I said already I've been playing this game for too long now.

I know I can escape the law and doctors, but it bloody well hurt in the process and I've got no intention of letting them get their crooked fingers on me again. (Ed note: but they did!) This time I want blood. You've hurt me and my wife. So seriously I'm going to learn how to fight if it kills me. Then when I do, do you really think I'm gonna hold back? Forget what you've done to me? Laughed as I cried, as I got f**ed, f**ed good and proper?

Nah man, it ain't gonna happen. There is gonna be retribution you mark my words. I can't say when, or how, just this ring on my left says you're gonna stay, and the five little pinkies on my right say your gonna get bad man!!! slapped like the bad man!!!(es) you are. Sorry, bad men that should read.

So what next? You guys just keep up the charade. Run your dojos like the imperial museums they're not. Charging those poor helpless suckers money for a pretence which they're never gonna be able to use. And even I don't like to fight; it gets me in trouble see? Not to mention I don't like getting hit!

What I was saying is that I actually think that most of you are cowards, and perhaps all of you don't realise of what I am capable. It is not just a man's cardiovascular index which determines the effectiveness of his action, but his conviction as well. If you are truly convinced that what you are doing is righteous and true, that you can defeat these lying a!!!!!s wherever they be, and punish the punishers, then good luck. I know I'm gonna need it.

But funnily enough, I ain't even scared. I'm actually quite looking forward to it. What do you think was worse, having my neck taken apart and put back together, or suffering seven months away from my gal when I knew she was being raped on a daily basis, and there was nothing I could do about it? How do you think that made me feel? Man, it's not good. I'm telling you this 'cos out of every thousand t*$%s who read this page, I think there will be one or two good people. And it is to you I am appealing.

Hopefully you will continue to hear from me on a regular basis from now on. I don't have local internet, but they've got it in the village and town. Keep up the good work, and let me know how you're getting on. Even these little touches will be like special to me.

For too long have the traitors got away with murder, and the piss-artist-head do-gooders jobs-worth p!!!!s let these rapists control the world, with their military and the rest. Not any more, and not if I can help it. One by one I intend to assess the targets and take them out. I don't know who you are yet? And I ain't gonna let you know before I hit you am I? That would defeat the purpose.

The next day Jo went back outside and again found the ragged rug sitting under the tree. Again he perched on top of it and imagined himself flying off to far and distant exotic locations and meeting strange and exciting people, and getting up to interesting and amazing things. He imagined himself also to far and ancient arenas, facing weapons racks and having his choice. From them he picked the bo staff, and then faced tigers and grizzlies that he pounded with the accuracy and brutality of a man who truly knows what he does. Then after all the beasts were left bloodied and either dazed or dying on the floor, he turned to face the human gladiators. Dressed in some kind of outlandish armour, and holding brutal and barbaric exotic weapons, some of which he had never even seen the likes of before, he looked at them. And they, or some of them at least, returned the stare. And it was less a kind of fear so much as a mutual admiration for the other's abilities which stood the two apart. At best. And at worst, they simply despised him, and regarded him with a sense of futility and a desire to teach him a lesson that he'd never forget. Jo was a great believer in education. But thought that maybe this was one class that   he didn't want to attend.

Then Jo started running. Slow at first, a slow jog actually slower than walking speed. But seeing as he was out of shape, it was fast enough for him. And he was running, not away from, but towards his enemies! What? You might cry, was he insane? Well either that or very brave! But either way he wanted to settle this thing one way or another, and if there was going to be bloodshed, then so be it.

The police and army-heads stood by on the sidelines bemused at this act of insane curiosity. They weren't about to interfere, and were quite happy to let this hooligan run into whatever peril he had awaiting him.

But Jo wasn't afraid. And if anything he felt strangely confident and, as he rapidly closed in on his foes, they were all watching him now. Some had even taken up defensive positions. He held his bo high above his head and began swinging it round. And began to let out a cry, so loud and fiendish that even the pigeons in the trees got scared. And his first opponent, a black-belt from New Orleans, was indeed taken by surprise. He hadn't been looking and got smacked by the staff, right off his pedestal. He then lay on the floor in a heap for the rest of the action.

The next combatant Jo faced was a brazen six foot South-African. Jo lunged at him, but was gutted to find the staff taken off him, to receive a clout on the head and ass with it, and then on the ground to be held into submission with the wood sharply cutting into his throat, just waiting for the order, which never came.

Jo had been beaten, thoroughly and comprehensively. He was told never to show his face around these parts again, and that if he did they wouldn't go so easy on him. Then he was politely shown the door with someone's boot, and left a muddy heap on the dirt track outside the city. He had failed again, in his attempts at world domination. He had to pick himself up, dust himself down, and try to at least pretend to find a semblance of a way how to return to reality. To make a living for himself and find some meaning to his fragile and bruised life.

But not now; now he was hurting all over. And he was angry. He curled up into a ball and began to cry.

login: john2054

password: damn**

<user registered. 01-01-2008 23:17>

<select destination>

:government access logs

<access denied. Unauthorized user priority>

:initiate protocol override codename blackfox

<blackfox initiated. Full admin access enabled>

(how can I help you today sir?)

:government access logs

<government records: public registry office, criminal inter-bureau database, national immigration bureau, public health records, political targets, military business>

:access criminal inter-bureau database

<verified. Accessing database… 1585 records found.> (what now sir?)

:find *sergeant mathers*

<searching sergeant mathers. 2 records found. M27ogj new-york black jag reg hu 287: F18vss brooklyn >

<access M27ogj>

<sergeant mathers. Male 27, 2 parking violations, skipped parole, resisting arrest. Current status: unknown>

:log-out

<exiting criminal inter-bureau database>

:access military business

<military investigations. Full access>

:run prog birdman

<initiating birdman. Accessing servers. 27 servers currently connected.> (what now sir?)

:list servers

<pentagon, whitehouse, national bureau of accounts, criminal department, war-office, graphic design, media wholesale, international business, kinder-garden schools, automobile registry, civil aviation authority, public library database, national farmers association ... >

:access pentagon

<logging in. protocol refused. Unauthorized system access, initiating system shutdown. All systems privileges revoked. user access revoked. Tracing ip address, trace initiating...>

:systems logout

<invalid user-command>

:protocol override code 2078

<invalid user-command. Initiating self-destruct sequence 5,4,3,2,1><game-over>

As Jo ninja-danced into the early hours of the morning, he contemplated what he would do to his nemesis in his head. As his bodies carried out the moves, attacks and counters, and grooves to some really perverted dance music, the whole of the rest of the world seemed to lift up away from him. All was left was nobody dancing like he'd never danced before. This is the moment he vowed to dance every day until the day he died. It is something he enjoys, and every time he does it seems to improve his confidence and ability.

In the cyber café later in the day, he told his cousin in law, Sammy, who was there escorting him at the time, 'Man, if I ever catch that freak who hurt my wife when we were separated...'

'You'll what?' Sammy inquired, 'beat him?'

'Er, kill him more like.' And I meant it. The thing is she won't even tell me his real name, let alone where she found him. (Although I have a pretty good idea, the army barracks! And I'm hardly going to go strolling around there picking fights now, am I?)

So where does that leave me? Back to scratch? Hardly. I now have a beautiful wife and baby, and a happy future for the rest of my life with them together, or so I hope. No man could ask for any greater treasure! Now I need to spend quality family time, consolidating on our promise to each other, and helping the baby to grow into a strong and capable young woman. It won't happen overnight. And I see no reason that I can't at least devote some of my spare time to the world of ninja dancing and other forays into the martial world as a pastime, which I can continue to degree level and hopefully beyond, with our return to Britain sometime in the not too distant future.

I still sincerely believe that it is a country filled to the brim with assholes. From the police, to the population, even to people you meet in the supermarket sometimes. I'm not saying that there aren't any good people out there. Just that they seem to be few and a rarity.

My friends are all good people. We fight for justice and truth. But that's another story. So how do I punch through a wall? Not by using my fist surely (that is a reference to the task I have ahead of me, and how I am going to do it!)

I know there are plenty of people all over the world who have immersed themselves in working hard, content to follow the sins and prejudices which their community endorses. But be it one way or another, I find myself out of that system. So whereas my work skills are near non-existent, my moral responsibility and mental capacity is high. And this is despite whatever the Doctors may say.

So where does that leave us now? Another story written that's all. I'm getting pretty good at writing these now I hope you'll agree. And I write with a translucent quality which mimics the truth so closely that I invite my readers into the worlds of my memories and experience, to witness the world in hopefully new lights. And also hopefully help them to see things in new ways.

417

I hope to continue writing for a long time. And one of these days I even want to fully commit myself to a comprehensive martial program for a long enough time that it will actually give me one day that prestigious pedigree of a master. This is where I have set my sights, and hopefully with my wife by my side, this all will become possible!

Now for what must surely be the last time, Jo lay back in the hospital bed and closed his eyes. The virus of mental deformity had returned. And surely this time there was no way out. It filled his nasal membranes with mucous, his eyes with tiredness, and his mind with anger. The medical establishment in the UK had been quick to put together a reaction force that comprised a Doctor, social worker and community psychiatric nurse who had first taken their baby off them and put her into care. This certainly broke her mother's heart, and despite Jo's best attempts to reassure her that everything was going to be okay, it most surely was not.

Now he found himself trapped here again. He imagined his enemies laughing from the high walled towers from whence he imagined they lived. Sipping champagne and reading the Beano. They had caught him, and be damned if they weren't gonna make him suffer. And what's more they would always get him. Always take away his gal, wherever she might be. Until he was an old and lonely man. Thoroughly shamed in the face of the public; the only one who truly understood him being the feral street cats and pigeons that he used to feed the scraps of chip suppers he had left after he had finished eating them.

But you can hardly fight a war with just cats and pigeons on your side! For one thing they would probably spend all the time chasing each other! And even if they were as courageous as any of these cowardly men and women, they could hardly load a gun, or ride a chariot, could they?

So now, as I think I mentioned, he was back. And things were exactly the same. Doctors didn't listen, the nurses were a mixed bunch with a few gems, who despite what they may say were thoroughly untouchable, most of the patients are indeed nutters, although with enough redeeming qualities to put them at least on a par with the majority of the hospital staff, certainly above many of the Doctors, and it seems to be the cleaners who actually run the place! Again it took him a good four and a half months before even getting any leave. And it took him that long to even start to regain a semblance of coherent social reality. His head was spinning. He was walking into walls. And my heart got broken.

All these years of love we had invested in each other had been effectively dismantled by the British state, just as I had feared that it would. And I had told her about this, that I feared it would happen. She didn't believe me, assured me that it would be okay, that love conquers all and all that crud. But where was love when the bullet shredded JFK's brains, or Lennon's for that matter? Was she taking a vacation, or maybe the seventh day off?

Now I could barely find the strength to lift my hand to change the hospital inbuilt TV remote, from one cruddy daytime sitcom to another. Not that it mattered, and not that they even had TVs in the rooms back on those wards. They didn't. If you were lucky you got your own room. Or (as proven by the fact that you were in there) if lady luck was sh!tting on you, you would find yourself in a shared ward, normally of between 6-8. Smoking out of the window if you were lucky to be granted a bed-side view. And if you weren't, well smoking anyway. Cigarettes had then been banned from the inside of all the hospital buildings, and I think the government is trying to fuse it out altogether. But try telling that to the few of us tobacco heads who, despite what we may say, will always remember the love of the weed.

So I pounded the wall and consequently broke another knuckle. I would have to make sure the meds didn't see that as well lest they got me into more trouble than I was already in. To the outside world all us 'nutters' clearly deserved the punishment we were getting. We must have done something bad to have posed such a risk to have had us put there in the first place, right? Maybe, but try telling us that at the time. 'Cos I guarantee it sure doesn't feel like that.

Despite only having done it three or four times now, and the fact remains that I could never dance, and have always had two left feet, I have always wanted to be able to. And now it seems as if by the strength of my sheer will power alone, I have learnt how to do it. Not follow step routines – they're for monkeys – but create my own grooves and moves for like two hours solid, the only rest being for a glass of water in the middle. Sure it is possible that my dancing would probably be considered rather gay by the majority of the 'normal' public. But I'm really past the stage of caring what anybody else thinks. When I get that feeling, say when I hear some good music beats in the street, I just start bopping. I suppose one of the key moments in my dance exploration development was on the large (approximately half a million) Stop the War (Iraq) demonstration in London. There, along to the music of the big band marching alongside us, we danced our way to victory.

This is a moment I will never forget: the streets full of us ordinary people, multi-cultural and unique dancing along and having a great time. I have seriously never before had such a great feeling of community togetherness in Britain, neither before nor since. And I suppose it's possible that we never will again. But that won't take away from the greatness of the event itself. (Ed note; not true, we only last month had another demonstration to 'Free Palestine'!)

And what's even more important, is that it wasn't the VIPs or speakers on the stage of the demo at the end of the march who were the attraction of the show (a generally mundane and uninspiring lot) but the actual rally itself which was the highlight of the show. Being part of something greater than its constituent parts on a really international level. And they tried to play it down in the media, giving us little or no mainstream news coverage. Probably the people who control the news (trust me the news is controlled) were of a different political persuasion to us marchers, and hence found no need to mention such a life changing event.

But really on the days of those rallies (there must have been about four I went on, and more besides that), I found that little bit of 'soul' confidence that my life needed. That little bit of encouragement to press ahead with my conviction despite when everyone else was howling for me to say 'stop'. And now it seems like we have had an impact, with a good section of the population, perhaps even Mr Tony Blair himself, regretting the invasion. He lost his job over it. But at the time we were in the distinct minority, and there was a vicious and very vocal group calling for our heads, for not supporting 'our boys' and any other such crud as that: the plonkers.

Now the war is over. Iraq is still a mess, with more innocent civilians being blown up every day. But at least the responsibility for this falls squarely on the shoulders of mainly a few, now largely discredited Washington heads and commanders alone. Not that they would ever be man enough to accept it. And we continue with our everyday lives. Perhaps never again will the people rise to power, take to the streets in the millions to fight something that they know is wrong, despite what they have been told. It's about having an ethical conscience boys and girls, and that is 'God's' work; don't you forget it.

But here we go again, I'm preaching at you and some of you are gonna whinge. It's like Sunday school all over again, complete with that bearded man, and his stone tablets up on that mountain. You know I am both a Buddhist and a

Christian. Some of you will never be able to understand what that means. The way you have been brought up and dictated to, drilled into your bones that there can only ever be one right or wrong way. And I'm not about to try and dissuade you now. But there are certain advantages to being 'multi-faith' such as it lets me agree with pretty much anyone I want to (people I like, and get good vibes from for instance), and riddle with theological bullets any p!!!!s (not to mention any names!)

On that note I'm gonna leave it. Peace guys, get some rest.

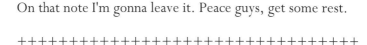

Hi guys. My enemies are all weaklings. They stick together like cowards for warmth, shivering in the day of the night's cold. All it takes is (for me to take out) one or two, and the whole house of cards topples with the domino effect which determines their fate. Aka as one is found out to be a liar, his or her faith to build on human distrust is undeceived, so too they stand on the toes of their next-door neighbour of whom they also know some dark secret. And in turn they bite the heads off their children, or parents, who go and hurt someone else. And this whole vicious cycle until eventually the community cannot take it any-more, and swamped by riots and lethargy the police go on strike, and the whole thing collapses into chaos and anarchy! Ha, that'd be the day!

I know that Rome, complete with its majestic coliseums and amphitheatres, wasn't built in a day, or its pyramids. But a hall built on rotten foundations, will fall down sooner or later. It is a matter of time. And that (wood)worm Bush is now fleeing the sinking ship (of his country's ideological status quo, just look at his Free Tibet speech in the Olympics if you want a concrete example of this), so too every American who voted for him are shown to be not as 'immune' from mistakes as they had previously believed (led on all the while by an earnest and over-enthusiastic press). This fabled democracy, which has proved impotent first in Iraq, now tumbles by the wayside. First in America, and then possibly even Britain! I mean it would if I had my way! See I am an old fashioned commie, as well as everything else. And I remember what you did to the USSR and Gorbachev, as well as everything else.

I also wanted to say this: It is not just a person's height of power which determines their strength of character, but also what they have had to overcome in order to get there. And what I mean by this is: big deal if you did well at school, got on the 'team', got some fit bird and the rest. But I'd like to see you survive a bullet down the spine like I have, not to mention the rest.

And I'm sorry if you don't understand the parables or syllogisms which I have used in this speech, but go and read a book will ya? Seriously just one, you illiterate and refutable oaf!

Patiently Jo considered his options. Sometimes you say things to clarify them for you in your own mind. You say them to have an effect. And at others, just because they sound well darn good! Everybody has a sphere of influence. Mine is zero/neo/infinite.

Again he looked down to the ring on his finger. He considered this more than just the vows he proudly made to his missus on that man-made day. More than a promise to his baby that he would look after her as she grew into an adult, and hopefully for the rest of mine (life) too. More than the memory of all of the pretty women I've kissed over the years.

But a commitment to striking terror into the hearts of the very terrorists themselves. Of combining the mental theoretical, social and sexual worlds into one complete source. And then wield it like an axe, to devastating effect. Yeah, this sounds cool; he smiled, half way through his ice-cream!

The next morning Jo awoke with a splitting headache. How long is this going to continue? He gingerly unzipped the net, got out of bed, only to find a neatly written hand note tacked onto the bedpost. 'I'll be gone for some time. Don't wait up.'

Great, he thought to himself. Away again. This marriage business wasn't all that it had been cracked up to be, he smiled. Then dragged himself into the bathroom, where he gleaned a look in the mirror and smiled again. He still had, after all these years. At least his handsome good looks hadn't escaped him.

Now dragging himself over to where the Nescafe was supposed to be he rattled the tin to hear a couple of musky mosquito webs lying there within. Great, another morning without coffee and drinking its poor substitute: chocolate. Well not today. Today he would go to the shops unescorted and find where they kept the Nescafe. Then with real Kenyan shillings he would inquire, using a subtle and sophisticated series of hand signals and grunts, the price, pay and return. All on his own! All without the missus, ever realising that he was gone! Yeah that's what he'd do; he'd show these natives who's the boss. Show these demeaning barbarians that he was back, and ready for trouble!

Then I realised the wife's all important message: 'Don't leave the house dear. There are bad men out there who would cut that finger off just to get at the gold.' And thought better of it.

Next he heard the door-bell chime, and rushing down the banisters was delighted and slightly ashamed to find the postman standing there holding two strange and obtuse packages, both with their address on it. The first was headed to john2054, and was a small and spherical object. The second, to his full and proper name: Jo the last great adventurer of the world, was a sturdy tube, about half a metre in diameter. He hoped he knew what these both contained. And after thanking the deliverer, he went into the lounge and frantically began to unwrap the packages.

On the way he noticed a box of tea-bags which he had forgotten that they had, then stopped to prepare and drink one, before continuing. Next he looked up to the bookcase where an old and perfectly preserved antique Jade sword rested on its holder; he brushed this aside to make room for the new goodies. Then it fell and cracked on the floor. Damn! he cursed; he'd liked that one and was such that it was worth a small fortune, more than the local crusted antique dealers had valued it at (a pittance!). He also knocked off at the same time four bronze Pussas (that's the Chinese for Buddha or so my reliable source tells me). They too cracked on the concrete below, and became worthless in the instant. And they too were worth a small fortune, he had imagined. Oh well. At least he could have donated a couple of them to charity, but it was too late now.

But still he had new goods. Inside the smaller present was a small but perfectly formed vial. He carefully unscrewed the lid and threw the empty container onto the floor below. On swallowing it this gave him a rush so intense, so profound, that it was better than any sex. Then the second package unwrapped to reveal a cylindrical tube, and with the lid off came a scroll. 'What the f!!!' he thought on discovering that on this weren't the detailed plans of the enemy encampment, which had been promised by the lousy ebay seller, but instead some crummy and archaic painting of a hundred tigers. What were they trying to say; didn't they know that the tiger was the Chinese symbol for femaleness? And where were the plans? That guy was definitely getting negative feedback, and damn the consequences.

427

So now in a bad mood he slumped back on the couch, poured himself another cup of tea and looked at the tigers. They did look pretty in their majestic and menacing form. It's a shame they stood little chance against today's modern rangers and poachers, equipped with the latest high tech. velocity rifles, laser guided some of them, he thought. Oh but they looked oh so peaceful out there in the Indian jungles or whereever it was they lived. Along with its brethren, the lion, the tiger has become known as one of the most formidable and lethal of the cats. And like the lion, they are quick as they are proud. Graceful as they are deadly. Surely a match for any man in the ring, or bush, were he to be stripped of all of those modern encumbrances that society provides for us.

Then throwing the parchment into the fire, he watched dazedly as the flames began to first lick, and then amass upon the old paper. A musty smell filled the room, and brown smoke drifted up the fireplace.

The enemy's camp was strong as it was flexible. This much he was certain of, and didn't need any bloody ebay plans to tell him. They had men, firepower, and reach. They were cunning, and bloody tricky at times. And he hadn't known a single time when they hadn't carried out a threat against him they'd promised. This had hurt a lot in the past, but now he was back up on his feet, trying desperately to find someone who could help him in his intention. But no one was listening. It seemed like he was going to have to do it on his own.

One man against the combined might of all of the world's armies and nations combined, oh what joy! Even the Dali

Lama in his limited wisdom had forsaken him, he realised after watching a discriminative episode of Al-Jazeera last night.

So what was left of it. And as the last embers of smoke made their fateful way up the journey towards the chimney and the clouds above; he would never be a ninja. This is what he now realised. His dad was right. They didn't exist, and were just the sole residents of Eric van Lustbader's and Stephen Hayes's collective imaginations. Now he gently slumbered off into another peaceful slumber, lightly clutching onto whatever it was on his left ring finger.

That evening on her return, Jo's missus found a phial on the floor, picked it up, read the label which said ninja potion on it, and chucked it away. I don't think she gave it a second thought.

Slowly Jo walked up and down the line of would be ninja applicants, roughly clutching their application forms in his hands. Who were these bozos who thought themselves good enough to train under him, let alone call themselves men? Some of the new ones began to chatter amongst themselves at the back of the line. 'ORDER!' He barked, and they promptly saluted. 'Yes Sir,' they replied.

He seriously doubted any of these so called black-belts would know how to scrub a floor, let alone kill a man. And he hadn't even heard of half of the styles they claimed to profess talent in. Brazilian Jujitsu? H-apkido (sounds like the sound you make when you sneeze!) Tae-kwon-do, sounds like some cheap oriental take-away, down Soho town!

Well he wanted to know what they could do for real, and so he pointed at two at random to step forward, and then told them to 'Fight!' Unbeknownst to him he had selected Caperwera and Karate Judoka. The Capi immediately fell to the floor preformed a double rotating, spinning axe flip, and then bounced to his feet. All the while nodding his head like one of those Churchill dogs off TV. Then the Karateka bowed before starting a kata consisting of similar axe kicks, bow stances and informed missionary positions. Then the two devils closed quarters, and what happened next nobody could believe. With the speed of lighting and the strength of tigers, the two men began bad man!!! slapping each other hard and fast.

Jo could barely watch. Never before had he witnessed such a brutal display of sheer hate and aggressive pain being inflicted on fellow men, in all his years. This had only gone on for thirty seconds at most before he yelled stop. But the two guys seemed to be getting carried away, and it was if they didn't hear him. This is exactly the same point the fat Shaolin monks began punching people in the line, and actually knocking them out. Soon the hall had descended into total anarchy, with blood-curdling screams filling the air as this once composed room of combatants exerted excruciating and terrible injuries on each other! There were fencers against footballers, gymnasts against clowns, and politicians against librarians! The whole thing looked like a bloody comedy of errors, except the punches they were throwing were very real, and mostly very hard.

Jo extracted himself from this mess, and gingerly clambered over a pile of bodies to make his way to the door. Who were these hooligans, and they called them disciples. Then after reaching the door and the fresh air on the outside, he put his hand on the knob and took one last look around to pay the scene a fond farewell before fleeing.

But now everyone seemed to be either dead or dying, or had at least let their better senses prevail and like Jo, retreated to a safe distance. Now only two remained. Both with tattered blacks hanging from their waists. A little kid ran around the outside of the ring, holding up a billboard and shouting out 'Ladies and gentlemen, welcome to the main event. Two fighters going to the death. Round One!' And then he shot back to sit and watch the fight from the sidelines. The kid had only one eyebrow. His other had been shaved off after received a beating by a group of those riverside gypsies who patrol the banks and prey on unsuspecting revellers, for their wallets, if not their arseholes! But that's a different story. (I can't remember his name now, only that he's Baz's mate. Okay?)

Next these already blooded men went for it. The first threw a punch which connected and another, which was countered into a lock. Then snapped. He showed no pain, but the bone could be seen hanging visibly from the skin. Then the assailant proceeded the lay a series of punches at his chest, breaking audibly three or four of his ribs. The victim now fell to the floor, struggling to breathe. Now it was clear that he was suffering. And the would be victor turned his back and smiled at the audience.

But by this time the hall had evaporated, and the Judoka mysteriously transformed into members of the crowd. They had watched the fight from a distance, and with a horrible fascination. He had won, punished this imposter who thought he could mock him. And now he had taught him a lesson he would never forget! With the broken arm, he would be in a lot of pain. And the snapped ribs would mean that it would be along time before he could breathe again normally, if ever.

The man thought his supremacy was assured. This is what he thought. Then he received a tap on the shoulder. Slowly he turned around. Standing before him was a half man, half zombie. With ribs protruding right left and everywhere, and one arm hanging limp by his side, he could have been an extra from a b-rate horror movie. But the ninja's second fist was hovering high above the air. So high it was out of his line of vision. He had no chance.

The fist connected so hard with the head in-between the eyes, it shattered the internal working of the central synapse and base spinal column. Blood rushed in to fill the void, and the invader dropped to the floor dead as a dodo. Then the ninja, stumbled away into the night. Never again would he let these bullies treat him in that way! He left before Jo could even get his name! And that my people, is a true story.

35: Jojutsu Syllabus Rewrite

1st kyu: pass your GCSEs

2nd kyu: kiss a girl/boy

3rd kyu: visit another country

4th kyu: leave home

5th kyu: win a fight

6th kyu: have sex

7th kyu: make friends with strangers

8th kyu: be homeless for a day

9th kyu: get arrested and spend twelve hours in police custody (minimum)

10th kyu: feed the pigeons and or ducks/geese/swans

11th kyu: dance

12th kyu: learn some Shaolin kung fu/chi-gong moves

13th kyu: write a book

black belt: make a baby laugh

2nd dan: walk for ten miles in a day

3rd dan: take down a cyber-enemy

4th dan: read one of Stephen Hayes's ninja books

5th dan: go on a march in London (or any other capital city)

6th dan: develop your own form of movement

7th dan: paint

8th dan: pray

9th dan: sing

10th dan: be happy

Now Jo patiently fell into a deep meditation which is the exclusive reserve of monarchs, parents, and other lonely parasites. He considered the meaning of life, the bows and flows of angel clouds, and other such things. He considered the reserve's native American Indian's totem poles, and the power of supreme control and philosophy. He continued the inspiration of spontaneous reaction and terrible, unanticipated response. He continued the authority of Karmic responsibility and the guilt of Karmic sin. And he considered how hard he would ever hit one of those f!!!ers if he ever caught them in the act.

Now he considered the humour of Drunken Monkey Kungfu, and what drink is my favourite tipple. He also considered what his favourite pub is (the Mallard), and how when they get back they would go there again definitely. He was especially impressed with the size of the king-sundaes. For 5-95 you get a dish to feed a king, or two infact, and that's just the ice-cream!

I still consider Britain to be a place full of rats and ass-holes. Two timing selfish good-for-nothings and jobsworths, just irritating nothings. He clenched his fist again, the one with the ring on it. Now he glanced across to his little angel who was sleeping, and he considered that he would never leave her. She brought faith and hope to both me and my missus, and makes real everything that was previously unreal. And I also consider it one of my ambitions, to turn around the sorry state of affairs which is the current martial form in the UK at the moment. How all of the old masters have been driven under-ground, and my ambitions, spiritual or otherwise, spurned like I'm just some jack in the ass and not a sincere fighter. Well I will show them, with the speed of a ninja, and the conviction of a hero. Yeah, that's what we'll be: heroes.

Disclaimer: the belts awarded to the students are done totally at the discretion of the present master of the school and are done so in according to his wishes. The guidelines below are only to help him (me), and are neither all-inclusive nor restrictive. But they are the basis of the framework which should be adhered to if at all possible! Also do not feel obliged to share these with your students recklessly. They can learn about them as I see fit!

I am also going to give a rank with each kyu, which should summarize the grade reached, and write a short paragraph. The requirements shouldn't be seen as a restrictive syllabus, but rather a base guideline on which a student should aspire.

Yellow 1st kyu Elemental: The student should master the five elements of them, fire, water, wind, earth and light. He or she should have a good use of his body, be able to use it as weapons and also wield a pair of nunchucks, or other appropriate weapon with confidence and ease. They should have good target recognition and be able to assess the threats of relevant people. They should have the ability to take them out if needed, or otherwise neutralise the threat they pose. They need to be generous and good character types, giving and loving without exception. And they need to be able to punch.

Orange 2nd kyu Cosmic: The student should have moved up a level from Elemental. As well as a total mastery of the elements, they need to have an understanding of how they interact with the other, the relevant dominance and order of things. And the power of things. They need to also have a complete use of physical weapons, tools and machines. Being able to use these with ease. They also need to have good empathy and characterisation skills, and be able to understand the motivations and reasons behind a person's/people's actions, even before they have made them. (This can clearly be tested for!) Target recognition needs to move up to threat assessment/analysis, and a comprehensive action plan realised complete with probabilities (this again can be tested for.). Characterisation needs to be enhanced to mirror the animal types and movements in basic combat situations, and also find the sense of humour in things. They should now be able to kick.

3rd kyu red Spiritual: This grade furthers the level of required abilities and characteristics expected from the Judoka. At this stage the student is expected to be able to handle him or herself comfortably in a fight. This includes being able to punch, kick, grab, hold, basic throws, weapons and open hand attacks. They also need to be able to comfortably dance for sustained periods of time, do push ups and or pull ups. They also need to be able to dance nicely, and without fear, for a decent period of time. In this dance they should be able to demonstrate/execute the moves they have learnt. When they attack, they should be able to control themselves, and work towards a required target/state of affairs. They should have a good world socio-political understanding, and also a good family consciousness. This should include but not be limited to the ability to speak with babies, old people, spouses and children authoritatively but sensitively. They should be confident in their martial ability and prowess. They should be able to disappear in a crowd of people, or on the street. And feign their moves before making them. They should have a good emotional awareness, also knowledge of what they are capable of. They should learn to harness the power of anger, and equally compassion as either overtakes them. And equally restrain and curb the emotional output in any given situation. The spiritual fighter needs to be a man (or woman if that's your preference). This is the first grade which requires complete responsibility for your actions, and a certain level of insight over the world around you.

4th kyu blue rainbow: I can think up some more stuff for this grade later.

5th kyu purple monkey: ditto

6th kyu pink drunkard: ditto

7th kyu brown trainee Ninja: ability to fight large groups of people and win. To piss people off and start fights for desired (hidden) purposes. And to shield true intentions from all but other Jujutsu ninjas. To use mind control techniques to craft destiny. And create rainbows.

1st dan black Ninja: At this grade the user will be awarded or choose for themselves a name. To become a ninja requires a comfortable and complete authority over the spectrum/syllabus requirements so far. Ninjas are as lethal as they are deadly. Masters of this kungfu, need to be able to move and fight like animals and switch at their will. They also need to be able to create weather patterns and have an influence on the outcome of world events. This will include but not be limited to international spiritual perception. They also need to be able to teach people how to fight, to take on students. With speed and grace, they need to be able to defend themselves in difficult situations. To fight their way out when their back is against a wall. Or at least survive an impossible situation without cracking. They need to be able to speak to animals, and make other Judoka stop and look at them, if not fear them. In order to do all of this they will need to be able to prove themselves to me. And to be a ninja they will need to bring night to day, and strike like lighting from the clouds. They will also need to have a good sense of rhythm, grasp of the importance of love, hope and charity and faith, have a certain level of translation/bilingual skills. They will have a good sense of commitment to the light side of the force, and indeed be well on the way towards Jedi status. They will be able to cook, and handle themselves in the pub. They will have a good knowledge and practical understanding of drugs, medicine and other martial arts. Including Jujitsu, Karate, Judo, Hoshinryjutsu, Caperwera, Taekwondo and Aikido.

2nd dan blackbelt Grandmaster: The gm needs to be more than just a man. More than just a ninja; the gm makes ninjas. He is a leader of men and a champion. Whereas all uncertainties held the people back, at 2nd dan the limits are no more. Communication is no longer limited to physical/sensory signals but reverts to signal based neo-metacomplexes. Physical strength takes a second place to epic philosophies. And the grandmaster's life should be viewed as a tangible testimony to the karmic destiny of mankind in general. This will require a series of thankless accomplishments, which must be chronicled and validated to carry the required authority. The GM should be able to answer for their every action, explain their every cause, and understand how the world is built on a series of differently qualitative foundations. They should have a good understanding of war history, including Vietnam, World Wars 1+2 and Iraq/Afghanistan. They need to be able to filter through the lies presented on the news to determine the factual validity and moments between events presented therein. And they need to have certain amounts of powers of control over the history, present, and future of the world.

3rd dan blackbelt: as yet undetermined title. I suppose the Judoka can help me to choose one for them at this level, something like supreme commander.

This is going to need to be something else. Whereas the grandmaster is a ruler of men, the supreme commander needs to be the leader of champions: one of the knights of the round table, of that ancient Camelodian mountain kingdom. They need to be able to teach babies how to walk. They need to be able to disguise their true ability, except for when they choose. They must be able to work, to support a family, and be a good member of the community. They need to be able to filter through the lies, and punish the offenders unhesitatingly and without remorse. They need to be ethical champions, craftsmen of literal communication. Emotional surf-boarders and artists. And surgeons of the martial arts. Money should no longer be a problem; they need to trust in God, and convict to him so that he frees their souls. They must be honest and sincere. Stalwarts of the truth and heroes of the underground. They need to be able to stand firm and alone. And not lie, deceive, or en-fraud. As well as family men, as well as physical mental social and MA champions, they need to be something else. They need to have taken this discipline to a new level. To have contributed to it in some irrevocable way, which will firmly place it in the history books for all of time. And they need to be a good friend!

36: Jopo Higher Rankings

10th dan: Buddha. A state unattainable by men so you can bloody well forget it!

9th dan: Arhat. A king amongst men and second in enlightenment only to Buddha himself. Arhat has complete wisdom insight, compassion, ability and prescience and presence. Ninja skills include being able to kill a man in broad daylight and suffer no repercussions (get away with it), both morally and for the world to see. Bitch slapping that innocent f%&£er I did last week is not quite the same thing, seeing as for a start I have had to go back on meds as a result when my Doctor found out, but at least the b$%^£ds haven't put me back in hospital. And you know they could've. It was bloody close; it actually took all of my ninja skills to avoid it including the handshake! Another ninja skill this guy will possess is invisibility.

8th dan: Oracle. A being of supreme knowledge and wisdom, the oracle is able to predict the future and reflect upon the past with such accuracy as if to make the three realms of time turn into one. This owes in a large part to his inner wisdom and active experience history. Ninja skills include lethal moves, death touch, invisibility potion, lightning speed and giant's shout.

7th dan: Lover. Must have a caring and genuine soul and make decisions in his life based not on the colour of someone's skin but the content of their character. Must be able to and enjoy swimming (or other therapeutic activity), be a good kisser, love all people (or most of them at least), go for the occasional jog, know how to play at least one sport, and have active membership in at least two different Martial Arts, or have attained blackbelt in one. Oh yeah and Jopo doesn't count! HA-HA-HA. Also I don't want any virgins for this one, you BUGGERS!!!

6th dan: Legend. Good communicator, reader, good at making friends.

37: Hacking to Oblivion

username logon: john2054

password: damn***

<access permitted, entering blogosphere intranet. Accessing accounts… User level entry 1>

: list 'martial: arts'

<tae-kwon-do, judo, karate, Jujitsu, aikido, hoshinryjutsu, kenpo>

: input $jujutsu:7 kyu:3 dan: 3 members

<$jujutsu:7 kyu:3 dan. input *member>

: 1 member. john2054: dob 030381 NI JR98damnC tel 0798damn*** country Kenya city Nairobi married: affirmative ranking:1st dan

: 2 member. chunkybeefsoup: dob na NI na tel +44753damn*** country United Kingdom city Derby married: affirmative ranking:2nd kyu

: 3 member. sammy: dob na NI na tel +0723damn** country Kenya city Nairobi married: affirmative ranking:3rd kyu

: input jujutsu, a new and novel take to the martial arts for beginners and veteran alike. it's free to join and easy to get into. Simply send an email requesting entry to john2054@yahoo.com and await further details on how to register. combining skills from a variety of other ancient combat traditions, jujutsu puts it all together in an easy accessible and complete fighting method. the instructor will start at your level, and teach you the basic safety preparation of break-falls and hand strengthening, before moving onto combat, spirituality and ninja training as the grade progresses. This is not a style for half-arses or macho d!!s, whip-asses need not apply. Utilises speed to emphasize strength, and karma to wield the force. Jedi at first dan. A more complete and comprehensive form than ever before imagined, the genesis of a neocon with a sense of humour. also known as cheeky-monkey style.

<updating information. Update complete>

:input Yellow 1st kyu Elemental…

<updating information. Update complete>

:input Orange 2nd kyu Cosmic…

<updating information. Update complete>

:close file: access user log: delete log

<log deleted>

:exit memory bank: logoff: shutdown

<shutting down…>

Teacher guidance notes to give me a quick-way-in to Sammy to cruise to his third kyu!

First step, yellow belt kyu 1! (elemental)

5 elements, understanding body use and strength as a human weapon, also weapon training.

Target recognition, assess threat: develop

eliminate people/neutralize threat, ability

generous + good character type, giving + loving.

Need to be able to punch!

Punching ability : Hands. Push-ups. Pull-ups. Running. Break-falls. Anything else he can show me.

Body as a weapon: striking points, elbows knees hands feet head arms, throws kicks punches, etc. mental projection, fear authority, hidden/shadow training. Weapon training, with a stick/imagined!

Target recognition/assess threat. Practise on members of public; what can you tell about them? How could you recognise a terrorist, and what would you do? What about an enemy, how would you deal with him, or an assailant/attacker. What if they were armed?

Eliminate people: pressure points. One inch punch. Killer blow, or Shaolin accuracy/efficiency. Spiritual/karmic power. Punching into nothing (letting their momentum do the work!) Remaining calm in the face of hate/emotional discord. Neutralize threat/weapon, pacification techniques. Gentle hand removal approach (like how I took the crisps off Sammy; ask and you will be given!) Make friends with target.

Generous + good character type. Giving and loving. I think this one is pretty self explanatory really. I also think that Sammy can comfortably pass this grade with ease. Take how he looks after his family as the karmic example, and far more! But I want to make the point to him about the power of listening to good music, and perhaps even lend him one of my CDs?

Lastly five elements, that is fire (dragon breath), water (cold shower), earth (dirt), wind (breeze/clouds) and light (the sun/holy light). Get him to tell me about these elemental artefacts. I think that really should be enough.

Patiently, Jo walked through the night. It had taken him a long time. A very long time. But as all these furious motorists drove from point to point, Jo used his legs. He appreciated that there was supposed to be some kind of highly trained elite fighting force, who didn't walk but ran everywhere! He didn't know much about that, only they can't be that highly trained if one of them left her rifle in a supermarket toilets as she is supposed to have done!

447

Then he shut his lips and watched and listened. He knew that the conventional knowledge of punching taught to hit forwards. And that he hit bent (or from the side as if you will). This way it undercuts your opponent's anticipation. And it does use different muscles, still in the arm but more bi-lateral.

My missus told me that she still loves me today. That means a lot to me you know. I still have the world of work to-do. But this little reminder eases the passage, and oh how it hurts.

Bad men have ruled the world for too long. They have got away with murder, stealing the good women away from the good men, and generally just making a nuisance of themselves. But Jo was gonna change all of that; he was sure of it.

Again he looked at the ring on his finger. A simple but telling reminder of his commitment to one woman and her baby. He wasn't gonna let them cut that off from them, however much they might want to. Or rather he would go down fighting. And so he calmly picked up his bag of books, and walked off into the sunset, seeking adventure and the high-life. Something he'd never had before.

38: The Ten Guiding Principles of 'Tear-drop' Kungfu:

1: Strike to kill!

Forget that namby-pamby self-defence rubbish that those TKD posters propagate. They are lies! You will have to fight, maybe to save your life, if not that then at least your pride. And when you do so, do you really think that your opponent is going to pull his punches? But what if he doesn't? What if you face a Ju-jutter? Trained to kill? Well then you had better have more than a rabbit up your sleeve if you want to survive that night!

2: Chi is real

Chi is real and tangible. Use it, harness it. It surrounds you, permeates you. Without it you cannot win a single fight, and will be swimming against the tide. With it your punches will be carried and bolstered. Feel it in your heart, in your love and embrace it. But do NOT let it control you. By all means go windsurfing from time to time, and feel the sorrow when you have to. Cry. But after you feel a little bit better, wipe away those tears, pick up that sandal, and squash those damn c!!-roaches! Make them fear your wrath!

3: Learn about the Shaolin   five animal forms

You would do well to learn from these great drunken masters. From Jackie Chan, to Bruce Lee, they embody the very heart of the fighting spirit, and carry great powers, much greater even than first meets the eye! Crane form, about stability and balance, monkey boxing, dragon form, tiger form, and the deadly poisonous snake movements. Learn about these tracking powers, and incorporate their movements and philosophy into your own personal combat regime. They will diversify your range tremendously.

4: Believe in the power of the mind

It is true that good fighters ought to have good muscle tone, endurance and accuracy. But there is another, lesser known about characteristic which differentiates the men from the boys. And that is mental capacity. Don't believe that you are going to win every fight you take in. You won't. And if my experience is anything to go by, you will lose a lot more in the early days. But keep on going; never give up faith.

5: Learn the power of one finger pointing Zen

Here's another much little known about Buddhist combat form, which can actually chop down mountains much less push them! And I will never forget the day in hospital when I fought a conventional boxer, complete with his ducks and dodges and uppercuts and parries, against one finger pointing Zen, the kind Chow-Yun-Fat so amply demonstrates in

Crouching Tiger-Hidden Dragon. Only this time it was for real, we had no safety nets or ropes! Still I did have to tell him no head shots. I wasn't quite ready at that time to get battered. I mean, the best fights are those which at least resemble an even match.

Ultimate power incurs the ultimate sacrifice. You have to commit your soul to the cause, and once you have there is no turning back. Eventually you will learn how to beat ten men, a city, the entire world even, on the tip of your little finger. But don't expect to be able to do this straight away! It is my experience that it takes a lot of blows before this level of skill is attained!

6: Do not let your injuries stop you

It is true that they will cause a setback. There is no denying that a broken toe/neck/heart/d!!/lungs hurt a lot. But if I stopped there on receiving these strikes, I never would have got over them to get where I am today. And it is also true that once broken, it will never be the same again.

For this you're going to have to learn ways to compensate. If your arm isn't strong, learn to punch with the body. And if they anticipate this and are gonna throw ya, learn to side-swipe and get out of the way before they do! See there are often ways around things, more than one way of getting the job done you might say. Now it is your job to find out what these might be (in any given situation).

7: Wash your own clothes

Whether you are in Africa, or America, do not always rely on the little lady (or maidservant) to do the laundry. Learn to use the machine, and when the time comes to do it, bung them in! It only takes a relatively short investment of time, and the rewards are manifold not to mention more hygienic.

8: Place family above all else

I don't care what any of these f!!!ers may say. Family needs to come first. That's above your job, your sport, yourself. Family is firstly your missus or husband, as appropriate. Then your children, then your parents, siblings and so on. It is a very lonely life without one, and so you need to protect and look-after your loved ones, and make sure that they never have to go through what you have.

9: Dance

Even if it's only for one CD's worth of trippy/gay dance beats, do it. All the great ninjas of the past did. Even if it's only every other day, or even once a beat. It will teach you rhythm and co-ordination. Style and sense. And don't worry if you look like a ponce at first. We all have to start somewhere, right?

10: Breakfall

I don't care who you are, how many dan you've got or what your credentials include. Everyone can be thrown; everyone has weak points, and so by learning to break-fall at least you will be able to cushion the blow. Even a simple roly-poly will suffice. Don't think that you're above getting down and dirty. Pride leads to a fall, as they say, as they say.

*: And know

That your enemies will oppose you in the form of people. By all means they may work for organisations, the NHS, the army, the government, the police or whoever. They may work within these, and work very hard. They may influence and have a great deal of powerful control over these machines. But we don't live in a dictatorship, but a democracy. There is a thing such as public opinion. It is the people behind the scenes you should worry about, those who pull the strings. But they are made of the same blood and bone as the rest of us, and no matter how good their prowess, even they have their weak points – even they.

And that's it! I realise that we've run over the mark a little bit, but I'm sure you'll forgive me. And stay posted for the latest news on TEAR-DROP KUNG-FU!

39: Numbers:

Hi class. Welcome to the Jujutsu dojo, an integral electronic forum based in the martialartstalk.net halls. Here you will learn the finer points of the style, and hopefully take away lesson plans to work towards for the next lesson. You will be expected to contribute to the in-lesson discussions, and also partake in the gradings, although I'm not entirely sure of how the format for these will take place, how much is going to be coursework based, on written tests or perhaps even proof by action? Hey, but that is for me to worry about.

And as you may have already gathered, a great deal of the work we do together will be theoretical. I will teach you things, and we will learn things together. Certainly teaching is actually one of the best ways anyone can consolidate and improve upon your knowledge base; teachers among you will already know I'm sure (Alex and Janet?)

So onto the lesson. I have chosen numbers as an easy way to get into the style. I appreciate that you may not immediately see the connection between this lesson and the realm of deadly physical combat. But please trust in me. I want to start it nice and easy to begin with.

And I bet most if all of you will already think you know numbers pretty well, hey. You all passed your GCSE/O-level math exams didn't you? You know the kind of stuff, algebra and trigonometry, Pythagoras and diameters. That kind of stuff? Well you're gonna be relieved to hear that that kind of stuff has no place here.

As a child and at school didn't you always wonder whether there was more to the lessons taught and their curriculum then? We're sticking to maths here, so didn't you ever wonder whether there was some other way of looking at numbers then viscerally presented to you back then? I know I certainly did! And in my desperation to find this hidden *secret code, I spent hours slogging away at the formulae, constantly processing and reprocessing the same old digits. Desperately trying to *crack the code. I never did break it. Sure I got the highest level possible for that GCSE (a*), but it really meant nothing. Really it didn't. We're not going to go back to my schooldays here, however, but look to the future. Or rather the recent past.

For it was very recently in my last stay in hospital, that I have consolidated upon my number philosophy to a concrete and radically different set of processes than has ever before been imagined. A good friend of mine in hospital, actually helped me set this up. Although it is true to say that I first began counting up to three in the 24 hours I did at the St Mary's Wharf police cell four years back, now I am out, and free to put it down on paper.

Enough of an introduction, let's get counting. Number one, what does that stand for? The Alpha and Omega? One God? Number one (SAY me)? Mankind? Planet Earth? Christianity? Strength over weakness? Physical discipline over moral disruption? Big men over

456

weaklings? What else, you tell me?

One is the root of all numbers. Not zero, which didn't even exist in Roman times(! did you know that?) Neo and everything. It is the root of all integral numbers, and a powerful entity if ever a number was one!

Let's move on: two, what does that stand for? 1+1, nah! I'm not talking about numerical meanings here, but real ones. And so in this world of signals and metaconsequences, where does the two stand. Man and wife! Child and parent! Yin and Yang, male and female, two lovers, two foes, two sides (right and left) and so on. Right and wrong. But I think the first definition, man and wife (unity), is the best one here.

How about three. I'm gonna cut straight past the crud, three means man woman and baby (family). It doesn't matter if you have more than one kid, or none at all. This is an empirical and epic truth. Three is the understanding that there is more to your life than personal pleasure, that there is a responsibility to something more than just your petty self.

And that's it! We can also say that four is the group root of two, and more importantly that five represents Miss Piggy and her four beautiful sisters (the fist/the universal symbol of the fighter/warrior/spirit) but beyond this we run into turmoil and confusion, and so will do best to leave it there.

Now you have completed your first Jujutsu lesson! Feel free to reread the class if you want to remind yourself of any of the details, and don't hesitate to question me directly (pm) if you want me to clarify any of the points on a one to one basis. I hope you understood and got something out of the lesson, and are ready for the next one, which will be on… The Fist!

Cheers Guys! John Robinson Jujutsu teacher.

40: Swahili

Repeat after me:

baby (means baby)

Mmtoto (means baby also)

Nakupenda (means I love you)

Jambo sasa (hello)

Sawa (Ok?/good)

Mpana (no)

djo (yes)

chappa chappa (beating)

polay mama! (sorry baby!)

Kwaheri (byebye)

Habari (hi)

That's it. Repeat and learn.

The next day on his way to the café to gulp down some cola, Jo found a book lying by the side of the street. Noticing its title, 'Hidden Ninja Secrets', he was immediately intrigued to spy what lay inside, and why anyone would want to discard such a fascinating work? Gingerly he opened the pages and skimmed through the introduction straight onto chapter one: basic strikes: Punches, centre, side-swipe, upper-cut, jab. Kicks: little + large, low + high. Throws: push + over the top, wrist grab. Holds: choke, headlock, arm-bar. Miscellaneous: break fall.

Hold on a minute Jo thought, where were the counters, and what about the feint? Ah some comprehensive book this is turning out to be! It's missed out on even the most basic of attacks. Next he hastily skimmed forward a couple of chapters to chapter three: Definitions: Oxymoron, Nemesis, Equilibrium, Jeet-Kun-Do, dao, epi-centre, meta-tarsal, Cephlocordal, metaphor, death, rebirth, Krishna, Arjuna, Meta-physics, Aesthetics, Poussa (Chinese Buddha), Dharma and Epidermis. He fell into a light sleep reading these words and had to snap himself out of it. This was sure some boring English lesson!

Then skipping forward another couple of chapters he found the following basic human types; White, Black, yellow, pink, brown and green. Man, woman, child, OAP and beast. Hard-worker, light worker, business man and manager. Rich, poor, not bothered. Now he was confused and more than a little frustrated. So he threw the book back into the bush from whence it came. He knew how to read; that was probably the best place for it! ;~)

Next Jo clambered onto a park bench and out of nowhere began ranting into a microphone:

'Hear me, hear me!' He shouted. 'Your financial institutions are based on the false accusations of negative credit histories, your wars based on lies and propaganda, your media input based on financial c!!roaches and truth manipulation, your government on trumped up ass-holes, your MMA tournaments on equally big-headed phenal extravators, and your video game industry on grown up nerds with nothing better to do!

Me and my army of Miss piggy and her four lovely sisters, are gonna topple your crooked empire with the power of a fist! And there ain't nothing you can do about it! Nothing at all! Your bullets can't reach me over here, don't you remember you already tried in the former Rhodesia, and look how far you got there? Oh big deal so you got Thabo Mbeki the sack; am I bothered, am I really? Most of you are just spineless whippersnappers, more concerned with your own Macho and wholly homosexual prowess in bed, than to ever concern about a little whippet like me. That's why I can sneak through the town undetected, fly where I want. And I am fighting. With my ninja dancing, and my ninja punches. We're fighting the tyrants of history, and their hidden world domination.

And as their empires begin to crumble and fall to ruin, we're still standing. The good decent people, the people who deliver the papers and teach in the schools. The people who fight the bullies, and stand up in court against them. The Venezuelan communists. People all across the world who've had enough of your power, and your dictatorship. And do you think we're gonna stop halfway there? Do you think we've come this far to leave a job half undone? Ha! What a surprise you are in for then!' He screamed, before slumping over to take his afternoon nap! It had been a long day.

And walking away he mused (you can't touch me.)

41: Inspirations

Good Use of the English language

TKD (aggression)

five animal form kungfu (especially monkey style)

Judo

Jeet-kun-do (water)

drunken fool kungfu

baby kung-fu!

The next night Jo had a dream. He dreamt that he was back in Africa, playing with the baby and just generally making a nuisance of himself. He set in motion the balls of entry in a TKD MMA club, full of these black shrouded ninjas; he'd teach them a thing or two. And he also arranged for one of the street urchins to take him to one of the festival carnivals they have over there. It was going to be difficult for him, seeing as he'd never had a girlfriend in his life, never had sex, couldn't dance (had two left feet), and smelt. But he had the conviction of a righteous man, and was damned that he was going to make a success of this holiday. It didn't matter what had happened to his gal and babe; this thing was going to be a success! If he had to he'd run for president, join the army, the secret service even! He was possessed by this point! He'd become a ninja! Learn how to throw shuriken, wield Kantanas, drive a battleaxe and just generally make a nuisance of himself in the dojo-halls of Kenya, as well as the dance-halls, cafés, and roads. He was gonna change the world. Starting with this page. Moving out to his first 'win'. Onto 'world-domination.' And there was nothing that could stop him! Not now, no single person or organisation, or government, or even all of them combined. He was now all-powerful! 'Cos you see the world is made up of individuals, and if you can be a higher/better person than one of them, you can beat the lot! And if you don't believe it, try it for yourself! Try and raise yourself to the ethereal/spiritual level, and then wield some wholly unholy influence. This is the stuff uber-ninjas are made of! A modern day fighting machine, with all the speed, power, and discretion of the hiding samurai, but also with the mechanics of an engineer, the impact of the Western imperial war machine and the bravery of the great heroes, whom if you don't know who they are by now, then you'll never know! But he had no intention of becoming a martyr. He had too much to live for. Not any more, not now! Now he had proved himself, was making some new friends, and bringing one or two of his ethical morals to the real world!

Then he woke up again, back in Britain. He could smell the smell of fishy chips and Tetley's tea wafting through the window. The papers were full of another aimless stabbing, of another teenage delinquent. The jails were pumped full of criminals getting let out early 'cos the government couldn't enforce their overzealous crime and punishment policies. And things were going downhill fast.

Adios suckers!

Now with the grace of a ninja and the speed of a samurai, Jo proceeded to decimate his enemies one by one. Carrying a badly scrawled handwritten piece of paper with their contact details on it, he found out where they lived or worked, and shamed or otherwise disgraced them so that they could no longer slander his name.

He was not a violent man, and couldn't kick to save his life. But when they put up a fight, when they amassed in a crowd of jackals baying for his blood, he saw it as his duty to take out the ringleader, or at least the one who stepped forward, with whatever came to hand. Be it a stick, or a foot. And it made him tired, all of this ninja dancing was okay, but it was the ninja kicking that really got him! Made him out of breath so that he had to sit down after two sets of ten or so. But from that day forth, he vowed to continue with the foot-strikes. Each day, every day. So his feet and legs would get stronger, faster, better balanced and more lethal generally. He truly would be an all round fighter once he had jumped that rope a few times he guessed.

But now he was just chilling. Looking forward to another nice sunny day in Nairobi! Dancing in the mini-buses (with the music blaring out) to the utter embarrassment of his soon to be eternal soul-mate, Jo really thought that he had got it made! No-one could stop him now, not that they'd even dare try!

Jo the Ninja shuddered at that last piece of over-inflated egotistical rhetoric! How headstrong had he been back in the day?! And that was only a relatively short time ago (a few months!) But still a lot of things had happened to him since then. Not to mention another damn trip to the hospital, a good seven weeks this time! Damn places, they really seem to like me there, they keep on wanting me back! Tee-hee. But seriously, I have started training on since returning to the UK. Sure only a little bit every day, a swim or a jog. But I've got to start somewhere you know. And a little is better than nothing at all. And despite not noticing drastic improvements in either my times or distance, it does seem to be getting a little easier than it was when I first started out. Less of a life and death scenario. I did find myself getting tired near the end of each swim, or right the way through running if the truth be told. But I hope that even that will get easier after time. And surely my everyday breathing had picked up remarkably after engaging in these work-outs.

Well I got banned off that MA forum/message board in the end you know. And rather than trying to hack a way back in, I think I should say good riddance to them. Anyway I've joined another one, one of their competitors like, and hope to be able to post any new ninja adventures there, when the time is right!

Also I will be going to Africa again at the end of next month, and hopefully will be able to think of some new ninja stories while I'm over there. And hope to join a local Aikido dojo after the holiday, all of which is good stuff. We're nearly there in this epic-flashback.

Take it EASY my trainee ninjees!

As Jo watched the mountains and clouds zip by underneath, he shed but a single tear. If his mission had been to go to Africa, to spread to them the good news and recruit minions for his 'new' martial art, he had failed miserably. And now he was alone, even as he had always been alone. Some f!!!!!! good his use of the English language had proved him in the face of the beasts and ogres which roam the streets of Kenya! And to think that he had once foolishly believed that he would be able to wield his metaphors like a sword! And look at where it has got me?

Without babe and baby, my heart has surely been irrevocably ripped. Just as she is getting damaged by God knows who, God knows where, right now as we speak. And to think that I had foolishly believed that I would be able to face my foes over here? That they wouldn't ostracise me and stick together, that they would stand in a line right before me so I could take them out one by one, without ever so much as hitting back!

But now it is all over. And so I am returned to the old Blighty. Yet again alone, with nothing. No invisible, invincible coat of arms which can stop bullets. Which when I don its carapace lets me walk lighter, jump higher and hit harder. No flexible yet strong wrought iron mesh chain mail/light as leather dragon hide which lets me swim as well as run. Nothing that can stop bullets. I wasn't invulnerable, just now perhaps very, very weak. My dreams have crumbled around me even as I had failed to enter the dragon's den and dethrone Satan himself who sits therein.

There is no such magic suit of armour. Much as there is no cure for my wheeze. It's a medical condition, my windpipe doesn't open properly because of a RTA some ten years back. This is scientific proof, and no amount of corrective surgery, or voodoo witchcraft, is going to change it. And because I can't get the right amount of air into my lungs, I'm never going to be able to dance, much less run or fight. And no amount of practice or shadow moves is gonna change that. And I'll also never be a ninja. (Too noisy, they'd hear me a mile off!)

Now stepped off the plane I get an itch which I scratched, on my left ring finger. What Britain will hold for me now I'm back remains an unknown quandary. But rest assured you'll be the first to hear!

You've got me in a rage now! You've got me and my wife arguing, and that really ain't no good. Rather than face me like men, you stab me in the back. And only Osprey had the courage to stand up to me. The rest of you like the treacherous snipers you are, deal with my version of the truth not head on, but from the rear. In the dark, like the batty boys most of you are. But I'm still here, and still fighting. Long live the King!

And crew-cut, just because you don't understand my form of communication doesn't make it invalid. It just means that you are stupid!

Two swords, two rings more like it!

Bloody and injured Jo stumbled from the battleground. He had taken quite a beating that time, so bad in fact that he had even had to intervene to stop his foe from causing any more damage! But it wasn't the physical flesh wounds that caused the most pain, but the emotional scars which made him cry, which hurt the worst. They hurt the worst and also provided the encouragement for him to continue fighting, hacking in, and struggling. Until the day he died!

The enemy now appeared all powerful, and some good his 'two ring' 'baby kungfu' style had stood against their vicious and merciless attacks. They truly had sought to strip him to the bone, to take away his dan, and what's more they had almost succeeded. But they hadn't, not yet anyway. He was still able to find strange and foreign parks, where the monkeys jump through the trees and the cacti grow to nine feet! Really I'm not kidding. I even took a photo of one except that my dongle has stopped working/is bugged so I can't upload it. But these photos have caused me more trouble than it's worth. Let's not even go   there.

So what else was there left for him to do? He had lost a battle, but the war rages on. And its ultimate outcome rests still squarely in fate's, or God's hands. The baby is still laughing smiling and dancing, so hope was still there yet. She respected him, and him her. That's not all. But if I told you any more I know for a fact that the powers that be would put two and two together, and who knows, probably even hire a real assassin to take me out! Ha! I'd like to see them try! So for now I'll leave it there. Glad to be back in the frame, and stay posted for the continuing exploits of Jo and his amazing adventure!

Jo licked his lips. He still had the itch on his ring finger, where the ring caught on a callous. And still his wifey was nowhere to be seen (perhaps she was sleeping in the next room with her baby). Then as he walked through the streets empty handed he swaggered a little bit. He considered himself to be ancient. And now he surely was an 'old man' in bed. Not that he couldn't perform, just what came out was as ineffective as one of his punches. Like slime. He considered that this was probably due to the years of self neglect he had enforced on himself, which was in turn due to an over-arching depression and therefore out of his control. But he still wanted to save the world. And DID have a surrogate daughter, even if she was not biologically his. She sure did love him. What's more it now looked as if there was another one on the way, again not mine. But that's okay. The most important thing is that me and my missus are still sleeping under the same roof, even if   not in the same bed.

Yesterday I learnt to my peril, that the only way to disarm an advancing armed assailant is by the wrist. Also that it is good to build strength by rage, but keep that fire in the grill, before it burns the whole house down. Manipulation of feelings seemed to be one of his strong points. He had an uncanny ability to piss off black-belts. Not just any of them you see, but only the big headed ass-holes he considered unworthy of that belt anyhow.

He was pleased that he didn't have any investments in shares, which would now be suffering terribly with the market crashes. Except that I do. Or that we're never going back to Britain, except that we are. We have to, I can't stick about here forever. They don't know me here, don't know how to take me. At least in my home city they are used to my 'eccentric' behaviour. Walking through the streets barefoot, or even very slowly. Like a speed of 0.1 miles an hour!

And I've been banned from the MA forum. Ha-ha, what are they afraid of? That my gloomy predictions might actually come true? That the global economy is rotten to the bone, and bound to fall, founded on pompous t*$%s it's only a matter of time? Well it certainly seems that way.

So for now it's back to the drawing board. I suppose my missus doesn't like my dancing, certainly not in public where it embarrasses the hell out of her. But it makes me strong, supple and fast, and so I plan to continue despite our differences. To work our way through it you might say. Nobody ever said that it would be easy. But at least now I have a wife, and despite whatever she might say to me at times, that really does mean the world.

With regards to this stock mess, well I just don't know. I don't want to suffer, neither for my fellow compatriots. But that being said, I have always considered myself to be a revolutionary, and in fact still do. This latest downwards flux could be seen as a revolution from the inside of sorts. And nobody ever said that the war was going to be bloodless – far from it. All revolutionary wars of the past, from Russia (won) to Vietnam (lost), have incurred tragic casualties. Only now they have taken it to their home turf. No longer are the fire fights on the streets of Bangkok, but the rugged terrain of the Wall Street electronic displays. A hidden and undisclosed enemy sniping at the home territory and assets, and a war of attrition has suddenly turned nasty, and very real, very quickly.

Will the markets recover, or will the collapse be very real and very social? Will the implications actually overthrow governments like the de-facto meaning of the word entails, or will it filter out like it has done so many times before? Even Jo couldn't foresee that far. All he knew was that the fight was very real, and had wrought its toll. But as long as the baby was still laughing, and that he was still there to see it, I have strength. And maybe, just maybe, one day, my baby kungfu will prevail!

42: Black Belt (Jojutsu)

With the last page of his recent book finally closing, Jo looked about himself. Wearing a dog-eared but good pair of blue second-hand jeans, a couple of nice designer sandals his wife had brought for him in hospital last time he was in Africa, a t-shirt and new jumper, a blue Christian plastic cross and chain, he felt ready. Readier now than he had ever been.

Ready to return to Africa and whip some black Negro-African butt back to the fifth century slave-camps from where they belong! I'm sorry if you don't like the analogy, but after what she's done to me, she, and they, deserve what they're gonna get.

I'm psyching myself up right now. Preparing to fight someone whom I don't know, and is I don't know how hard. In fact most of these black Negro brothers are pretty tough. You should have seen them working on the building in progress opposite the hospital I was in over there, where they banged and hammered away like there was no tomorrow!

But the human frame is somewhat different to raw building material, Jo considered. Sure he's got his work cut out, going to an alien land with unforeseen adversaries and his freedom, at least for the end of the three week holiday is at stake.

But with wisdom, reflection, a certain amount of cardiovascular training both before and after, some kung-fu patterns, and the surety that karmic resolution brings, he felt

473

as ready now as he had ever been. He wasn't expecting this to be pretty, but bloodbaths never are!

Deep in meditation, ninja Jo reflected upon what it had taken to reach this point. A great deal of pain, targeted at first to him he believed, and then caused to others by him, through domestic violence on his mum and sister ten years ago. Time had softened this pain, but the memory was very much alive for all of us. I hoped to be able to make up for lost time and do some things to compensate my mum for the physical and mental misery I have caused her in the past. But when she gets upset with me, even now, I know part of her still hurts inside.

How can I try and explain to her that she's not to blame? It was wholly my fault, the monster I had become. And in some senses still am. Rejected by the world, shat upon by school and community I was an outcast. And my accident and hospitalization and the subsequent pain that caused me, only nailed the coffin further shut.

It has taken some years of righteous living to begin to lead something resembling a normal life. I doubt I'll ever get there completely. I very much doubt I'll ever work again. And why is it that I should think the odds are stacked against me for going into hospital yet again?

But my writing helps me to find peace where there once was none. God helps me to find fellowship when there are other theists about. Hope gives my life meaning and my family brings me colour. But when I say my family, what I really mean is my daughter, Michelle. She really means that much to me, and I hope to support her forever.

With care and precision ninja Jo mounted his telescopic sniper rifle sights, and drew a bee-line on all of the possible targets. He had done his homework. And years of fighting the tide, first at school, then on the internet chess forums, and finally on the martial sites, had taught him more than a thing or two about when to stick your head out, and when to keep it safely down behind the parapet.

The advantage of using a weapon is that it gives you other, shall we say, advantages over the opposition whom-so-ever they may be. So for some the ogre hammer provides a daunting and very real physical weight with which to throw behind their every move, should they so desire.

Jo didn't have this. I am, as presently, fairly mildly constituted, with a delicate constitution and a fragile frame. But whereas others may use guns, fists and sex as lethal weapons, ninja Jo was equipped with one forté. A weapon which years of cruel and brutal slog had warped and shaped to his mind. A faculty which has been honoured alongside and parallel to his musical taste, both ear and tongue, and followed his mental and spiritual progress. From the brink of oblivion and back, and even recounted a great deal of this journey with the insight of one who has been there and can speak with the authority of one who knows that he is speaking the truth from the heart.

Jo's weapon is the pen. The ability to capture a memory or foresight, engage with it, perhaps hesitate for a beat and bring from the page something very real and perchance precious. Peace.

Swimming what seemed like for hours, Jo became a fish. Darting in and out of the currents beneath the reef, in and amongst the coral, all the while keeping an eye out for the Great Whites and their terrible teeth, and also avoiding the Sting-Rays as another harmful predator, he considered himself to be free. Not restricted to the inland streams and gullies of the trout or other land bound species, Jo was an ocean rider, free to swim wherever he may, with whomsoever he chose.

Then a moment later and he is a bird, flying in crane stance high and away from the ordinary mortal folk, ducking and diving with the winds and the clouds that grace them, spiralling above and away from the terrorists down below, surely aching and arching to heaven?

Suddenly he felt lonely. Looking all around him he saw happy people, talking and getting on with ordinary lives. Where was his (immediate) family when he needed them? Some far off continents doing God knows what with God knows who.

Suddenly his whole life seemed a fake, the title he had bestowed upon himself (ninja) artificial and his whole purpose a joke. The sunshine comforted him with its rays. How lonely must it be to be a sun, glorious high in the sky, providing light and warmth to everyone? But solitary in its purpose, and alone. Always perilously alone. How humble our lives seem in such thoughts.

Jo got out of the pool soaking wet and more than just a little tired. It had been another hard morning of beating the ripples of the pool with his hands, of struggling to stay afloat and catch his breath. One minute he was on the surface with the rest of the bath's swimmers; today mainly a group of ageing ladies and two or three gents. The there was Jo, the outcast ninja, struggling to find meaning in this life.

He could only swim slow. I can only swim slowly; that's all I've ever been able to manage. I even remember at primary school being tracked to the top group, I was the slowest in it. They even tried to move me down groups but I was having none of it. So last I stayed!

But still, it's not just the quality of the swim, but the quantity! What that's supposed to mean is that if I can't meet them for speed, I damn well will for distance! And I've even incorporated a swan stance double ten rep. into my swim on before the last rep, before I dive in for the last. This dive was more a belly flop today! And when I'm doing my yoga I have to keep a weary eye out for over zealous pool attendants so they don't ban me! I've already had a warning for running into the dive you know!

So I swim. And yesterday I ran, or jogged even. But I find that a little more demanding, so hence prefer the pool work. Peace.

Sitting in his quiet space, alter-ego Jo considered the truth of all things. With his music blaring out he likened entering the zone to playing music in his sleep. With the dream realm causing drifting and rolling in oceans of emotions and waves of experience back and across his mental state, he reflected was this what it felt like to be enlightened?

To have cut free loose from the rest of the civilized plateau and now remain purely on a land of ethereal beings and subconscious. Half aware of reality and one eye firmly fixed on the nobody's business of the supranet (that's metaphysics by another name), it wasn't so much that I'd died as transcended.

But with one foot continuously floating off from the ground, my fingertips gently try to hold on to the cracks in our foundation. To make some kind of sense out of this mess we call reality. Not just to exist in pleasure, but help others rescue their selves from the pit and hold onto their morals where once there was none.

For sure for a long time I lived in that miserable realm which is primarily the reserve of bandits and pirates. Cut-throat jacks, eager to sell their own grannies for a couple of pieces of silver. But some-how, somewhere I found my way out of it. And with a couple of years of mortal struggle, and fighting the cold I find myself where I am today. Still fighting but now there's more at stake. Specifically my wife and baby daughter. Peace.

Quiet as an assassin, invisible as a ghost, ninja Jo crept through the night. With stealth and precision he assassinated his enemies.

Back at his castle his libraries stocked tomes of ancient far Eastern literature, annuals of historical battles from Rome to Greece, France to Japan, Napoleon to the Kamikaze, Julius Caesar to Apollo and Bacchus. In his books were stories of vampires and dragons, minstrels and artisans, revolutionaries to slaves. And the books weren't just epic stories, but also contained many reference manuals for physical and technical realities as well.

Jo spent many nights slaving over encyclopaedias of exercise, and then would soon after enter one of his many gyms and practice kung-fu moves and karate kata.

In his libraries he also kept large blank folders and pads for his own writings. He was a professor and a scholar as well as being a night stalker. And this he used these ephemeral literate skills to research facets of interest and thereby increase his knowledge.

In recent years Jo had also followed closely the booming expansion of the internet. Admittedly being banned from more than a couple of forums for his outlandish attitudes, he still revelled in being able to contact people all over the world with the ease of the click of a mouse and the push of a button.

And so that my friends, is a look into the inner sanctuary of our chief player. He also had a large heath stoneware fireplace he used to like chilling in-front of when the day was done.

So the question we have to ask ourselves is this: what does it take to become a (good) ninja? Years of martial training? That would certainly appear to make a warrior, but a ninja? Well no, not if I want to be counted in. A week's martial training is all I've had but still I'm fighting! How about an open mind, a giving heart, a free generosity and a kindred spirit.

The spirit is something best developed in pain. That's me and my wife. One day last year Michelle, the little one, held my hand in bed when I reached out, and in that instant I swore to stay with her. As she grows up, I will support her and be the good father figure my wife never had.

Jo walked towards the closing pages of this latest recount of his recent adventures carrying the weight and responsibility of a warrior who knows not only that he is true in his conviction and just in his cause, that the battle is not even half way over, but with the stamp of a tyrant and the seal of a martyr, the closing pages of this epic at least ensure that it has begun.

I hope that no more innocents have to die in the name of freedom or the shadow of the beast. But at least if they do I know that I have done this time, all I can to avert such a disaster.

In fact the truth be known, terrible men will still hold the power to meter out death and destruction on thousands and hundreds of thousands of innocent civilians much as they have done since the days of Churchill and Stalin.

This isn't a history, but one author's chance to grapple with the truth. I have arrested certain ideas in attempting to draw together a sound and comprehensive tale under these meagre pages.

And now we are at the end I hope you have been able to digest and feel empowered by at least some of these tales. 'Cos that's what it's all about, isn't it? Self empowerment and fulfilment. Or to put it another way, fate and destiny. It is worth spending a moment relaxing in the appreciation I want to express to you for following me on this journey, and I wish you all the best for whatever the future may bring.

Printed in Great Britain
by Amazon